BONNIE HONIG

DEMOCRACY
AND
THE FOREIGNER

Princeton University Press

Princeton and Oxford

**The Library of Congress has cataloged the cloth edition
of this book as follows**

Honig, Bonnie.

Democracy and the foreigner / Bonnie Honig.

p.   cm.

Includes bibliographical references and index.

ISBN 0-691-08884-5 (alk. paper)

1. Democracy. 2. Immigrants. 3. Nationalism.

4. Internationalism. I. Title.

JC423 .H748   2001

325.1—dc21   2001016373

British Library Cataloging-in-Publication Data is available

This book has been composed in ITC Garamond Light

Printed on acid-free paper. ∞

www.pupress.princeton.edu

Printed in the United States of America

5   7   9   10   8   6   4

ISBN-13: 978-0-691-11476-7 (pbk.)

ISBN-10: 0-691-11476-5 (pbk.)

For my parents,

David and Schewa Honig,

whose foreignness shaped their lives

and mine

———✦———

Politics exists because those who have no right to be

counted as speaking beings make themselves of some

account, setting up a community by the fact of placing

in common a wrong that is nothing more than this

very confrontation, the contradiction of two worlds

in a single world: the world where they are and

the world where they are not, the world where there

is something "between" them and those who

do not acknowledge them as speaking beings

who count and the world where there is nothing.

—*Jacques Rancière*

Contents

Acknowledgments

"There's no place like home." The magical phrase, repeated three times while she clicks together heels gripped by hard-won ruby slippers, returns Dorothy home from her nightmare-dream in the land of Oz. On its face, the phrase expresses a heartfelt home-yearning, as in "There's *no* place like home, [sigh]." Here the phrase suggests that home is so unique, wonderful, and irreplaceable a place (a "place where people know me, where I can just be," in Minnie Bruce Pratt's phrasing), that no other place ever lives up to it. However, the selfsame phrase unmasks this yearning for home as a fantasy. Switch the emphasis to "There's no place *like* home," and the phrase now seems to suggest that there is no place as wonderful as home is mythologized to be, and that includes home itself. The uncanny, punlike character of the phrase combines an unrelenting yearning for home together with an awareness that the home so yearned for is a fantasy.

Such ambivalence—its political-cultural organization into the separate, distinct desires we call home-yearning and escapism—is one of this book's points of departure. The desires for "a place where people know me, where I can just be" and for a place where I can never "just be" because my sense of my self is always challenged and expanded often drive the politics of foreignness traced here. Or better, perhaps these desires are themselves the effects of the politics of foreignness, symptoms of larger issues in democratic theory having to do with the freedom, agency, community, and solidarity that are the daily work of life in a more or less democratic polity.

⸺◦⟞⟝◦⸺

Little did I know when I wrote the above scene-setting sentences several years ago that by the time this book was truly finished I would have written it in thirteen different studies in four different states. Such nomadism has enabled me to present my work in progress to a wide range of audiences who generously shared their perspectives with me at talks and conferences. Many others read all or parts of the manuscript along the way and provoked me to think further about issues I thought I had already settled. First and foremost, for giving me the gift of their time, and for reading drafts of chapters with an intellectual generosity to which I have already grown happily accustomed, I am grateful to some of the members of my new Chicago circle of theory colleagues, Eric Santner, Patchen Markell, Peter Fenves, and Sara Monoson. Our newest member, Miguel Vatter, arrived in time to make me attend once more to Machiavelli. Also in that circle, Linda Zerilli has been my partner in thinking about this book since its inception, and to prove it I have a stack of emails from her that is taller than I am. I thank her for her many, many, many contributions to the project.

Amy Gutmann and Sanford Levinson read the manuscript for Princeton University Press and provided helpful guidance and encouragement for the last stages of revision. Others who heard or read parts of the manuscript and commented on them to my profit include Seyla Benhabib, Lauren Berlant, Josh Cohen, Bill Connolly, Mo Fiorina, Richard Flathman, Jill Frank, Marcie Frank, Marjorie Garber, Ruth Grant, Barbara Johnson, Michael Jones-Correa, George Kateb, Steve Macedo,

Harvey Mansfield, Pratap Mehta, Martha Minow, Bruce Robbins, Michael Rogin, Michael Sandel, George Shulman, Rogers Smith, Michael Warner, Patrick Weil, Stephen White, and Iris Marion Young. Late in the day, Joan Cocks graciously made time to read almost the whole manuscript and helped give it its final contours.

I have had great good fortune in research assistance over the years: thanks to Patchen Markell, Michaele Ferguson, Arash Abizadeh, Michael Bosia, Torrey Shanks, and Ella Myers.

Drafts of all the chapters were presented at various colloquia, panels, and conferences: at the Ford Foundation, MIT, several APSAs, Harvard, Rutgers, and Duke Universities, the University of Iowa, ICA in London, the American Studies Association in 1998, among others. Some of the chapters appeared in much abbreviated form as articles, and I am grateful to Sage Publications, *Strategies* (http://www.tandf.co.uk), and *Social Text* for permission to reuse material here that was first published there.

I am especially grateful to the students at Northwestern University. The first to join the new graduate program in political theory, in particular, Torrey Shanks and Ella Myers, have inaugurated here a new and exciting theory conversation of which I am fortunate to be part.

My recent association with the American Bar Foundation made me appreciate the forceful role of the iconic lawgiver in the symbolic politics of foreignness. Chapter 2 exists because of the ABF. The ABF also provided me with research funding, teaching relief, and intellectual company. I am grateful to John Comaroff, Bryant Garth, Carol Heimer, Chris Tomlins, Joanne Martin, Beth Mertz, Annelise Riles, Vicki Woeste, and, briefly, Janet Gilboy, as well as such visitors as Felicia Kornbluh, Michelle Landis, Ronen Shamir, Saskia Sassen, and Kunal Parker. Also at ABF, Renee Brown prepared the manuscript for publication with courtesy and professionalism for which I thank her.

At Princeton University Press, Ann Wald first acquired the manuscript, and Ian Malcolm adopted it as if it were his own. I am very grateful to both—to Ann for her early interest in this project and to Ian for the great care he took of it.

Michael Whinston designed and oversaw the construction of the last three studies in which this book was written, thus doing literally in those moments what he always also does figuratively: supporting my writing, work, and personal life with characteristic warmth and good planning. He also helped hammer into shape the final drafts of chapters 1 and 5. My son, Noah Whinston, was born at the start of this project, and my daughter, Naomi Honig, arrived five years later at its close. It seems to me appropriate that they should sandwich the project in this way because they teach me daily one of this book's most vital lessons: how to live with alienness. Noah also provided several key insights into the *Wizard of Oz* and the biblical story of Moses, for which I thank him most sincerely.

Finally, I am enormously indebted to Tereza Almeida, Audra Jestes, Jane Merriam, and, most recently, Carol Paine for caring for my children while I worked and for teaching me some of the skills of child care upon which I now rely. I cannot thank them enough.

Evanston, Illinois, and Warren, Vermont

December 2000

DEMOCRACY
AND
THE FOREIGNER

Would it still make sense to speak of democracy when it
would no longer be a question . . . of country,
nation, even of state or citizen?
–Jacques Derrida

What is a foreigner? A [wo]man who makes
you think you are at home.
–Edmond Jabes

1 NATIVES AND FOREIGNERS:
Switching the Question

"How should we solve the problem of foreignness?" The question under-
lies contemporary discussions of democracy and citizenship. Proposed
solutions vary. Political theorists deliberate about whether or to what
extent social unity is necessary to sustain social democracy. Courts
rule on the extent of government's obligations to its noncitizen residents. Economists debate the costs and benefits of immigration. Sociol-
ogists argue about the (in)effectiveness of multilingual education.
But, notwithstanding their differences, participants in contemporary debates about foreignness all reinscribe foreignness as a "problem" that
needs to be solved by way of new knowledge, facts, or politics. In so
doing, they reiterate the question that has dominated political theory
for centuries.

In classical political thought, foreignness is generally taken to signify
a threat of corruption that must be kept out or contained for the sake

of the stability and identity of the regime.[1] This somewhat xenophobic way of thinking about foreignness endures in the contemporary world, though other options—from assimilation to the many varieties of multiculturalism—are now also considered viable.[2] All of these options persist in treating foreignness as a problem in need of solution, however. Even many of the most multiculturally minded contributors to diversity debates treat foreignness as a necessary evil and assume that we would be better off if only there were enough land for every group to have its own nation-state.[3]

There are some who take a more positive view of foreignness. In *Nations Unbound*, Basch, Glick Schiller, and Szanton Blanc endorse a new transmigrant politics that is, in their view, bringing to an end the nation-state's privileged position as the central organizing institution of modern cultural, political, juridical, and administrative life. In the same spirit, James Holston and Arjun Appadurai claim that in many places "the project of a national society of citizens . . . appears increasingly exhausted and discredited."[4] Analogously, for Iain Chambers, increased encounters with transnational others have the following, desirable consequence: "The earlier European intertwining of national language, literature and identity is unpicked, and the epic of modern nationalism is forced open to meet the exigencies that emerge from more complex patterns."[5]

For celebrants of postnational politics, foreignness does not seem to be a problem in need of solution. It is a welcome agent of welcome changes. But these thinkers, wittingly or unwittingly, rearticulate the classical position on foreignness noted above. That is, on the postnationalist account, too, foreignness is a threat to the stability and identity of established regimes. Postnationalists differ from their predecessors only in their valuation of that threat. They celebrate it and valorize the very fragmentation that earlier political theorists took to be a problem.

Motivated by these ongoing debates, I take foreignness as a topic, a question, rather than a problem. What does it mean? What sort of work does it do in cultural politics? In the chapters that follow, I read texts of democratic theory looking at the roles (often heretofore unnoticed) played in those texts by strangers or foreigners, and I read popular and high cultural stories about strangers or foreigners, looking for the lessons they might have for democratic theory. Again and again, I find foreignness used in familiar ways, as a device that gives shape to or threatens existing political communities by marking negatively what "we" are not.[6] But I also find foreignness operating in a less convention-ally familiar way, with a seldom-noted positive content and effect.

Sometimes, the figure of the foreigner serves as a device that allows regimes to import from outside (and then, often, to export back to out-side) some specific and much-needed but also potentially dangerous virtue, talent, perspective, practice, gift, or quality that they cannot pro-vide for themselves (or that they cannot admit they have). This supple-ment of foreignness gives receiving regimes something different from the novelty, cultural breadth, and depth identified by theorists of immi-gration and multiculturalism such as Bhikhu Parekh.[7] Indeed, it is often their foreignness itself—not, as Parekh suggests, the culturally inflected talents, skills, or perspective that individual foreigners happen to have—that makes outsiders necessary even if also dangerous to the regimes that receive them. Indeed, sometimes foreignness operates as an agent of (re)founding.

In the classic texts of Western political culture (both high and low), the curious figure of the foreign-founder recurs with some frequency: established regimes, peoples, or towns that fall prey to corruption are restored or refounded (not corrupted or transcended) by the agency of a foreigner or a stranger. Moses appears as an Egyptian prince to lead the Israelites out of Egypt and bring to them the law from the mountain. The biblical Ruth's migration from Moab to Bethlehem reanimates the alienated Israelites' affective identification with their god while also be-ginning the line that will lead to King David. Oedipus arrives from else-where to solve the riddle of the Sphinx and save Thebes (temporarily) with his wise leadership. In *The Statesman*, it is the Eleatic Stranger who teaches us how to know the true statesman. In *The Republic*, the founding dialogue of political theory's interminable debate about jus-tice takes place in the house of a foreign merchant, Cephalus, who is originally from Syracuse. Why is this the setting? Does Plato mean to imply that justice, or perhaps philosophical dialogue itself, is occa-sioned by engagement with foreignness?[8] Later in *The Republic*, Plato has Socrates say casually that the myth of the metals, the Republic's founding myth, is a "Phoenician thing," not unfamiliar and yet of foreign origin. In the *Social Contract*, Jean-Jacques Rousseau's lawgiver comes from elsewhere to found an ideal democracy. And in the contemporary United States, a variety of American institutions and values, from capitalism to community to family to the consenting liberal individual, are seen to be periodically reinvigorated by that country's newest comers, its idealized citizens: naturalizing immigrants. Again and again, the cure for corruption, withdrawal, and alienation is . . . aliens.

This finding invites us to switch the question that has long dominated our thinking about foreignness. Rather than *"How should we solve the problem of foreignness?"* and "What should 'we' do about 'them'?" (questions that never put the "we" into question and this, surely, is part of their point and attraction), the question that animates this book is: *What problems does foreignness solve for us?* Why do nations or democracies rely on the agency of foreignness at their vulnerable moments of (re)founding, at what cost, and for what purpose?

As we will see in the chapters that follow, foreign-founder scripts use foreignness in a dazzling variety of ways: the foreign-founder may be a way of marking the novelty that is necessarily a feature of any (re)-founding. The same mythic figure may be a way of illustrating a psychological insight that stale or corrupt patterns cannot be broken without the injection of something new. The novelties of foreignness, the mysteries of strangeness, the perspective of an outsider may represent the departure or disruption that is necessary for change.[9] The foreignness of the founder might also be a way of marking and solving a perennial problem of democratic founding in which the people must be equal under the law and cannot therefore receive it from any one of their own number. Some theorists, such as Julia Kristeva, speculate that stories of foreign-founders are a culture's way of marking its inextricable relation to otherness, its strangeness to itself. Finally, the foreignness of the foreign-founder might be a way of modeling the impartiality, breadth of vision, objectivity, and insight that a founder must have. Who but an outsider could be trusted to see beyond the established lines of conflict and division that make shared governance difficult?[10]

Some might argue that none of these hypotheses is really needed because the reason we tell stories of foreign-founding is quite simply that they are true. For example, in answer to the question: "Isn't it curious that some stories of founding feature a foreign-founder?" they might say: "Not really. Or at least not necessarily. After all, some origin stories feature foreign-founders because some peoples really were founded by a foreigner. Take Russia, for example."[11] They might then go on to detail the events that led up to the A.D. 862 invitation by quarreling Slavic tribes to the Varangian Rus': "Our whole land is great and rich, but there is no order in it. Come to rule and reign over us!"[12]

But can the facts of a foreign-founding story decide the question of its meaning and power? The facts do not explain why the story is retold and recirculated, nor to what effect. The truth and meaning of Russia's origin story have, for example, been heatedly debated for centuries. Historiographers date the inauguration of the debate to September 6, 1749, the day Gerhard Friedrich Müller gave a lecture on the origins of Russia to members of the Imperial Academy. Omeljan Pritsak captures what must have been a dramatic scene: "Müller never finished his lecture. As he spoke, tumult arose among the Russian members and 'adjuncts' of the Imperial Academy in protest against the 'infamous' words they were hearing." Müller was charged with dishonoring the nation, and a special committee was appointed "to investigate whether Müller's writings were harmful to the interests and glory of the Russian Empire." The result? "Müller was forbidden to continue his research in Old Rus' history, and his publications were confiscated and destroyed. The intimidated scholar eventually redirected his scholarly work to a less incendiary subject: the history of Siberia."[13]

This academic exile to Siberia did not put the matter to rest, however. Following these events, eighteenth and nineteenth-century anti-Normanists denied the foreignness of the Rus', claiming they were really Slavs, not Swedes. One Slavophile even rewrote the founding story: in Khomiakov's long poem, *Vadim*, the foreign Rus' leader, Riurik, is driven out of Novgorod by a good Slav, Vadim. In *The Chronicles*, Vadim is mentioned only in passing, as having led a *failed* resistance to Riurik. But Khomiakov was "one of the leading spokesmen for the Slavophile view of history." For him, Andrew Wachtel explains, "the undesirability of a foreign-born ruler and the need for a native Slavic element to triumph over him becomes clear."[14]

Unsurprisingly, a century earlier, Catherine the Great, herself a foreign ruler of Russia, gave the story a rather different spin, in which the foreign Riurik is an enlightened ruler and in which (in Wachtel's words) "Russian patriotism and national pride are not incompatible with borrowing from the outside."[15] Others insisted on the incompatibility that Catherine tried to minimize, but their agenda was neither nationalist nor xenophobic. Nineteenth-century Normanists such as Vladimir Solovyev affirmed and valorized Russia's foreign-founding because, they argued, it meant that Russia was particularly well positioned for a cosmopolitan or universalist mission.[16]

Pritsak suggests that these debates are ongoing because each side of the argument has its weaknesses. The problem, he says, is a problem of knowledge: "[H]istorians have too often substituted political (or patriotic) issues for improved techniques of historical methodology in their discussions; they have had a limited knowledge of world history; and they have been biased in their use of source materials."[17] It is not clear, however, whether the objective and thorough history that Pritsak calls for could put a quick end to the centuries of to-ing and fro-ing on the question of the Rus'. Do historical facts have that kind of power? Even if the empirical question regarding Riurik's foreignness could be put to rest, the question of his expressive significance as a foreign-founder would still be an open question whose debate would arouse passions and land some unfortunate souls in a Siberia of one kind or another.

Confronted with the fact of Riurik's foreignness, nationalists would undoubtedly engage in a symbolic politics of foreignness: How foreign was he? What does his foreignness mean for Russia? In all likelihood, the fact of Ruirik's foreignness would drive some to argue that Riurik, though really a Scandinavian, was possessed of Slavic features and temperament. Alternatively, scholars might redate what they take to be the beginning of a Slavic people, so that Riurik would be removed from his position of central importance in the Slavs' origin story. In short, the questions raised by the foreignness of the founder are not, *pace* Pritsak, empirically soluble; they are symbolic questions. Similarly, in contemporary debates about immigration, the facts can inform but they cannot resolve the question of whether immigrants are good or bad for the nation because the question is not, at bottom, an empirical question. The question of why the founder (or the refounder) is a foreigner points not to the origins of the origin story in question, but rather to the daily workings of that story in the life of a regime.[18]

Similarly, when I ask why a (re)founder is a foreigner, I am asking not "Where does he or she come from and why?" but rather "What symbolic work is the story of foreign-(re)founding doing for the regime in question?"[19] Of what practices and programs of renationalization and legitimation are the symbolic politics of foreignness a part? And, in the cases of *democracy's* foreign-(re)founders in particular: Is foreignness a site at which certain anxieties of *democratic* self-rule are managed? At bottom, these questions are not about foreignness per se, but about the work that foreignness does, the many ways in which it operates as a way to frame other issues of democratic theory and citizenship.[20] The answers to these questions vary in relation to different texts and contexts.

In Chapter Two, where I read Rousseau's *Social Contract* together with Freud's *Moses and Monotheism* and Girard's *Violence and the Sacred*, I find that the figure of the foreign-founder may be a way of managing some paradoxes of democratic founding, such as the alienness of the law, an especially charged problem in democratic regimes. In Chapter Three, the foreignness of Ruth is what enables her to supply the Israelites with a refurbishment they periodically need: she chooses them in a way that only a foreigner can (and the more foreign the better) and thereby re-marks them as the Chosen People. She also domesticates by way of her apparently freely felt love for the law the alien and violently imposed law that Moses brought to the Israelites from the mountain. In Chapter Four, I trace how foreignness works, in the American exceptionalist literature, contradictorily and simultaneously to reinstill popular but always shaky beliefs in a meritocratic economy, heartfelt community, patriarchal family structures, and a consent-producing liberal individualism, all of which undergird the sense of choiceworthiness that immigrants are positioned and required to enact for the United States. Immigrants' new membership in the United States is not only celebrated, it is also endorsed as iconic of good citizenship, with problematic consequences for the native born and for all would-be democratic citizens.

All of these uses of foreignness are double edged, however. Foreignness operates in each instance as both support of and threat to the regime in question. Moses' foreignness and that of Rousseau's lawgiver, the biblical Ruth, and America's immigrants do not only solve certain problems. In each case, their foreignness is itself a problem for the regimes that seek to benefit from its supplement. What I find, therefore, and what I call attention to in each of the chapters below, is what we just saw at work in the case of Russia's origin story: a *politics* of foreignness in which different parties to the debate try to mobilize a founder's foreignness on behalf of their ideal, while also striving somehow to solve or manage the problem of the founder's foreignness.

The cultural organization of foreignness as threat and/or supplement is not exhausted by the types of foreignness examined here. To the foreigner as founder, immigrant, and citizen, one could add other categories—the foreigner as refugee, boundary crosser, terrorist, outlaw, repository of irrationality, erotic excess, madness, anarchy, and so on. But my goal is not to offer a complete catalog of the symbolic figurations of foreignness. Instead, my goal is to study in depth some of the uses to which foreignness is daily put on behalf of democracy. Since democracy is still thought of in predominantly national terms, this means we must look not only at texts of democratic theory in which foreignness figures, but also (as in Chapter Three on the Book of Ruth) at texts in which foreignness is put to work on behalf of national or subnational communities. Since much of the contemporary democratic theory literature theorizes democracy as a form of liberalism, we must look also at texts in liberal theory that use foreignness to shore up specifically liberal institutions and values such as consent (as in Chapter Four, when I discuss Peter Schuck's and Rogers Smith's part in American immigration debates).

It is worth mentioning here, however, that one counterimage of foreignness does keep surfacing in each of the chapters: that of the *taking* foreigner. This taking is not the criminal activity of an outsider (though it is not immune to such depictions) but an honorific democratic practice—that of demanding or, better yet, simply enacting the redistribution of those powers, rights, and privileges that define a community and order it hierarchically. Here the iconic taking foreigner puts foreignness to work on behalf of democracy by modeling forms of agency that are transgressive, but (or therefore) possessed of potentially inaugural powers. Carried by the agencies of foreignness, this revalued "taking" stretches the boundaries of citizenship and seems to imply or call for a rethinking of democracy as also a cosmopolitan and not just a nation-centered set of solidarities, practices, and institutions. One might object that such a move to locate democracy also on cosmopolitan registers itself amounts to a "use" of foreignness on behalf of a political aspiration. The point cannot be denied. But the hope is that this particular use might better serve the needs of democracy than the mostly nation-centered alternatives whose promises and insufficiencies I track in the chapters that follow.

In Chapter Five, I raise the issue of genre, which provides one way of understanding why political theorists have not heretofore attended to the politics of foreignness as I cast them here. Most readers of democratic theory tend to bring certain romantic genre expectations to texts, often treating the narrative as a series of arguments intended to bring about a reconciliation, a happy (or at least resigned) marriage between a people and their law or institutions. In Chapter Five, I ask: What if we read democratic theory gothically instead of romantically? Gothic novels depend on the reader's uncertainty as to whether the heroine's would-be lover is really a hero or a villain. Similarly, a gothic approach to democratic theory presses us to attend to the people's perpetual uncertainty about the law and their relation to it: Is it really part of us or an alien thing, an expression of our intimate will or a violent imposition? That gothics tend to represent and deepen our uncertainty about the hero by making him a foreigner, and the setting a foreign (often a Catholic) place only adds to the appositeness of this genre to democratic theory, in which anxieties about empirical foreigners and (in more abstract terms) the alienness of the law are always at work, even if seldom in a way that is noted by many scholars.

Another genre choice also shapes this book. What unites texts as disparate as Rousseau's *Social Contract*, Freud's *Moses and Monotheism*, the biblical Book of Ruth, Michael Walzer's *What It Means to Be an American*, and Schuck and Smith's *Citizenship without Consent: Illegal Aliens in the Polity* with one another and with the various films I discuss as well, including *The Wizard of Oz*, *Strictly Ballroom*, and *Shane*, is that all are—whatever else they may be—*myths of foreign-(re)founding*.[21] Reading them as such makes certain salient but heretofore relatively unnoticed characteristics of the texts rise to the surface, while others, though perhaps more often noted, recede into the background.

For example, the Book of Ruth is usually read as a conversion story, so Ruth is often compared to Abraham, the first convert to Judaism.

Reading Ruth as a myth of foreign-founding invites a comparison instead to Moses, the possibly foreign lawgiver who formed the tribes of Israel into a people of the law. That new comparison calls attention to the fact that Moses died in the land where Ruth was born: Moab. Suddenly, it seems possible that one of the many effects of this great short story is its implication that the law may be reborn as a woman, that one of Ruth's many functions may be to rescript our affective relation to the law from a relation of violent imposition or awe to one of loving devotion, from the sublime to the beautiful.[22] The justification for reading Ruth as a myth of foreign-founding is that she is, indeed, the agent of a (re)founding. Her virtuous example returns the Israelites from a period of corruption to devotion to the one true God. Through her son, Obed, she inaugurates the monarchic line of David.

My analysis of foreign-founder scripts is motivated by several goals. It is not my intention to make a general claim about the necessity of stories of foreign-founding to successful refoundings, nor, indeed, to recommend the telling of such stories. Not all regimes tell such stories, and those that do retell them with varying frequencies and intensities. I aim merely to ask what sort of work is done by such stories where they do exist. The genre is a curious one and seems to beg for some sort of explanation. Why do regimes tell stories of themselves in which they are depicted as dependent upon the kindness of strangers? What effect might such stories have on the democratic aspirations of a regime? Aren't democracies particularly threatened by such accounts, given the still widely held belief that democracy presupposes and requires social unity?

Second, entering into the interpretative fray over the significance of myths of foreign-founding is a way to vie for the political-cultural capital that such stories offer the interpreters that claim them. One of the most interesting things to come out of this study is the fact that foreignness in and of itself is neither a cosmopolitan nor a nationalist resource. A foreign-founder is not, as such, an obstacle to a national project. Nationalists find in the figure a vehicle of renationalization. Cosmopolitans find in it a resource for denationalization. Since the symbolic powers of foreignness are capacious enough to be mobilized by both sides, those who would like to expand the reach of democracy beyond the nation's borders must enter the interpretive fray and not just count on the facts of foreignness to do the world-building work of politics.[23]

Third, this genre, in which foreignness does positive work (even if not *only* positive work) for a regime, might be a useful resource for those who would like to address tendencies to xenophobia that are part and parcel of modern democratic life. But how? Will attending to the iconic foreign founder open up democracies to the foreignness we now encounter, not for the first time, as part of the processes of globalization and migration? Maybe, but as I argue in Chapter Three contra Julia Kristeva, such an awareness all by itself is not a sufficient condition of generating a more open and magnanimous democratic politics. In truth, it may not even be a necessary condition. There is no logic that requires that relatively homogeneous societies are less tolerant than relatively heterogeneous ones, and there is no empirical evidence to support such a claim, either. If the foreign-founder helps us to combat xenophobia, it is by inviting us to see how a fraught relationship to foreignness may be generated or fed by certain needs and demands of democracy itself (in different ways in its various settings, theorizations, and practices) rather than, say, stemming exclusively from deep psychological needs or from separate, independent tendencies to nativism or xenophobia.

With this last phrase, I take issue with Rogers Smith's argument in *Civic Ideals*. In that book, Smith advances what he calls a "multiple traditions thesis" according to which the United States is not—contra Alexis de Tocqueville, Louis Hartz, and other American exceptionalists—a purely or essentially liberal democratic regime. Instead (as evidenced by its citizenship laws, whose history Smith traces in detail), the United States is a regime constituted by many competing, incompatible, sometimes cooperating ideologies such as liberalism, republicanism, racism, patriarchalism, and nativism. Liberalism and republicanism are, according to Smith, egalitarian, while the other traditions are ascriptive. This pluralization of America's ideological base allows Smith to argue against critics of American liberalism, and also against critics of liberal theory more generally, that the shortcomings of liberal theory and practice do not stem from liberalism per se. The admirable moments of progress, liberation, and justice that punctuate American history are attributable to its liberal or republican commitments, on Smith's account, and America's less fine moments can be traced to its ascriptive traditions.[24]

What is striking about Smith's reading of American liberalism is that its structure replicates the very mode of thinking that the author seeks to criticize. Out to discredit "ascriptive mythologies that can easily become demonologies," Smith produces an argument that is itself demonological in structure. The many violent crimes and injustices that mark American national history are not essential to its character as a partly liberal democratic regime. Those violences come from elsewhere, from other parts of the American polity. Ascriptive ideologies distinct from liberalism are responsible for the nativist, sexist, and racist citizenship laws and arguments catalogued by Smith. Thus, liberalism is insulated from implication in the unsavory elements of American political history. The real culprits, those other "traditions," are set up as Girardian scapegoats. Made into the bearers of all that liberalism seeks to disavow, they can now be cast out of the polity, which is then (re-)unified around this purging of its pollutants.[25] That is to say, they are rendered foreign to the would-be, still-hoped-for, liberal democratic body politic.[26]

My point is not that, contra Smith, liberalism is in fact the real culprit, after all. What evidence could decide *that*? On the contrary, my point is that setting the problem up as a search for the single, causal culprit is misguided.[27] Rather than join this argument, pro or contra, I want to point out how Smith's multiple-traditions thesis works to direct our critical scrutiny away from the object being defended (in this case, liberal values and institutions), while encouraging a demonizing attitude toward the objects of critique (in this case, more explicitly ascriptive forms of life).[28] The foreign-founder invites us to set the problem up differently. Because the figure puts foreignness at the center of some democracies' daily (re)foundings, the foreign-founder presses us to look beyond xenophobic beliefs to explain xenophobic politics. What if such politics are *also* driven by pressures that come from within democracy itself, as it is variously practiced and theorized?

By inviting us to switch the question—from "How should we solve the problem of foreignness?" to "What problems does foreignness solve for us?"—the foreign-founder gives us a more promising way to proceed in our efforts to study the diverse, intimate relations between liberal democracy and its would-be others. Such an alternative analysis shows how certain anxieties endemic to liberal democracy—the paradox of democratic power (given up just as it might have been gained), the alienness of the law, the lack of a sense of choiceworthiness or the periodic need to have that sense refurbished, the distance or inaccessibility of consent—themselves generate or feed an ambivalence that is then projected onto the screen of foreignness. This ambivalence is testified to by Rousseau's curiously foreign lawgiver who is both loved and feared by the people he founds.

The iconic foreign-founder also presses us to ask whether democracy, in its origins and daily refoundings, may presuppose not only the reconstruction of the national (as theorists such as Smith, Beiner, Miller, and others assume) but also the violation of the national.[29] To counteract the still deep-going assumption that democracy is necessarily a national form, I refer occasionally in the pages that follow to an alternative conception of democracy: democratic cosmopolitanism. Nationalists often resort to the specter of an international government in order to discount cosmopolitanism and reprivilege the state as the center of any future democratic politics.[30] But democracy is not just a set of governing institutions.[31] It is also a commitment to generate actions in concert that exceed the institutional conditions that both enable and limit popular agencies.

At their most successful (as with some international human rights, labor, and environmental organizations), such actions in concert open up and even institutionalize spaces of public power, action, and discourse that did not exist before. In short, democratic cosmopolitanism is a name for forms of internationalism that seek not to govern, per se, but rather to widen the resources, energies, and accountability of an emerging international civil society that contests or supports state actions in matters of transnational and local interest such as environmental, economic, military, cultural, and social policies.[32] This is a democratic cosmopolitanism because democracy, in the sense of a commitment to local and popular empowerment, effective representation, accountability, and the generation of actions in concert across lines of difference, is its goal. In that sense it is also a rooted cosmopolitanism, rooted not (contra a range of cosmopolitans from Julia Kristeva to David Hollinger) in a national ideal but rather in a democratic ideal, one that seeks out friends and partners even (or especially) among strangers and foreigners.

Jean-Jacques Rousseau, himself the great theorist of democracy as a national form, makes a surprising gesture in this direction when he refs in passing to the apparent doubles of his domestic foreign-founder, the "few great cosmopolitan souls" who are the last remaining persons in the modern world to be moved by the pity and the natural goodness characteristic of the Rousseauvian state of nature:

> The law of nature no longer operated except between the various societies, where under the name of the law of nations, it was tempered by some tacit conventions in order to make intercourse possible and to take the place of natural commiseration which, losing between one society and another nearly all the force it had between one man and another, no longer dwells in any but *a few great cosmopolitan souls*, who surmount the imaginary barriers that separate peoples and who, following the example of the sovereign Being who created them, include the whole human race in their benevolence.[33]

The analysis developed here of the intricate relations between democracy and foreignness just might open up more room for the admirable impulses personified by Rousseau's few great cosmopolitan souls and today enacted by such admirable groups as Médecins du Monde. But I am motivated most centrally by a more humble and academic desire. How shall we understand the following puzzles? The texts that I read, from the *Wizard of Oz* to *Shane*, from Rousseau's *Social Contract* to the Hebrew Bible and American liberal and democratic theory all suggest in one way or another, that democratic citizens (not the Bible's original audience, but definitely Moses' and Ruth's contemporary readers), are often threatened and supported by dreams of a foreigner who might one day come to save us and enable us finally to abdicate or perhaps reassume the abundant responsibilities of democracy. Why? Why do these fears and hopes take shape through the figure of a foreigner? And what can that foreigner, the iconic foreign-founder, teach us about the insufficiencies, challenges, dramas, and dreams of democracy?

> What good is a legend to a people that makes
> their hero into an alien?
> – *Sigmund Freud*

2 THE FOREIGNER AS FOUNDER

Dorothy and the Wizard

In a book about *The Wizard of Oz*, Salman Rushdie offers a fresh reading of that canonical American film as a tale not of home yearning—
the conventional reading—but of adventurism. Rushdie's Dorothy is an
eager émigrée, anxious to be off and away from the stultifying gray of
her Kansas home.[1] Boredom and colorlessness (but also a certain felt
neglect at the hands of her Aunt Em and Uncle Henry ["Not now, Dorothy!"]) prepare the way for Dorothy's eventual home leaving. But injustice and felt powerlessness provide the final push. Dorothy finally
leaves because her aunt and uncle bend helplessly before the force of
a law that serves the wealthy, powerful Miss Gulch, allowing her to

take away Dorothy's dog, Toto. Home is not only an uninteresting place, Rushdie rightly stresses, it is also unsafe, unfair, and unjust.[2]

But Dorothy is not only an adventurous émigrée.[3] She is also (both wittingly and unwittingly) the vehicle of a welcome regime change. The injustice and unfairness that marked the Kansas home from which Dorothy fled in frustration are no less present in Oz. And the well-intentioned are for the most part as ineffective in Oz as they were in Kansas. The peoples of Oz and its environs are far removed from democratic self-governance. Dwarfed by arbitrary and unaccountable power, the Munchkins suffer deeply under the tyranny of the Wicked Witches of the East and West, against which the curtained, bureaucratic rule of the Wizard is no match. They are left dependent for occasional unpredictable salvation upon good witches with limited powers. Dorothy, the émigrée, the stranger, the foreigner who arrives inexplicably from elsewhere, becomes the vehicle of Oz's peoples' reempowerment. She kills two ruthless witches and unmasks the well-meaning but distantly inept and fraudulent Wizard, whose departure she also occasions. Her final gift to the peoples of Oz is her own departure.

The conventional view of the *Wizard of Oz* sees Dorothy's departure as a testimony to the value of home which, complicated as it is, never stops tugging at Dorothy's heartstrings. This is the reading Salman Rushdie is out to offset. But Dorothy's departure acts out another quite different script at the same time, that of the foreign-founder, a figure that pops up repeatedly in Western culture, high and low. It is by virtue of her power as a stranger and a naive that Dorothy can do what no native of Oz would dare to. Unsocialized by the reign of terror that has molded the locals into servile abjection, Dorothy topples the forces of corruption and alienation. Then, to top that off, she leaves the people to sort out the terms of their own self-governance. Rather than stay to rule this grateful population, she leaves them under the loose charge of the Scarecrow, Tin Man, and Lion, three characters who represent the virtues necessary for successful self-rule: brains, heart, and courage.[4]

Dorothy does not turn the local population's debt to her into an opportunity for domination.[5] The Wizard in his day did just that, and the consequence was the alienating governance whose weaknesses and blowhard corruptions made Dorothy's adventure so necessary for Oz. Between them, then, the Wizard and Dorothy may be seen to represent two sorts of foreign-founder and the uncertainty of the gifts they bear for the regimes they (re)found.

But what about the peoples whose founding is at stake? We can learn more about them by contrasting Dorothy's fantasy and its fulfillment in Oz with the peoples of Oz's fantasy and its fulfillment by Dorothy. In Oz, Dorothy is big rather than little, she has power (represented by the ruby slippers), and she is looked up to and worshiped rather than ignored. Hers is a child's fantasy of being as important and powerful as a grown-up, and the mostly diminutive peoples of Oz (even the Wizard is short) satisfy her longing.[6] For their part, the various peoples of Oz and its environs (from the Munchkins to the enslaved soldiers of the Wicked Witch of the West) are likely moved by a rescue fantasy. They are infantilized and, although they dream of being liberated, their dream includes the fantasy of being relieved of the adult responsibilities they have thus far failed to live up to. Dorothy, this magical foreigner who fell like manna from the sky, does their dirty work for them.

The two fantasies meet on common ground: in both, the local peoples are infantilized. Like good Tocquevillians, they belong to many leagues and civic associations, and they have a lot of offices (as well as some officiousness: recall the comic scene in which the Munchkins insist that the death of the Wicked Witch of the East must be legally, officially, verifiably certified—"Is she really most sincerely dead?"). But the Munchkins take no democratic responsibility for freeing themselves from the forces that dominate their lives. What does this mean for their political future? How likely are they to take up the democratic self-governance that could follow in the wake of Dorothy's rescue of them and her timely departure?

The people's paradoxical dependence upon a founder at what could be the very moment of their assumption of democratic power and responsibility is a deep and knotty problem in the history of political thought and culture. By what magic are dependent, not yet fully formed followers supposed to become the responsible, active citizens that democracy requires? The problem is crystallized at the moment of founding, but it recurs daily in a regime as new members enter fully into citizenship (whether by reaching adulthood or crossing the border to resettle) and as established citizens are renormalized into accepted expectations of belonging. Might the figure of the *foreign*-founder, who appears not just in such popular-culture texts as *The Wizard of Oz* but also in such high-culture texts as the Hebrew Bible, Rousseau's *Social Contract*, and Freud's *Moses and Monotheism*, be a way of working through this and other problems that plague democratic political culture?[7]

Rousseau's Lawgiver

"What good is a legend to a people that makes their hero into an alien?" asks Sigmund Freud in *Moses and Monotheism*, the book in which he unmasks Moses as a foreigner (make that two foreigners).[8] A legend that makes a people's hero into an alien is no good at all—this is the implied answer to Freud's rhetorical question. But what if we suppose otherwise? Might the foreign-founder's foreignness be, perhaps, a necessary condition of his performance of his founding functions?

The lawgiver of Rousseau's *Social Contract* is a foreign-founder. This foreign-founder's seldom-noted figuration of foreignness at the heart of Rousseau's ideal democracy invites us to ask whether democracy itself—at its origins and in its daily refoundings—might require not just the (re)construction of the national (in order, say, to broaden the sympathies of the masses for one another, as Benedict Anderson might argue), but also the violation of the national. In contrast to neo-Rousseauvians like David Miller, who argue that democracy depends upon socionational unity, Rousseau's foreign-founder invites us to ask whether democracy might not also presuppose and require some deep relation to foreignness.[9] Is there some deep connection between democracy and foreignness? If so, the figure of the foreign-founder might serve as a political-cultural resource for those seeking to open up the reach of democracy in late modernity, to multiply affinities with others both here, in the temporal space of the nation-state, and elsewhere.

When Rousseau introduces a foreign-founder to the *Social Contract*, he reiterates a classic script familiar to readers of founding myths from Greece to Rome to the Hebrew Bible. But Rousseau's reliance on a foreign-founder is particularly curious given the xenophobia for which he is otherwise quite famous, and given his belief that a legitimate regime, a regime in which the people are sovereign, presupposes and requires social unity. So what is a theorist of socionational unity, like Rousseau, doing relying on a *foreign*-founder?

Moreover, why would a radical democrat like Rousseau turn to a lawgiver at all? Why not allow a people to constitute itself, as such? What problems of founding are managed by the introduction of a founder? What problems of founding are managed by way of the founder's foreignness? Are there any problems of democracy, in particular, that are being worked through, symbolically, by way of the device of foreignness? And why doesn't Rousseau, for whom social unity was a most important goal, worry that the introduction of a foreigner into his ideal polity might undermine rather than animate his experiment in radical democracy?

Rousseau comes to perceive the need for a lawgiver when he considers for the first time, in Book II, Chapter 3, of the *Social Contract*, the possibility that the General Will can err. Although he insists that the General Will as such cannot err (if it erred, it would simply not be the General Will), Rousseau's consideration of the possibility opens up a troublesome gap between the people doing the willing, and the General Will that is supposed to be the effect (but also the cause) of their willing.

"[T]he general will is always right and always tends toward the public utility. However, it does not follow that the deliberations of the people always have the same rectitude" (ibid., p. 155). Here Rousseau evidences an anxiety that plagues most radical democrats who agitate to give the people power. Popular sovereignty is supposed to *solve* the problems of (il)legitimacy and arbitrariness. But once the people have power, that "solution" suddenly looks like a problem, for the people, too, can be a source of arbitrariness. The rhetorical dynamic goes something like this: "We need to give the people power! The people must have power! Omigod, the people have power! What are they *going to do* with it?"

Rousseau tries to maintain his faith in the people even under the pressure of his anxiety—"the populace is never corrupted, but it is often tricked"—but he cannot finally fend off the concern that the people, upon whose will the legitimacy of the regime is supposed to rest, will not necessarily exercise their will in the *right* way.[10] At the same time, Rousseau seems both to trust in the ability of ideal circumstances to secure a mutual transparency for the populace (necessary for the emergence of a General Will that can be known as such), and to despair of ever overcoming the stubborn opacity and mutual strangeness that mark human relations even under ideal circumstances. When under the sway of the former assumption, Rousseau characterizes the process of general willing as a process of public deliberation and debate. But under the sway of the latter assumption, responding to the conditions of mutual opacity and mistrust, Rousseau insists that discussion will only fan the flames of factionalism, and concludes that the General Will will be produced, if at all, only by way of silent introspection (Book IV, Chapter 2).

Either way, Rousseau does not believe that the people can be the solution to arbitrary, illegitimate, and coercive rule without also becoming a problem that rules or laws must solve.[11] You cannot have good laws without good people, and you cannot have good people without good laws, he says as he presents the problem as a problem of founding (though in fact it recurs daily as subjects are [re]socialized into citizenship): "For an emerging people to be capable of appreciating the sound maxims of politics and to follow the fundamental rules of statecraft, the effect would have to become the cause. The social spirit which ought to be the work of that institution, would have to preside over the institution itself. And men would be, prior to the advent of laws, what they ought to become by means of laws" (Book II, Chapter 7, p. 164). A *deus ex machina* is necessary to solve the problem, and this *deus ex machina* arrives in the figure of the founder, a good person prior to good law, a miraculous lawgiver.[12]

From what Rousseau says about the founder, others have concluded that he must be a god, a divinity. Indeed, Rousseau himself seems to say as much:

> The discovery of the best rules of society would require a superior intelligence, who saw all of men's passions yet experienced none of them; who had no relationship at all to our nature yet knew it thoroughly: whose happiness was independent of us, yet who was nevertheless willing to attend to ours; finally one who, preparing for himself a future glory with the passage of time, could work in one century and enjoy the reward in another. Gods would be needed to give men laws. (Ibid.)

But Rousseau does not himself depend upon gods. He goes on to give a great deal of advice to the "one who dares to undertake the founding of a people" and it is here that he mentions, as did Aristotle before him, that "it was the custom of most Greek towns to entrust the establishment of their laws to foreigners."[13] Rousseau adds to Aristotle's list, noting that "the Republics of modern Italy in many cases followed this example; Geneva did the same [here Rousseau is thinking of Calvin as a founder] and profited by it."[14]

Rousseau's mention of famous foreign-founders at this crucial point in his text suggests that he sees foreignness as a way to manage some of the challenges that face a founder: Who besides a god or a godlike man would be able to discover the best rules for a society, see all of men's passions yet experience none of them; have no relationship at all to our nature yet know it thoroughly and, perhaps most important of all, have a happiness that is independent of us? These characteristics might be found only in a man of perfect virtue. But they—or something enough like them—might just as well attach themselves to a foreigner.[15] Someone who comes from somewhere else is familiar with human nature, intrigue, and ambition but is not himself captivated by the particular intrigues at work here, in this new place, in which he has no investment or history. A foreign-founder's foreignness secures for him the distance and impartiality needed to animate and guarantee a General Will that can neither animate nor guarantee itself.[16] Moreover, because he is not one of the people, his lawgiving does not disturb the equality of the people before the law. And finally, his foreignness may well add to his charms and enhance his leadership. No known genealogy demystifies his charismatic authority.[17]

But this solution comes at a price, particularly for a democratic founding. The lawgiver leads the citizens to a legitimate set of arrangements, but he also positions citizens in a relation of heteronomy that is deeply at odds with Rousseauvian legitimacy. As Alan Keenan puts it, "Rousseau's recourse to the legislator" is "surprising, even farfetched," because it appears "in a text devoted to laying the foundations of popular autonomy."[18]

The problem is not unique to Rousseau's democratic ideal. The dependence of weak, dependent, democratic citizens upon strong, heroic, independent strangers is played out repeatedly in American popular culture as well, most noticeably and ritually in movie Westerns. As in one classic of the genre, *Shane*, a heroic stranger arrives from elsewhere to save a weak town from powerful and corrupt bandits.[19] (In *Shane*, these bandits are led by a man named Riker.) The hero saves the town through the sheer power of his exemplary if flawed personality, innate sense of justice, and his mighty prowess with firearms. By the film's end, the sources of corruption have been excised (Shane kills Riker), and the townspeople are restored to virtue and reempowered for self-governance. Although the people usually beg him to stay (sometimes with no small degree of trepidation), the hero moves on when his (re)founding work is done.[20] In *Shane*, the hero explains that he cannot stay because murder never goes away.

Similarly, in Rousseau's *Social Contract*, the founder leaves after founding the polity. There is no provision for the office of legislator in Rousseau's *Social Contract*. "This function, which constitutes the republic, does not enter into its constitution." The relief experienced by the locals when the foreign-founder, whom they may well have begged to stay, decides rather to leave recalls the "terror" which, according to Jacques Derrida, attends the eternal waiting for the Messiah: "Who has ever been sure that the expectation of the Messiah is not, from the start, by destination and invincibly, a fear, an unbearable terror—hence the hatred of what is thus awaited?"[21]

If the fortuitous arrival of the foreign-founder seems too good to be true, his timely departure seems almost beyond belief.[22] This timely departure is one of the conveniences of the classic foreign-founder script, and it is necessary for several reasons. The energies of the foreign-founder, so valuable and much-needed in a time of (re)founding, are threats to established regimes. In the case of Shane, the very mysteriousness, individuality, audacity, charisma, passion, violence, and power that enable him to save the town he passes through also make him dangerous to the community on a daily basis. The violence he used to excise the town's oppressors was indispensable to the fragile community, but that same community, still grateful, is now endangered by the continued presence of that violence in its midst.

Shane's threat to the restoration of the ordinary is figured as a threat to the nuclear family at the film's center. The wife-mother is attracted to Shane, and the son clearly prefers the stranger to his own father, who is less manly, more human-all-too-human, than the visiting hero. As long as Shane stays in town, life cannot be restored to its routine hetero-normative safeties.

A distinctively republican perspective on the matter is articulated by Abraham Lincoln, who notes that the same men who are great founders in extraordinary times are fated to be criminals in ordinary times. From a republican perspective, the danger posed by would-be founders stems not so much from their individuality, per se, as from their great-ness and ambition, which can be boundless. "[M]en of ambition and talents . . . naturally seek the gratification of their ruling passion."[23] However, this particular republican concern is not evident in *Shane* nor in the other foreign-founder texts examined here, and this raises a question about what exactly this founder "ambition" is supposed to signify. Is the problem always with the founder, as the republican ac-count seems to suggest? Or is it possible that what gets characterized as a founder's ambition is in fact (also) a projection of the people's own (illicit and therefore denied) desire to submit in a very nonrepublican way to the will of the inspiring and charismatic founder rather than to the law he founds?

Either way, whether it is he himself who desires to rule or the people themselves who desire to be ruled over, the lawgiver must leave. Rous-seau's lawgiver must leave not so much because he represents a danger to the community (as in the case of the stranger of the classic Westerns), but because the people must at some point be left to their own devices. This is supposed to be a democratic people. Law and order may be put (back) into place by way of the founder's agency, but the regime now depends upon his departure (and, indeed, upon his disappearance, lest he develop a posthumous cult following. This is the significance of the fact that, as Harold Bloom points out, "No one knows [Moses'] burial place to this day").[24] The founder must leave (or, as in the worthy exam-ple of Lycurgus, he must abdicate),[25] and he must not return. In Rous-seau's *Social Contract*, the lawgiver's foreignness may even function to reassure the people that he really will leave when his time comes. Why should he stay? He has no ties to this place.

But there is surely something too neat about this script. Can the for-eignness of the founder only serve the regime well and not also unsettle or disturb it at the same time? The foreignness of Rousseau's lawgiver may stand for his ability to—it may even even enable him to—found wisely, but wouldn't that same foreignness also make him (and perhaps also his law) a threat to the social unity that is a necessary condition of Rousseauvian democracy?

Rousseau's assumption of a timely departure is problematic at the level of theory because it seeks to prevent the foreignness of the founder from ever becoming a problem for the regime that profits from it. A greater sensitivity to the dilemmas of the foreign-founder's position and the limited efficacy of timely departures is exhibited by Yasushi Akashi who, as U.N. Special Representative to Cambodia, was himself a kind of foreign-founder. Akashi's job was to enter into the "wreckage of [a country] trying to start over after civil wars" and provide ways out of political impasses that warring parties could not resolve for themselves. Responding to criticisms that he ought to have been more zealous in "razing Cambodia's Communist-dominated government departments to clear space for more democratic institutions," Akashi explained that during his tenure in Cambodia a certain foreign-founder from America was always at the back of his mind: Douglas MacArthur. The MacArthur-led American postwar occupation of Japan was "enlightened and generous and liberal," Akashi said. "But some of the democratic policies were changed, some even abolished by subsequent, more conservative, Japanese governments—not because they were opposed to the policies, but because they were given to us by foreigners."[26] For Akashi, the foreign-founder is a radically undecidable figure. His foreignness may benefit the regime he (re)founds, but it is also a threat to the regime at the same time.[27]

The biblical Moses, one of three lawgivers most admired by Rousseau, was also a foreign-founder, and he, too, was marked by this undecidability.[28] Raised in Pharaoh's household, Moses was thought initially to be an Egyptian. True, Exodus explains that Moses was really an Israelite, abandoned by his mother in the hope that he might escape the death sentence decreed for male Israelite infants. But even if Moses' origins can be so neatly purified by genetic fiat, it remains the case that he was brought up as an Egyptian, not an Israelite. He must have spoken differently from the people he ultimately led. (Freud suggests that Moses' famous stammer, his "heavy tongue," might not be a simple "historical truth" but rather a way of recalling, in "slightly distorted" form, "the fact that Moses spoke another language.")[29] Moses must have carried himself in a foreign way. This may have enabled him better to represent the Israelites to Pharaoh, who had until recently been a member of Moses' family, after all.[30] And Moses' foreignness may have contributed to the Israelites' willingness to be led by him. After generations of slavery, how could the Israelites not think that an Egyptian accent, bearing, and affect bespoke authority and perhaps even superiority? Surely, following the lead of an Egyptian was established habit by now.

But that same foreignness, so enabling to Moses' leadership, must also have attenuated Moses' relation to the Israelites. Indeed, it may well be that it was only Moses' timely death, before the Israelites entered the Promised Land, that prevented these awkward questions about membership and identity from coming up for a real interrogation. "Is Moses really one of us, or not?" the Israelites might well have asked once settled in the Promised Land. Either way, Moses would have been in trouble, of course. As a mere member of the people, his power to found them and give them the law might have been undone. As an alien, he and perhaps even his law might have had to have been immediately ejected from the Israelites' midst.

Rousseau never confronts the problems that might be posed by the lawgiver's foreignness and its undecidability. His assumption of a timely departure allows him to avoid the issue, and he never asks about the effects the founder's foreignness might have on a regime even long after the founder's departure. Nor does Rousseau inquire into the particular circumstances of the lawgiver's departure. Does he jump, or is he pushed? For a consideration of these issues, we have to turn to Freud, who sees the foreignness of Moses as the object of one of the greatest cover-ups of all time.

Freud's Moses

Notwithstanding Rousseau's idealized version of the foreign-founder script, the founder's foreignness does not only reassure. If the foreign-founder must leave after the work of founding is done, that need stems from the very foreignness that so enables foreign-founders, and not just from their necessary but denied violence, not just from their structurally awkward role as lawgivers in an otherwise egalitarian democracy, and not just from the founders' off-putting personal quirks, ambitions, or vices. Sigmund Freud, in *Moses and Monotheism*, offers a reading of the Moses story in which the foreignness of Moses runs much deeper than in the speculative account I offered above; and, sure enough, in Freud's version, Moses' leadership ends not by natural, if ordained death (as in the official version), but by his murder at the hands of the people he founded.

According to Freud, Moses is "an Egyptian—probably of noble origin—whom the myth undertakes to transform into a Jew" (ibid., p. 13).[31] Beginning by noting that Moses' name is not Hebrew but Egyptian (pp. 4ff), Freud goes on to draw on the structural similarities between his own account of the Family Romance (in which the child, disappointed in his parents but especially in his father, fantasizes that he is adopted and that his real family is one superior to that from which he is presently trying to escape) and Rank's account of exposure myths, in which the hero, such as Cyrus or Romulus, is thought to be of low birth but turns out to be of high birth.[32] In both the Family Romance and the exposure myths, Freud points out, it is the supposedly adoptive family that is the real one; the supposedly real (lost and hoped-for) family is a figment of the individual or cultural imagination. Moses' story reverses the chronology of humble and noble, but it is otherwise structurally similar to these other fantasies and myths.[33] So, Freud concludes, here too the supposedly adoptive family must be the real one; Moses is really a member of Pharaoh's household. Moses is foreign to the people he founds.

Rousseau's foreign lawgiver is guided by his removed judgment when he decides which mores are best suited to a people given their histories, cultures, territory, climate, population size, and other similar considerations. Rousseau assumes that the biblical Moses was similarly guided, attentive to considerations of fit and proportionality when he gave the law to the ancient Israelites.[34] But Freud's Moses is guided by a quite different agenda.

Freud's Egyptian Moses is not primarily interested in looking for the mores that will best fit a group of individuals and help mold them, lastingly, into a people. Instead, Freud's Moses is looking for a people to vivify a moral code bereft of followers, the suppressed religion of Ikhnaton to which he, Moses, remained loyal. An Egyptian follower of Ikhnaton's monotheism, Moses was deeply affected by the Egyptian rebellion against that religion after Ikhnaton's death: "If [Moses] was not to recant the convictions so dear to him, then Egypt had no more to give him; he had lost his native country." Homeless at home, Moses stumbled in his "hour of need" upon "an unusual solution." He "conceived the plan of founding a new empire, of finding a new people, to whom he could give the religion that Egypt disdained" (ibid., pp. 31–32). Moses molds the Israelites into Ikhnaton's religion, passing on to them mores that are utterly foreign to them; he imposes upon them alien customs (such as circumcision, a practice that was associated with the ancient Egyptians, Freud argues);[35] and he commands them to obey a god that is not theirs.

In sum, Rousseau tells the story of a people in search of religion, while Freud tells the story of a religion in search of a people: it's a great image—a homeless religion wanders around Egypt and its environs looking for followers. While the foreignness of Rousseau's founder is a sign of his ability judiciously to find the right fit between a people and the mores that will bind them together, the foreignness of Freud's founder is a sign of the harsh ill-fittedness of the religion whereby he founds his people.[36] While there is violence in both foundings—Rousseau's lawgiver forces people to be free and soon introduces a death penalty; Freud's Moses suppresses resistance with "savage chastisement"—Rousseau treats that founding violence as both justified and incidental, while Freud sees it as savage, and significantly so.[37] The violence of Rousseau's founding is not a sign of the law's ill-fittedness to the people; rather, it is a sign of some people's recalcitrance even when faced with good law. Freud, however, sees the violence of the Mosaic founding as a sign of his law's fundamentally impositional, harsh, and foreign character. Monotheism is too abstract to satisfy the instinctual longings of this people, and it is also a foreign import. Or, better, abstract monotheism, because it is so strict and renunciatory, is experienced and represented as an alien (and, more concretely, a foreign) thing.

We might capture the difference between Rousseau and Freud in psychoanalytic terms: Rousseau's foreign-founder is like the good father whose primary concern is his children and their needs, which he is always trying to serve.[38] Freud's foreign-founder is like the bad father who uses his children to fulfill needs that are his own.

As it happens, these good and bad fathers correspond to the rather different natural fathers imagined by Rousseau and Freud, respectively, in *On the Social Contract* and *Totem and Taboo*. In Rousseau's state of nature, "children remain bound to their father only so long as they need him to take care of them. As soon as the need ceases, the natural bond is dissolved." But who decides when the "need ceases," and how? And what if the parties disagree about this?[39] (One cannot help but recall here the plaintive cries of the young boy in *Shane* as he watches his hero ride away: "Shane, come back!")[40] Rousseau never raises these questions. They probably never occurred to him since he would have assumed that these things are decided uncontroversially in a state of nature. But the pattern of timely withdrawal is repeated outside of the state of nature. The idealized father, who withdraws at the indisputably correct time (and who always knows what the indisputably correct time is) so his children can live as independent beings, free of paternal authority, is Rousseau's model for the lawgiver who makes his appearance thirteen chapters later in the *Social Contract*.

By contrast, Freud's natural father, who makes his appearance in *Totem and Taboo*, has excessive desires, and the needs of his children are the last thing on his mind. He is in no way self-limiting, and he rules over his sons with authoritarian force. He does not leave when his sons reach maturity, and, finally, when they can no longer tolerate his prohibitions, particularly those against sharing the women of the clan, they murder him. Even that does not rid them of his overbearing presence, however. They internalize the very prohibitions against which they chafed in his lifetime—they eat him—and they are haunted by his will and their violence ever after.[41] Freud's Moses reperforms this script: "The great deed and misdeed of primeval times, the murder of the father, was brought home to the Jews, for fate decreed that they should repeat it on the person of Moses, an eminent father substitute" (ibid., p. 113).

There can be no adjudicating the "truth" of these two imaginings. Indeed, the issue here is not about "fathers" per se but about how these different imaginings of the natural father shape our thinking about the problems of authority, freedom, and founding that foreign-founder scripts are intended to manage. In both Rousseau and Freud, the paternal figure—the natural father—stands for the law, authority, or powers by which we are governed but which we have not ourselves authored and to which we have never consented. For Rousseau, theorist of the general will, paternal power represents the very problem he is trying to solve, the problem of the law's arbitrariness and illegitimacy. ("Man is born free and everywhere he is in chains" [Book I, Chapter 1].) But rather than solve that problem, Rousseau merely avoids it by imagining that fathers whose will is impositional and never justified will both recognize the moment of departure when it comes and then obligingly disappear. For Freud, that obliging disappearance is a fantasy, at best a screen memory behind which the murder of the foreign-founder, the man Moses, is concealed.[42] Rousseau's account of the natural father who leaves when his sons are ready invites us to imagine that arbitrary and impositional powers simply withdraw when children—or citizens—reach the age of majority. Freud's account promises us that paternal authority never withdraws voluntarily; we always have to take it rather than wait for it to be handed over, and even if we think we have rid ourselves of its power, it will return to haunt us.

That haunting occurs in Rousseau as well, however. Indeed, we might see Rousseau's foreign-founder as a kind of return of the repressed father. On this interpretation, the felt but unacknowledged alienness of the law of the natural father by whom we were governed, however benevolently, without our consent finds expression in the curious foreignness of the founder who also governs us without our consent until, in his judgment, we reach the age of political maturity.

In other words, Rousseau teaches us that even when the terms of our governance are good for us, we cannot but experience (paternal) authority as alien (it does not come from us). Perhaps the concept of *foreignness* is a way of symbolically marking and making sense of that alien experience, a way of giving it cultural organization while also displacing it outward and disowning it; it comes from somewhere else. If the founder—who shapes our identity as a people, who ushers us into maturity and enables us to be autonomously self-governing—is foreign, that is because the law by which we were founded is always lingeringly alien to us since we did not (indeed, we could not) will it for ourselves.[43] (That is why we needed a founder in the first place!) And we never will—at least not in the full, unvarnished sense required by would-be radical democrats like Rousseau.

Such a reading of Rousseau offers one possible explanation for the more general frequency and circulation of foreign-founder scripts in political culture. On this account, the foreign-founder script both domesticates and preserves in its entire uncanniness the alienness of the law. That Rousseau, a xenophobic theorist of self-identity, should himself rely on the figure of the foreign-founder shows just how inescapable and thoroughgoing is this sense of the law's alien character, even in a particularly well-ordered regime, which is what Rousseau thought he was theorizing in the *Social Contract*.

Indeed, Rousseau knew this: noting that the task of the legislator is to "change human nature," Rousseau says that in order to do this the legislator must "deny man his own forces in order to give him forces that are *alien* [in another translation, the term—"étrangères" in the original—is rendered *"foreign"*] to him and that he cannot make use of without the help of others" (Book II, Chapter 7; emphasis added). Might the foreignness of the foreign-founder, his alienness, be a sign—and a vehicle—of the (self-)alienation that is the necessary basis of life among others under law? It may be that one function of the mythic foreign-founder (in this context) is to make some sort of sense of that felt alienness of the law, marking that alienness but domesticating it at the same time by way of a story of a nice (if somewhat short-tempered) foreign-founder, which is what Moses was before Freud got his hands on him.

In short, contra *Freud*, *it is not because the tablets were handed to the Israelites by an Egyptian Moses that the Israelites experienced the law as alien and impositional (which is why Moses had to use force to secure its implementation). Rather, it is because of the law's alien and impositional character that the story of the law's origins had to be one in which it was an Egyptian—a foreign-founder—who handed the tablets to the Israelites.*

(Freud misses this point because he is so intent in *Moses and Monotheism* on trying to prove that Moses was *really* an Egyptian, as a matter of empirical fact, that he never poses the symbolic question: *Why* was Moses an Egyptian?[44] What cultural, symbolic or political work was accomplished by way of his "foreignness"? This omission is astonishing coming from the author of *The Interpretation of Dreams*, though it is understandable given the exigencies that must have driven the Jewish Freud's project of writing about Moses and monotheism in the 1930s, first in Austria and then, as an exile, in England.)

But the law is not just alien; it is both strange and familiar at the same time. And that is why the foreignness of Moses is not simply concealed, as Freud assumes—it is *poorly* concealed, poorly concealed by way of a genetic fiat that had to fail: Moses' foreignness is concealed in order to signal and secure the people's identification with the law; but it is poorly concealed in order to preserve a marker of the law's alienness to the people who live by it.[45]

There is no way to avoid this sense of the law's alienness. But its character as a problem is severely aggravated when we are dealing with *democratic* law (which is supposed to be coming from the people, after all), and when democracy is conceived of in Rousseauvian republican terms as a politics of radical self-authorship and self-identity.[46] However, there are good, radical democratic reasons for wanting to preserve rather than heal the sense of alienation that Rousseau—and certain contemporary theorists of legitimation and deliberation[47]—try so hard to overcome.

Legitimation theorists worry that alienation can be a source of civic cynicism and withdrawal. It can. But it can also be a source of civic activism, unrest, and protest. The positive side of "alienation" is that it marks a gap in legitimation, a space that is held open for future refoundings, augmentation, and amendment. That gap is closed by those who read alienness out of Rousseau's text (whether by ignoring or domesticating the foreignness of the lawgiver), are blind to the haunting opacity of the people to one another in Rousseau's polity, and are inalert to the ambiguity of the law that both is and is not the product of the General Will, produced both by public deliberation and by silence, generated by the people but also imposed by the lawgiver.

———

In sum, Rousseau and Freud together present a fuller picture of the symbolic functions of foreignness than does either theorist alone. From

Rousseau, we learn that foreignness models founding virtues such as objectivity, disinterestedness, and impartiality, while also symbolizing a denaturing self-alienation that life under law enacts and requires. From Freud we learn that foreignness signals and maybe also aggravates the trauma of norm transmission or the imposition of law. These perspectives are not necessarily in conflict. What is (allegedly) impartial and objective invariably appears alien and violent from the vantage point of the particular. But these perspectives are not necessarily compatible, either. What is allegedly impartial and objective may also appear alien and violent from a vantage point that understands itself to be impartial and objective, too.

Similarly, Rousseau's and Freud's respective theorizations of the figure of the foreign-founder together produce a more complete picture than does either alone. Rousseau imagines that the supplement of foreignness is entirely successful and not also unsettling to the order founded by its agency. Freud, by contrast, sees the founder's foreignness as entirely unsettling to the nation and as an aggravator of the already traumatic process of norm transmission. Each thinker provides an important corrective to the other. Taken together, they teach us that the supplement of foreignness is undecidable: it both shores up (Rousseau) *and* unsettles (Freud) the people or the law being founded.

As I argue in the chapters that follow, the foreign-founder's undecidability is inescapable and, indeed, necessary (even if also threatening) to his founding mission. In the case of the biblical Ruth, for example, it is simply not possible for her to shore up the nation without also unsettling it at the same time. This undecidability sets in motion a politics of (re)founding, which involves the plural efforts by postfounding generations to (re)define their collective identity by retelling their origin stories or by inventing new ones. For those whose origin stories feature a foreign-founder, the politics of refounding often involve a contest to erase that figure from memory or to position him as *either* foreign to *or* founder of the nation. Rarely is the foreign-founder celebrated as such. The political-cultural struggles to mark or resolve the undecidability of the foreign-founder figure are a major focus of the chapters that follow. For now let us complete this stage of our analysis of the foreign-founder figure by putting it into proximity with another liminal figure who is also a vehicle of social or political reconstitution: the scapegoat.

Girard's Scapegoat

The setting for the foreign-founder's appearance may be described, in René Girard's terms, as a sacrificial crisis, a crisis in which "the whole cultural foundation of the society is put in jeopardy" (*Violence and the Sacred*, p. 49). What Rousseau saw as the threatening divisiveness of factionalism or self-interest, and what *Exodus* describes as a lapse into idolatry, Girard describes as a loss of common distinctions, a loss of communal unanimity. The loss of unanimity returns the community to an unending cycle of violence. Rousseau and Girard both think the solution is renewed social unity or unanimity and both see an outsider as a necessary vehicle of that solution. But for Rousseau, social unity is achieved in response to the leadership and direction provided by an outsider, a foreign-founder, while for Girard, unanimity is achieved by way of opposition to an outsider—a sacrificial victim or a scapegoat: "The scapegoat is the innocent party who polarizes a universal hatred" (*Job, the Victim of His People*, p. 5). What counts is not the hatred but—as in Rousseau at the founding of the social contract—"the communal gesture of unanimity" (*Violence and the Sacred*, p. 101). In Girard, that unanimity is achieved only in relation to an outsider because "otherwise the community might find it difficult to unite against it" (ibid., p. 102).[48]

Sacrificial victims are chosen from among those "who are either outside or on the fringes of society," such as "prisoners of war, slaves, small children, unmarried adolescents, and the handicapped." The list, which "ranges from the very dregs of society, such as the Greek *pharmakos*, to the king himself," covers a diverse group, but its members have something in common: all are "exterior or marginal individuals, incapable of establishing or sharing the social bonds that link the rest of the inhabitants."[49] The scapegoat's outsider status ensures that the violence performed against him will not be avenged: "Between these victims and the community a crucial social link is missing, so they can be exposed to violence without fear of reprisal. Their death does not automatically entail an act of revenge"(ibid., p. 13).

Girard repeatedly emphasizes the beauty and completeness of the scapegoat solution, noting that violence is symbolically expunged or absorbed by a ritual that never exceeds the economy to which it is assigned. But this account, no less than Rousseau's vision of a lawgiver who leaves at the perfectly right time, is surely too neat.[50] Moreover, Girard never inquires into the outsider status of those taken to be safe objects of violence. It is as if their empirical marginality is what causes their scapegoating. And yet Job, perhaps Girard's lengthiest example of a scapegoat, was not an outsider. He was a member of the community that came to despise him, probably because his run of bad luck made his neighbors nervous about their own fate.[51] Then they cast him out. With this turn of events, he *becomes an outsider.* As he himself says, "The serving maids look on me as a foreigner, a stranger, never seen before" (quoted but not commented upon by Girard, *Job*, p. 4).

Now, this suggests that the scapegoat need not be an actually existing foreigner but rather anyone whom the community can successfully and unanimously cast as one. And, indeed, in his book on Job, Girard tracks the social processes that produce Job's marginalization. In that book, if not in *Violence and the Sacred*, Girard seems to understand that the individual is not a scapegoat because he is a foreigner; instead (as Job found out), he is (or becomes) a foreigner because he is a scapegoat. Or, better, these two of Girard's books in tandem rightly teach us that the practice of scapegoating sometimes chooses its objects from an already existing, available pool of outsiders and at other times produces its objects from among the members of the community in crisis. The important point here is that scapegoating is not caused by scapegoats— an already existing pool of outsiders. Scapegoating is a social practice that finds or produces the objects it needs.

A scapegoat is a figure made to represent some taint borne by the community as a whole, in particular, the loss of distinctions that defines the sacrifical crisis from which the community is trying to recover. The attribution of that taint to a scapegoat allows the community unanimously to disavow it, and the ritual murder of the scapegoat cleanses the community and reestablishes the lines of proper order that had become so dangerously attenuated. Girard's scapegoat theory is valuable to an analysis of the politics of foreignness because it presses us to attend to the *politics* of foreignness—the cultural symbolic organization of a social crisis into a resolution-producing confrontation between an "us" and a "them." Moreover, Girard offers us a new angle from which to reread our foreign-founder texts.

In a Girardian retelling of the Moses story, Moses would be a scapegoat (especially if we take seriously Freud's suggestion that Moses was murdered by his people), and Moses' foreignness would be a projection (not, contra Rousseau, Freud, and Girard in *Violence and the Sacred*, an empirical fact, or at least not necessarily so). Such a retelling might go like this. In the desert of Sinai, the Israelites long for the "fleshpots of Egypt" and worship idols while awaiting Moses' return from the mountaintop. After Moses returns and reinterpellates them into the law of monotheism, the Israelites seek to disavow and expunge their forbidden lapse into identification with Egypt. They project that forbidden identification onto Moses, calling *him* an Egyptian, later inscribing him into their cultural narratives as a (n adopted) son of Pharoah. Then they kill him in order to cleanse themselves of their sin, and they say he died of natural causes.[52] Poor Moses is a good candidate for scapegoating not because he is a foreigner (on this reading, he isn't . . . yet) but perhaps because, as a leader, he is, as Girard points out, a liminal figure, a quasi insider who is already in violation of the social links that scapegoat rituals seek to shore up. Alternatively, in more Freudian terms, Moses may be chosen out of the group because it was he who instituted the law that occasioned the Israelites' collective transgression and violence.

Girard's account suggests new readings of our other texts as well. Earlier, we thought that the Munchkins need Dorothy to do their dirty work for them because they are not bold enough to take on the witches that terrorize them, and we thought of Shane as a hero who comes in to save weak, would-be democratic citizens from bandits or bullies like Riker. We took these accounts at their face value, and we worried that citizens in need of rescue at their origins (*or, more pointedly, citizens who tell themselves such stories about themselves*) could hardly be prepared for the daily challenges of democracy in which, after all, bandits or bullies surface all the time while powerful rescuers do not. But what if neither the Munchkins of Oz nor the local citizens of *Shane are* weak? What if the stories they tell about themselves suggest instead that they are actually quite powerful, powerful enough to do the violence that their (re)founding requires (let us say they do take on the wicked witches or face off with Riker's men), and powerful enough to blame a scapegoat for it, even generating a cover story that almost conceals their implication in the violence and seeks to relieve them of responsibility for it?

The people's unwillingness to take responsibility for their (re)founding violence might be psychological, but it might also be political. Another way of putting Girard's point about the need to perform sacrificial violence in order to end cyclical violence without inaugurating a new cycle of violence is to say, as many democratic theorists do, that ordinary democratic life demands a measure of stability and routine that might be impossible to secure for citizens known to be capable of great passion and violence.[53] It was in the spirit of this belief that Abraham Lincoln said of the first American founders: "Passion has helped us; but can do so no more. It will in future be our enemy."[54] What if, believing this, the locals invent a scapegoat, a Shane or a Moses or a Dorothy, who is then said to have been the agent of the violence that was really committed by the would-be citizens but which they now need to disavow? Or perhaps the Shane or the Moses or the Dorothy figure is indeed one of their number and a party to their collective violence but is then said to have been the leader and even (in an effort to externalize the problem) the outside agitator of it?[55] Whether wholly invented or chosen out of the collectivity, or a little bit of both, the figures that personify the violence take it upon themselves (or suffer its projection onto themselves) and thereby, Christlike, absolve the collectivity of implication in it.[56]

Now what if we apply this approach to Rousseau's *Social Contract?* We might see the arrival of the figure of the lawgiver not (contra William Connolly, Alan Keenan, Geoffrey Bennington, and others, including myself above)[57] as a sign that the project of General Willing has failed, but rather as a sign that it has succeeded. Think of what the lawgiver is said to bring to the people—not just perspicacity but also a death penalty, not just heroic beneficence but also stern discipline. What if these are in fact willed by the General Will, generated by the people themselves, imposed upon themselves, and exacted from among their own number? What if the too-good-to-be-true arrival of the lawgiver is just a story we tell ourselves so we can disavow, rather than take responsibility for, those violences, those ritual and nonritual sacrifices on which the founding and daily maintenance of our democratic polity depends?

This interpretation of the *Social Contract* may seem a bit far-fetched, but there are several things that can be said in its favor. First, it allows us to treat as continuous the aspiration of *The Government of Poland* and the *Social Contract*. In *The Government of Poland*, Rousseau advises us to build national unity by telling and performing stories of heroes we admire. What if the *Social Contract* is just such a story, the story of our valiant but failed effort to legitimate our chains by willing the General Will and our happy rescue by a fortuitous foreign-founder?

Another virtue of such a reading is that it solves a problem that has puzzled Rousseau's readers for ages: Why does this radical democrat for whom popular sovereignty is the only solution to the problem of legitimacy turn, at the last minute, to a founder, and to a *foreign-*founder at that? Not (contra Connolly, Keenan, Bennington, and myself above) because he needs an external source to animate a General Will that cannot animate itself. Rousseau himself certainly never admits *that*. True, he puzzles over whether the General Will can err. But were the General Will really unable to set itself in motion, that would mean the whole project of the *Social Contract* had failed, and that would be quite an admission to make only halfway through the argument in its favor. Instead, what if the lawgiver is brought in because of the General Will's *success*? What if Rousseau calls on the lawgiver because he seeks to externalize the General Will's violence, the willed violence of (re)-founding?

That externalization may be best achieved by way of a story, and a figure, rather than by way of an analytic argument. Perhaps, rather than being a philosophical justification of political violence (most famously answering the question: Under what circumstances can a person be "forced to be free"?), Rousseau's text is performative in character. What if, rather than *argue* for the legitimation Rousseau seeks, Rousseau's text tries to *bring that legitimacy into being with an origin story*? ("Rousseau had always considered texts about politics to be political acts," says Neil Saccamano in a reading of Rousseau that has great affinities with the one developed here.)[58] Taken as a public myth of origins, Rousseau's *Social Contract* performs the exorcism of a local violence on which citizens depend, but which they must disavow lest it consume them.[59] The price of that exorcism is high: the introduction of the lawgiver-scapegoat and the erasure of the people's miraculously successful willing of the General Will.

Perhaps the greatest virtue of this reading is that the foreignness of Rousseau's lawgiver suddenly makes sense. No longer is that foreignness a puzzling departure from Rousseau's famous xenophobia. Instead, in keeping with that xenophobia, the founder's foreignness can now be seen to enhance his effectiveness as a lawgiver-scapegoat. What quality, other than foreignness (viewed from a xenophobic perspective like Rousseau's) could better secure the lawgiver's role as scapegoat?

As is now clear, this new take on the *Social Contract* switches our sense of the lawgiver. No longer is he a repetition of the idealized, independence-granting father of the state of nature (Book I, Chapter 2). Instead, the lawgiver, on this account, is the mirror opposite of that first father. Where the first, natural father's self-limiting nature absolved us of implication in any violence against him by making such violence (unbelievably) unnecessary, the second father figure absolves us of implication in violence by appearing to do our dirty work for us. Moreover, his timely departure or murder helps to sustain the fiction that whatever violence we are involved in is confined to the generation of founding. Thus, we tell ourselves, the violence that touches our regime is contained and final rather than boundless and cyclical. Our clean hands come at a price, however. The price is our own democratic power, the power to act in concert as a sovereign people. The story we tell ourselves about ourselves is an infantilizing origin story in which we abdicate democratic responsibility for our common life together. Also on this reading, then, Rousseau's introduction of a paternal figure continues to puzzle, even if its foreignness does not.

Democracy and Foreignness

As we shall see in the chapters that follow, a thorough analysis of the symbolic politics of foreignness draws upon the multiple, sometimes conflicting insights of all three of the thinkers addressed here: Rousseau, Freud, and Girard. But what if we treat these authors' texts not just as analyses of a problem but also as alternative origin stories? Which of these texts would serve most effectively as a generator of democratic agency? Curiously, given that Rousseau was theorizing democracy and given that Girard is trying to understand sacrificial violence for the sake of our collective life together, it may be Freud, the one most removed from democratic theory, who provides the best resources out of which to generate a model of agency for would-be democrats.

If we treat Freud's *Moses and Monotheism* as itself an origin story (that is to say, if we treat that text as a countermyth and not just as a study of an origin story), and if we set aside for a moment Freud's severe demand that the subject renounce instinctual life for the sake of a rational life under abstract law, then certain salient elements of a potentially democratic agency emerge from Freud's account: here we have subjects who exist in agonistic relation to a founder whose alienness is a poorly kept secret; subjects who do not expect power to be granted to them by nice authorities with their best interests at heart; subjects who know that if they want power they must take it and that such taking is always illegitimate from the perspective of the order in place at the time;[60] subjects who know that their efforts to carve out a just and legitimate polity will always be haunted by the violences of their founding; subjects who experience the law as a horizon of promise but also as an alien and impositional thing.

Such subjects are, I would argue, better prepared for the ongoing, always changing demands of democracy than those Rousseauvian sons of kinder, gentler fathers who expect the reigns of power to be handed over to them when the time is somehow objectively, impossibly right. Such modified Freudian subjects seize power themselves and convert their experience of alienation into a source of transgressive (because unauthorized) democratic energy. They are prone to repeat and relive their originary traumas. They do not expect their father figures or their own violences and transgressions to confine themselves to preassigned locations or economies.

Democracy is always about living with strangers under a law that is therefore alien (because it is the mongrel product of political action— often gone awry—taken with and among strangers). Even at its very best, or especially so, democracy is about being mobilized into action periodically with and on behalf of people who are surely opaque to us and often unknown to us. We can see this, as Rousseau himself usually did, as a problem that needs to be solved. For example, we can, in the spirit of Rousseau, focus, as Benedict Anderson does, on how our mutual strangeness is overcome by technologies of simultaneity (like mass, national newspapers). Or, like René Girard, we can tell ourselves that those scapegoats—often cast as foreign—that used to check the rupturous tendencies of our social violence have been effectively replaced by modern legal institutions.[61] Or we can focus on our lingering alienness to one another even in the face of such technological and institutional remedies and even in the face of our actions in concert.

If we take the last position, then the strangers with whom and on behalf of whom we struggle, and the felt strangeness of the institutions that aim to define the terms of democratic contest, might stand not simply as obstacles to a democratic project. They might also stand as markers of the fact that democracy's energies and origins always point beyond the (national) borders and commonalities that have heretofore presented themselves as democracy's necessary conditions. Insofar as he compels us to this insight, the figure of the foreign-founder (perhaps like one of Rousseau's "few great cosmopolitan souls"?) might be an agent of one more (re)founding, inaugurating and animating a democratic politics that seeks to broaden the distributions of goods, freedoms, powers, accountability, and justice within and across borders without presupposing a unified demos stabilized by a metaphorics of national kinship.[62]

In the next two chapters, I look at two other multiply and contestably retold origin stories, the biblical Book of Ruth and the myth of an immigrant America. Both of these origin stories reiterate the foreign-founder script analyzed here. I map out the field of contesting interpretations and iterations and then offer my own. My interventions are motivated by a desire to redirect and harness the energies of foreign-founder scripts on behalf of a democratic politics that does not renationalize the state. This is a democratic politics that seeks, instead, to multiply the sites of affect, coordination, and organization that move people into (and sometimes out of) politics on their own behalves and on behalf of others.

And we Americans are the Israelites of our time.

– Herman Melville

3 THE FOREIGNER AS IMMIGRANT

The Book of Ruth as a Foreign-Founder Text

The Book of Ruth is not usually thought of as a foreign-founder text, but all the basic elements are there. The Israelites are in a period of corruption. A foreigner arrives and her presence among them works to effect two significant changes. Ruth, the Moabite, is the vehicle of a regime change from rule by judges to rule by kings. In that sense, she is a kind of founder, even if not exactly a lawgiver. But Ruth is also a (re)founder in Rousseau's other sense: she (re)founds a "people." Traditional Jewish readers see in Ruth a shining example of virtuous devotion to the one true God or to her Israelite mother-in-law, or both, and Ruth's example is said to be so powerful as to return the Israelites from corruption and set them again on their own true spiritual path. That happy outcome is represented in this text by a return to plenitude: the end of a famine and also the end of barrenness. The Book of Ruth ends with the birth of a boy, Obed, whose line will lead to David, the first line of kings to rule Israel. (That same line will later produce Jesus.)[1]

Ruth is different from Rousseau's foreign-founder in that she is not a lawgiver per se, and her foreignness is not a way of modeling distant impartiality, objectivity, or neutrality. Her function is not to lead a people nor to address directly the narrowness of a people caught up in corrupt factionalism and self-interest. Ruth is different from Girard's scapegoat, too. If she (re)generates communal unanimity, it is not by serving as a magnet for a unifying hatred that takes her as its object. Rather, through indirection—through her example—Ruth inspires and reenchants a jaundiced nation. Foreignness as distance does play a role in Ruth's ability to do that. Her ability to inspire is in direct proportion to her distance (conceptual, epistemological) from the people she joins. The more foreign she is, the more apparent is the universality of the divinity and the people to which she is drawn.

Ruth does introduce two new wrinkles into the foreign-founder script. She is a woman, not a man, and she does not leave when her work of refounding is done. She stays and so becomes an immigrant. Is there any connection between these two departures from the more standard foreign-founder texts? Why does Ruth stay, and does her staying support or subvert the (re)founding she enables? Ruth's status as not just a foreigner but also an immigrant means that she poses for us some slightly different questions than those posed by our other foreign-founders: Is there some sort of connection that we might grasp through Ruth, not just between foreignness and founding, but between *immigration* and founding?

Ruth

The Book of Ruth begins with a flashback. A few years earlier, a man named Elimelech, his wife, Naomi, and their two sons left Bethlehem to escape famine. They moved to Moab, having heard that Moab was flourishing while Bethlehem suffered. The move to Moab is controversial. Elimelech has abandoned his community in a time of need, and

worse yet, he has gone to live in Moab, the home of the historical enemies of the Israelites. This terribly forbidden move, and the famine that
occasions it, suggests that the Israelites have fallen away from their
fundamental moral principles. Elimelech's emigration, in particular, signals a loss of social unity among the Israelites, and his emigration to
Moab, of all places, suggests a diminution of respect for proper boundaries. Both are signs of what René Girard calls a sacrificial crisis.

The Moabites are corrupt as well, but in their case the condition is
not temporary. They refused water to the Israelites as they wandered
in the desert from Egypt to the Promised Land. And when the Israelites
camped at Beth Peor, some Moabite women are said to have tried to
seduce the Israelite men into illicit relations and idol worship. For this,
the prohibition in Deuteronomy against marrying Moabites is uncom-
promising: "None of the Moabites' descendants, even in the tenth generation, shall ever be admitted into the congregation of the Lord."[2]

Elimelech dies soon after settling in Moab. His sons, Mahlon and
Chilion, marry two Moabite women, violating the biblical prohibition
against such marriages. These men also die within ten years, leaving
behind three childless widows, Naomi and her Moabite daughters-in-
law, Ruth and Orpah. Naomi hears that the famine in Bethlehem is over,
and she decides to return home. Her daughters-in-law accompany her
initially, but she soon tells them to "turn back, each of you to her mother's house" in Moab.[3] They refuse, Naomi insists, and finally Orpah,
weeping, agrees to return to Moab; but Ruth remains. And when Naomi
tells her again to leave ("See, your sister-in-law has returned to her
people and her gods; return after your sister-in-law"),[4] Ruth responds
poignantly:

> Whither thou goest, I will go
> Whither thou lodgest, I will lodge
> Thy people shall be my people
> Thy god shall be my god
> Whither thou diest, I will die, and there I will be buried.[5]

Naomi says nothing in response, but she stops protesting and Ruth ac-
companies her on her journey.

In Bethlehem, Naomi is welcomed back by the women of the community. She announces her losses to them and declares her name

changed from Naomi (which means "pleasant") to Mara (which means "bitter").[6] Naomi and Ruth establish a joint household. Ruth supports them by harvesting the remnants left in the field of a man named Boaz, who, as it turns out, is a relative of Naomi. Having heard of Ruth's remarkable loyalty to Naomi, Boaz welcomes Ruth to his field and sends her home with extra grain.

But Naomi and Ruth conspire together to achieve a more certain protection than that. Ruth seeks out (and perhaps seduces) Boaz one night on the threshing-room floor and calls on him to extend his protection to her through marriage, while also redeeming a piece of land that was left to Naomi by Elimelech. Boaz notes that there is another male relative who has prior right or obligation to redeem the land, but he promises to do what he can for Ruth. He goes the next morning to find the next of kin and convenes a meeting of the town elders to resolve the question of Elimelech's land. The next of kin's interest in redeeming the land dwindles when he hears that Boaz intends to marry Ruth. Knowing that if they have a son, the child could claim the redeemed land as his own inheritance without recompense, the next of kin offers his option/obligation to Boaz.[7]

Boaz and Ruth marry and have a son who is given to Naomi to nurse. The women's community celebrates, proclaims the child Naomi's son and protector in old age, pays Ruth the highest compliment, declaring her to be of more value to Naomi than seven sons, and names the child Obed. Ruth never speaks again, and she is, of course, absent from the Book of Ruth's closing patrilineal genealogy which ends with David, later to be the king of Israel. Ruth's precarious position in the Israelite order is stabilized by a marriage and birth that provide the founding energy for a new monarchic regime. In turn, Ruth's migration seems to be the vehicle of this welcome regime change. The Book of Ruth opens "In the days when the judges ruled," a time of famine, barrenness, and corruption, and closes amidst plentiful harvest and a newly born son with a genealogy anticipating the coming monarchy. This is a community in dire need of the inspirational example of Ruth's virtue and perspicacity. The emigration of Elimelech and the intermarriages of Mahlon and Chilion suggest that the Israelite character has been corrupted under the rule of the judges. Ruth helps to solve the problem, not only with her inspiring example but also by founding the line of

David, a single monarchy that claims to be superior to the plural juro-cracy it replaces.

But this regime (re)founding leaves us nonetheless uncertain about Ruth's status as an immigrant. How should we read Ruth's closing silence? Has she been successfully assimilated, or has she been left stranded? More generally, what connections between foreignness and founding and between immigration and founding are presupposed and consolidated by this great short story? What is a Moabite woman—a forbidden foreigner—doing at the start of the line of David?

Immigration and Founding

According to two representative readers of the Book of Ruth—Cynthia Ozick and Julia Kristeva—Ruth is a model immigrant.[8] Ozick reads the Book of Ruth as a tale of reinvigoration by way of conversion or assimi-lation. (This is in line with the dominant, traditional reading of the story.) Ruth's conversion to Judaic monotheism from Moabite idolatry testifies to the worthiness of the Jewish God. Ruth's devotion to Naomi exemplifies Ruth's virtue, which is an example for everyone and a ground for the rule of David. Ruth, the model immigrant and convert, supplements the Israelite order and saves it from its wayward rule by judges by beginning the line that will lead to a new sovereign monar-chy. Ozick's Ruth exmplifies the universal appeal of monotheism and its progress in time, while also marking the compatibility of a now both promisingly and dangerously unlocatable monotheism with a particu-lar, located, statist, and royal lineage.

For Kristeva, by contrast, Ruth unsettles the order she joins. A new monarchy is inaugurated by Ruth, but it is also riven by her, by the moment of otherness she personifies as a Moabite. While Ozick's Ruth completes the Israelite order, Kristeva's Ruth makes it impossible for the order ever to attain completeness. And this, Kristeva argues, is Ruth's great service to the Israelites: she disabuses them of their fanta-sies of wholeness and makes them more open to difference and oth-erness, preparing the way for a welcome cosmopolitan identity. But Kristeva's Ruth does not only disrupt the order she joins. She also adopts its customs and rituals and tries to get along. From Kristeva's perspective, that makes Ruth a valuable model for those contemporary Moslem immigrants who are seen as resistant to absorption into their receiving regimes.[9]

Ozick's and Kristeva's redeployments of the Book of Ruth exhibit two of the dominant and enduring responses we have to immigrants. Either immigrants are valued for what "they" bring to "us"—diversity, energy, talents, industry, innovative cuisines, and new recipes, plus a renewed appreciation of our own regime whose virtues are so great that they draw immigrants to join us—or they are feared for what they will do to us: consume our welfare benefits, dilute our common heritage, fragment our politics, undermine our democratic culture. Both responses judge the immigrant in terms of what she will do for—or to—us as a nation.

The first (welcoming) response models immigration as an occasion for citizens (who are perhaps jaded) to reexperience the fabulous wonder of founding, the moment in which the truth or power of their regime was revealed or enacted for all the world to see. Notably, Moab is (as President Bill Clinton put it in a speech in the Middle East in the fall of 1994) "the land where Moses died and Ruth was born."[10] Ruth is a vehicle through which the law comes alive again generations after the death of the lawgiver, Moses. She repeats the foreign-founder script first acted out for the Israelites by Moses. She returns this people to their origins but without the violence that Machiavelli thought was a virtually necessary feature of such a return. In so doing, she occludes the violences of this people's origins. Her immigration reperforms the social contract of Sinai and allows the Israelites to reexperience the official version of their own beginnings: not the "savage chastisement" of Freud's Moses, but rather the wondrous experience of awe before the law. With Ruth, the law is not violently imposed, it is instead lovingly chosen. And Ruth's choice of the Israelites re-marks them as the Chosen People, a people worthy of being chosen.[11] Here, the immigrant's choice of "us" makes us feel good about who we are.

The second (wary) response to immigrants also suggests a reexperience of the founding. Highlighted here, though, is the impulse to secure a new regime's identity by including some people, values, and ways of life and excluding others.[12] By moving into Bethlehem, Ruth reverses the trajectory of the Girardian scapegoat. She brings pollutants in rather than carrying them out. But she serves the same purpose as the Girardian scapegoat, nonetheless. She manages or conceals the violence of founding and reinstalls the unanimity that grounds the social order. By way of her conversion, the Israelites are brought back from corruption not, as at Sinai, by a stern Moses, but by a kind and virtuous woman who, without violence, makes visible to everyone the universally magnetic power of the one true god. Through Ruth, we might say, the sublime law is made beautiful. But this immigrant foreign-founder is nonetheless also deeply threatening to the people she (re)founds. Her choice of the Israelites and her presence among them *endangers* their sense of who they are. If a Moabite—the most foreign of all foreigners, a member of an idolatrous and murderous people—can move to Bethlehem, does that mean that Israel is now a borderless community open to all comers?[13]

The Israelites turn to a scapegoat to help solve the problem. The text's contrast between Ruth and Orpah highlights the extraordinariness of Ruth's border crossing, as Ozick points out.[14] But the contrast also has another effect: it makes clear that Israel is not open to all comers. It is open only to the Moabite who is exceptionally virtuous, to the good Ruth but not to the threatening Orpah. (Is Orpah not threatening? Traditional interpreters give expression to their fears when they claim that Goliath is her descendant.) The Book of Ruth invites readers to project Ruth's frightening foreignness onto Orpah, the one who leaves to return to her gods, the one who did not choose the Israelites. Orpah is the vehicle whereby the Israelites expel outward to Moab a foreignness that is inside their social order (Moses might have been an Egyptian, Jahve might be an alien god, Ruth is surely a Moabite).

Together, Ruth and Orpah personify the coupling of wonder *and* fear, opportunity *and* threat, the sense of supplementation *and* fragmentation that marked the foreign-founders of Chapter Two and that immigrants often excite in the orders that absorb or exclude them. Personified by the two distinct characters of Ruth and Orpah, these impulses may seem to be attached to different objects—the good immigrant versus the bad, for example, or the welcome newcomer versus the frightening stranger. But what if we read Orpah as part of Ruth, a personification of the part of Ruth that cannot help but remain a Moabite even in Bethlehem?[15] There are grounds to do so. *It is, after all,*

Ruth's very foreignness—her likeness to Orpah—that enables her to choose the Israelites in a meaningful way. Indeed, the more radical Ruth's foreignness, the more meaningful the sense of chosenness that results from her choosing.[16] The more deep the enmity between Moab and Israel, the more profound the friendship that is declared in its midst. The more radically particular the convert, the more obviously universal the divinity that compels her to join up. The Israelites' own insistence that *their* god is uniquely universal is what puts them in need of periodic new testimony to his charms. Even as they eschew converts, they rely on them in this deep way. The most powerful testimony to Judaic monotheism's attractions is the testimony provided by the *most* unlikely person, the one coming from the most radically particular and hostile culture. It is because Ruth is a Moabite that her conversion—if a conversion it was—is fabulous. Indeed, were the scapegoating of Orpah really to work, were it somehow possible to cleanse Ruth of her foreign Moabite identity, the price of such a cleansing would be the very gift Ruth has to offer. There is no way around it: with all of its good resonances and bad, a *Moabite* has come to live in Bethlehem.

Ozick's Ruth: Convert or Migrant?

For Cynthia Ozick, the Book of Ruth illustrates the choiceworthiness of the (now, once again) Chosen People, the universal pull of their monotheism and the force of its assimilative power. Ruth is a model émigrée because she leaves behind the idolatry and barbarism of her native Moab. When she says to Naomi "thy god shall be my god," Ruth announces her fidelity to a god more advanced than those of the Moabites, one that cannot be seen and may not be physically imagined or represented.[17]

Ozick's reading of the Book of Ruth is indebted to the rabbinical interpretations but departs from them significantly. "I mean for the rest of my sojourn in the text to go on more or less without [the rabbis]," she says at one point.[18] Where earlier readers interpreted Orpah in terms of her unfavorable comparison with Ruth, Ozick pauses to look at Orpah in her own right. "Let us check the tale, fashion a hiatus, and allow normality to flow in: let young stricken Orpah not be overlooked."[19] Orpah is noteworthy not just for her failure, by contrast with Ruth, to emigrate to Bethlehem for the sake of Naomi and monotheism. Orpah stands out for her own admirable action: she married an Israelite in Moab (not a popular thing to have done, certainly) and came to love Naomi. Orpah may not have been up to the tests of monotheism and emigration, but she was an "open-hearted" woman,[20] beyond the confines of "narrow-minded," conventional prejudice.[21]

Ozick's Orpah is special, but ultimately, in the crucible of the decision to emigrate and convert or not, the true principle of her character is revealed. She represents "normality," not "singularity."[22] Her wants are mundane; her imagination does not soar. In returning to her mother's house, she returns also to her idols. Orpah "is never, never to be blamed for" her choice, Ozick says, but she suggests nonetheless that history has, indeed, judged Orpah ("Her mark is erased from history; there is no Book of Orpah").[23] Ozick resists the judgment of history by pausing to reflect on Orpah. But Ozick also consolidates history's judgment by depicting Moab's (and Orpah's) disappearance from the world stage as deserved rather than contingent, and by figuring Orpah's decision, as ordinary and immature by contrast with Ruth's decision, which is "visionary."[24] "Ruth leaves Moab because she intends to leave childish ideas behind."[25]

The contrast between Ruth and Orpah, though softened by Ozick's appreciative hiatus, instantiates Ozick's distinction between the normal and the singular. But it also does something else. Ozick's contrast between Ruth and Orpah effectively works to undo the undecidability of the immigrant who both supports and threatens to undermine the order that both depends upon and is threatened by her. Ozick positions Ruth, the immigrant, to reinvigorate the Israelite order without at the same time threatening to corrupt it. The threat of corruption, along with the specter of unconvertible foreignness, is projected onto Orpah, whose failure to emigrate symbolizes a failure to convert (and vice versa). If by staying home Orpah stayed with her gods, then by leaving home Ruth left her gods behind. The contrast leaves no doubt about Ruth's conversion. There is no danger in her presence in Bethlehem. She is surely one of "us."[26]

The unthreatening character of Ruth's reinvigorative immigration is further consolidated by another moment in Ozick's essay. In a lovely insight into Naomi, Ozick sees her instruction to Ruth to follow Orpah and return to "her people and to her gods" as evidence that Naomi "is a kind of pluralist," *avant la lettre*.[27] Naomi is not a zealot, Ozick says. Orpah has her gods, Naomi has hers, and Naomi knows and accepts that. But Ozick stops short of noting the significance of the fact that Naomi's acceptance of Moabite idolatry is tied to the fact that Moabite idol worship occurs in Moab. Her pluralism is territorial. When Naomi says that Orpah has returned to her people and to her gods, Naomi implies (and Ruth surely picks up on this) that it is not possible to go to *her* people in Bethlehem with Moabite gods. In Naomi's pluralism, people and their gods are tied together and positioned in their proper territorial places. Ozick is right that this is a valuable pluralism by contrast with the forms of imperialism and zealotry that tolerate difference nowhere on earth. Its limits are more evident, however, by contrast with forms of pluralism that demand a more difficult toleration, that of differences that live among us, in our neighborhoods, right next door, in our own homes.

Ozick's positioning of Ruth and Orpah as personifications of singularity and normality, combined with her territorialization of cultural difference, establishes a safe and secure distance between Ruth and Orpah. This distance (intentionally or not) works to enable Ruth to serve as a vehicle of the reinvigoration Ozick seeks without also jeopardizing the identity of the Israelites. Ozick's Ruth is able to supplement the Israelite order without at the same time diluting or corrupting it because the undecidable figure of the (Moabite) immigrant, both necessary for renewal and dangerous to the community, has been split in two: Orpah—the practical, material, Moabite who stayed at home with her idols in her "mother's house"[28]—figures the other whose absence keeps the community's boundaries and identity secure; while Ruth—loyal, devoted to Naomi, possessed of the mature, abstract imagination needed to be faithful to the one invisible god—refurbishes the order's boundaries through her conversion to it. This splitting protects the Israelite order from the corruptions of foreignness while allowing the regime to profit nonetheless from the supplement of Ruth's migration.

But Ruth's incorporation into the Israelite order is less complete and more ambivalent than Ozick suggests. Where Ozick sees virtue, conversion, and assimilation, the text of the Book of Ruth suggests complication, recalcitrant particularism, and prejudice. The following four examples illustrate how this radically undecidable immigrant resists Ozick's decisive narration.

First, the Book of Ruth repeatedly refers to Ruth as "Ruth, the Moabitess,"[29] suggesting that she in some sense *stays* a Moabite, forbidden, surely noticed, and perhaps despised by her adopted culture even while also celebrated by it.

Second, the Book of Ruth makes a point of the fact that Naomi takes Obed from Ruth to nurse. Why?[30] The taking is reminiscent of the story reported by Herodotus of the "Pelasgian inhabitants of Lemnos, who carried off Athenian women from Brauron and had children by them. When their mothers brought them up in the Athenian way, the fathers became afraid and killed both mothers and their children."[31] The Israelites' appreciation of Ruth's reenchantment of their way of life finds expression in the women's community's celebration of her. But when Naomi takes Obed from Ruth, that signals the community's continuing concern about Ruth's foreignness. Ruth, the Moabite, cannot be trusted to raise her son properly, in the Israelite way.[32]

Third, another pivotal scene, this one misread rather than ignored by Ozick: What happened that night on the threshing-room floor? Most commentators, including many of the rabbis, treat the scene as a seduction. Ozick, however, says that the scene depicts "a fatherly tenderness, not an erotic one—though such a scene might, in some other tale, burst with the erotic."[33] Indeed. Another commentator, Jack Sasson, does better. Focusing on Boaz's initial fright upon awakening, Sasson speculates that Boaz mistook Ruth for a "Lillith." A Lillith is a demonic woman/spirit thought to be responsible for nocturnal emissions and male impotence. "[U]pon awakening, Boaz discerns the figure of a woman. Fearing that it might be that of a Lillith, he shudders in fear. The storyteller's joke is that Ruth turns out to be equally as aggressive in her demands to be accepted as a mate. In this case, we shall be shortly reassured (if we do not know it already) that matters will turn out well for all concerned."[34]

The "joke" of the scene depends upon Boaz's "mis"identification of Ruth as a Lillith. But the joke of the scene is not on Boaz. It's on this commentator. Because of course Ruth *is* a Lillith. What Sasson does not note is that Boaz's "error" is overdetermined not simply by Ruth's sex-gender but also by her Moabite identity. Moabite women were seen by the Israelites as fearsome temptresses and seductresses. This scene is much more (or less) than a joke, then. In it, Boaz is allowed to experience his worst fears about Ruth: that, her conversion/immigration notwithstanding, she is truly a Moabite after all, a bearer of desire that will not respect the proper boundaries of male, Israelite subjectivity.

The key to the scene is Boaz's question upon awakening: "Mee at?"—"Who are you?" as in "Who goes there?" It is a border guard's question. Boaz may ask it because he really does not know who this figure is. It *is* dark. But we know he can see *some*thing, because he says "Mee at?" which addresses the question to a female. He would otherwise have asked "Mee atah?" or "Mee zeh?" using the universal masculine.

Still, Boaz may ask because he really doesn't know. Or, he may ask because in this nighttime encounter it occurs to him for the first time as a really pressing concern that he really does not know *who Ruth is*! Is she a new Moses, risen from the dead in Moab, come to save and inspire and regenerate the Israelites? Or is she a Moabite? Is she friend or enemy? Founder or foreigner? Who *is* she? The answer comes: "I am Ruth, your handmaid." Not just "I am Ruth" but also "your handmaid." She tries to reassure. Nothing to fear here, she seems to say. But what does she know? She can hardly reassure in this matter. Besides, if the rabbis are right, Boaz will soon die, on the night of his wedding to Ruth. It seems there was something to fear, after all.

Finally, let us turn to the most famous scene of this short story, the scene in which Ruth declares herself to Naomi. *What* is Ruth saying when she says: "Whither thou goest, I will go, Whither thou lodgest, I will lodge, Thy people shall be my people, Thy god shall be my god, Whither thou diest, I will die, and there I will be buried"?

Some commentators, such as Julia Kristeva, treat this speech as a declaration of woman-to-woman love and friendship. Ruth will stick with Naomi, no matter what, 'til death does them part. (Indeed, in our own time, this speech serves as a wedding or commitment vow for many lesbian couples.) For Ozick, however, it is noteworthy that Ruth is saying not only that she loves Naomi *but also that she* feels the pull of the one true god. Why would Ruth say "Thy god shall be my god" if she were not moved by faith? Why would she even move to Bethlehem?

"Everything socially rational is on the side of Ruth's remaining in her own country."[35]

Ozick's reading is not implausible, but there is nothing *in the text* to rule out other rival readings: the social rationalities of the situation are unclear, after all. It cannot have been easy to return to Moab as the childless widow of an Israelite.[36] Desperate to get out of there, Ruth may have spoken to Naomi neither out of love, nor faith, but rather out of immigrant practicality: please take me with you, she pleads, knowing that Naomi does not want to. Naomi has just said to her, "See, your sister-in-law has gone back to *her people* and to *her gods*; return, too, as your sister-in-law has done." Ruth may detect in this instruction a concern that she, Ruth, a Moabite, with her own people and her own gods, will be unacceptable and unassimilable in Bethlehem. Do not worry, Ruth responds. I may not know all the customs but I will go where you go, live where you live, *your people shall be my people* and *your god shall be my god*. As far as the text is concerned, Ruth may simply be reassuring Naomi—as so many immigrants have reassured their hosts and sponsors before and since—that she will be no trouble.

These three readings of Ruth's speech—Kristeva's, Ozick's, and my own—suggest that it traffics in all three of the kinds of friendship distinguished by Aristotle in the *Nicomachean Ethics*: virtue (Ozick's version, in which Ruth's declaration is a conversion), pleasure (Kristeva's version, in which Ruth's speech declares a deep love for Naomi), and use (my own reading, in which Ruth's speech is an expression of immigrant practicality). Aristotle claims that only friendship as usefulness is *political* friendship, but in *Politics of Friendship* Jacques Derrida suggests instead that what marks friendship as a political relation are the perpetual confusions among its three registers.[37] Enmities arise "between friends who, as it were, have been misled, and have misled each other because they have first mistaken friendships, confusing in one case friendship based on virtue with friendship based on usefulness, in another, legal and ethical friendship, etc." (p. 206).

Reading Ruth under the sign of virtue and pleasure, respectively, both Ozick and Kristeva seek to position Ruth's relation to Naomi on a single register of friendship. They want Ruth to be only a friend, not an enemy at the same time. Or better, they want her to be only one kind of friend, not another at the same time. Ozick maps Ruth's relation to Naomi as one of strictly virtue friendship for the sake of a pure Israelite monotheism, which is reliable and universal, in Ozick's view, only to the extent that it is untainted by eros (hence her rejection of any erotic quality to the nighttime meeting with Boaz) and untouched by any instrumental calculations of usefulness. Kristeva privileges the woman-to-woman eros reading for the sake of a cosmopolitanism that needs the animation of an erotic motivation but seeks to avoid an overly universalizing virtue, on the one hand, and an inadequately passionate—merely instrumental—regard for others, on the other hand. In both of these readings, Ruth's Moabite identity is transcended, whether by the pull of virtue or love. Without the continuing taint of her foreignness, however, Ruth's capacity to (re)found the people, or as in Kristeva's case, Ruth's capacity to model any meaningful kind of cosmopolitanism, is severely diminished.

Reading Ruth's speech to Naomi as an expression of friendship as usefulness—as I do—may serve as an antidote to these other readings insofar as it resists the impulse to transcend Ruth's foreignness and seeks not to overstate her membership and acceptance in the Israelite community. But this reading is also too univocal. For the *undecidability of Ruth's speech*—the fact that the speech is precariously perched simultaneously on all three registers of friendship (virtue, pleasure, and use)—is what accounts for the deep uncertainty that surrounds her. Convert, devoted and loving daughter-in-law, practical and reliable immigrant—which kind of friend is Ruth to the Israelites? Ruth is always, undecidably, both friend and enemy (in Derrida's sense of the wrong kind of friend) at the same time. That is what positions her possibly to inaugurate a politics, not just a monarchic line but a politics, a set of struggles about meanings and powers and futures, a reconfiguration of "the space [or spaces] where parties, parts, or lack of parts have been defined."[38]

The nuances of Ruth's speech are absent from Ozick's reading because she positions Ruth on only one register of friendship (virtue-conversion) and because she splits the undecidable figure of the immigrant into two distinct figures: the one who shores up the order (Ruth), and the one who might corrupt it (Orpah). Ozick sees things this way because she counts on Ruth, the immigrant, to perform a function not unlike that of the foreign-founder in Rousseau's *Social Contract*: he, too, comes from elsewhere to return a wayward order to its forgotten first principles. He, too, as Neil Saccamano puts it, enacts the "scene" of lawgiving and "ravish[es] the assembled public with a passion for law that gives them all the virtues they do not have."[39] As we saw in Chapter Two, Rousseau tries to solve the problem of the foreign-founder's unsettling foreignness by having him leave when his restorative work is done. Ruth is less accommodating. She cannot leave without undoing the very gift she has to offer, that of refurbishing the Israelites' sense of chosenness by choosing to live among them. So she stays. And her foreignness—so necessary to her refounding function—remains a problem.[40] Ozick tries to solve the problem as many multicultural Western democracies have done: by having the helpful (part of the) foreigner (Ruth) assimilate and by ensuring that the dangerous (part of the) foreigner (Orpah) leaves or stays behind.

Kristeva's Ruth: The Ideal Immigrant

The true opposite of Ozick's reading of the Book of Ruth is developed by Andre Lacocque in *The Feminine Unconventional: Four Subversive Figures in Israel's Tradition*. Playing Freud to Ozick's Rousseau, Lacocque presents a foreign Ruth that is all bad, providing an effective counter to Ozick's presentation of the foreign Ruth as all good. As his book's title suggests, Lacocque sees only the *un*settling and none of the supplementary effects of Ruth's inclusion in the Davidic line. According to Lacocque, Ruth could not have been intended to help found the line of David, nor could that text conceivably have been used to support his reign, for "[o]n the basis of Ruth, the great king could . . . be considered as an alien, a mongrel, a parvenu, the outcome of unspeakable mating affairs." Lacocque concludes, therefore, that the Book of Ruth must have been written much later, not as an ad hoc legitimation text for David but rather as a "post-exilic parable," a "lesson to the Temple-based ideologists in Jerusalem" who opposed intermarriage or marriage to converts.[41]

Julia Kristeva tries to move beyond the simple poles represented by Ozick and Lacocque in an appreciative reading of Ruth that sees her as both a supporter and a disrupter of the regime she (re)founds. In *Strangers to Ourselves*, Kristeva reads the Book of Ruth as a potentially alternative and disruptive model of a founding myth. (It is disruptive, but it still founds.) Noting Ruth's love for Naomi, Kristeva calls attention to the woman-to-woman passion at the base of the Davidic line, a passion that flies in the face of structuralist assumptions about the order-constituting function of the male homosocial exchange of women.[42] And she points out, further, that Ruth's disturbing foreignness has a positive and generative effect on the regime she joins.

Kristeva does not look to foreignness as a way to model objectivity or impartiality. Instead, echoing another aspect of Rousseau as well as Freud in her appreciation of the fact that life under law requires a degree of self-alienation, Kristeva argues that the sense of strangeness and self-difference excited in the self by an encounter with an other is an important experience for would-be democratic and cosmopolitan citizens. Ruth personifies an otherness that is said to make impossible the identitarian nationalism to which Kristeva's cosmopolitanism is opposed. Ruth, "the outsider, the foreigner, the excluded," founds a monarchic line that is riven by difference from the beginning. The rift is generative: "If David is also Ruth, if the sovereign is also a Moabite, peace of mind will never be his lot, but a constant quest for welcoming and going beyond the other in himself."[43]

There is, however, little trace of Kristeva's idealized ("welcoming") relation to the other in David's lament, cited by Kristeva, that "the people often speak to him wrathfully, saying 'Is he not of unworthy lineage? Is he not a descendant of Ruth, the Moabite?' " nor in David's wish, also cited by Kristeva, to be rid of his Moabite ancestry so that the people might properly revere him.[44] David's impure origins are unsettling to him and to his people. David was more zealous than Kristeva suggests in dealing with others. He certainly outdid Saul in his willingness to destroy his enemies. And later rabbinic interpreters imagine David complaining about being identified with Ruth because he thinks (certainly the later interpreters think) the foundation of his regime will be more stable and more secure without her. Like Sophocles' Creon, who thought the stability of his new regime depended upon building it on one figure and not two—Eteocles without Polynices—David thinks that if he can build on one figure, Boaz without Ruth (as in the Book of Ruth's closing genealogy), then the foundation of his regime will be secure.

Contra Lacocque, David does need Ruth, however. But not to "worry" his sovereignty, as Kristeva puts it.[45] Instead, he looks to Ruth to supplement his own well-known deficiencies of character with her exceptional virtue. Moreover, David's genealogical connection to a Moabite likely suited him in another respect, too, given his and later Solomon's efforts to expand Israel's sphere of influence to include Moabite territory. In short, Ruth's position in relation to the Israelite order is neither unambivalently supportive (contra Ozick) nor unambivalently subversive (contra Lacocque).

This thoroughgoing ambivalence suggests that the Israelites are far less comfortable with their undecidable foreign (re)founder than Kristeva suggests. Kristeva argues that Ruth's gift to the regime *is* her foreignness and its worrying of Israelite sovereignty. But this misses the fact that the Israelites, and Ozick, think that Ruth's virtue is in spite of her foreignness or apart from it. Her gift to the regime is her exemplary character, faith, and conversion-immigration. Ruth's foreignness is what makes her choice of the Israelites so powerful, but her foreignness per se is no gift.

I note these textual and historical details not just to correct Kristeva on matters of fact, but to raise the political-theoretical question of whether the simple fact of a divided sovereignty or subjectivity, riven by differences (that are perhaps personified by others), is a sufficient condition (as opposed to being merely a necessary one, *if that*) to secure a properly open relation to strangeness in ourselves and others. Kristeva's use of the Book of Ruth is reminiscent of the strategy used by the Russian westernizer, Vladimir Sergeyevich Solovyev, who looked to Russian history to ground an outward and universal orientation for Russia. As we saw in Chapter One, Solovyev claimed to have found that ground in the ninth-century request for a foreign-founder made to the Norse by several feuding Slavic communities. But what is the significance of this supposed Scandinavian origin for Russia, an origin that is much disputed to this day? The mere awareness of our own internal divisions may make us more tolerant of others (who may personify those divisions for us). But it may just as well engender and feed a determination to extinguish or contain that strangeness, to scapegoat it, in order to (re)establish the unity and, as in Girard, the unanimity we crave. Something *else* is needed to propel the move from divided subjectivity to an acceptance of strangeness in others.

Like Solovyev, Kristeva seems to count on the ethics-generating power of stories about strangers to move us out of our inward-looking national or ethnic identities. But, in the end, Kristeva's own acceptance of strangeness turns out to depend upon the stranger's willingness to affirm the existence and the worth of the order she supplements and disturbs. As we shall see below, when she discusses Ruth again, this time in the context of contemporary French immigration politics, Kristeva makes it quite clear that for her, no less than for Ozick, Ruth is a model immigrant because of her willingness to leave behind Orpah and all she represents.

Gender and the Foreign-Founder

The Book of Ruth does not only celebrate Ruth, as we have already seen, it also expresses the Israelites' fear of her. But the fact that Ruth—a frighteningly foreign Moabite—is an Israelite heroine would not have surprised Freud. Freud was aware, after all, that the foreign Moses who governed the Israelites so savagely is also celebrated by them. Freud might have seen the celebration of Ruth as a sign that her dangerous foreignness, her character as a much-feared Lillith, had been massively repressed, just as was the Egyptianness of Moses for so long. But Freud also has the resources within his account of Moses both to see that the Israelites need to have their sense of choiceworthiness periodically shored up by a foreigner, and to know that a frightening Moabite would be best positioned to provide the Israelites with what they need.

In *Moses and Monotheism*, Freud argues that the Israelites covenanted under Moses with an "alien" god, Jahve, whose alienness was then hidden by Jahve's retrodictive claim that "he had been the God of those patriarchs," Abraham, Isaac, and Jacob (p. 53). Freud finds "astonishing" the idea of a "god suddenly 'choosing' a people, making it 'his' people and himself its own god." He says: "I believe it is the only case in the history of human religions. In other cases the people and their gods belong inseparably together; they are one from the beginning" (pp. 54–55). (Also astonishing is the fact that Freud never asks whether these other peoples' original unitariness is any truer than that of the Israelites. He only questions the latter's.) "Sometimes, it is true, we hear of a people adopting another god, but never of a god choosing a new people." Freud interprets this unheard of divine choosing as a way of remembering the repressed choice made by the Egyptian Moses, who "had stooped to the Jews, [and] had made them his people" (p. 55). Whatever its real source (whether Jehovah, the original alien god of Abraham or the foreign god of Ikhnaton, or Moses, the foreign law-giver), Ruth replays the script: rising from the shadow of Moses' unknown grave in Moab, this frighteningly foreign Moabite chooses the Israelites as her people and thereby reperforms the original choice that made them "chosen." This is a repetition with a difference: Ruth is seen to model a relation to the law that is one of loving choice, not violent submission. Either way, however, she re-marks for the Israelites, as Moses did generations before, the alienness of the law under which they live (although, as we saw in Chapter Two, that felt alienness will be most salient, most problematic, and most in need of cultural organization in a democratic regime).

But Ruth reiterates Moses' script with another difference as well. She does not die a timely death, nor is she killed by the people she (re)-founds. Instead, she seems to be absorbed by them. As we saw earlier, she cannot leave without undoing the gift she brings: she cannot re-mark the Israelites as choiceworthy unless she sticks to her choice to live among them. And thus her foreignness—always with them and forever the condition of the meaningfulness of her choice—seems to be even more difficult to repress or manage than was that of the foreign-founders of Chapter Two. There, the problem of the foreign-founder's foreignness (and of the regime's founding violence, which the founder's foreignness masked) was solved (if it was solved) by the founder's timely departure or murder. In Chapter Three, thus far, we have seen how the problem of Ruth's foreignness is solved by the contrast between the bad foreigner (Orpah) and the good (Ruth), which works to reassure members of the receiving regime that the latter's foreignness (and maybe also the foreignness of her predecessor, Moses) is not really threatening.[46] But in the case of Ruth and her readers, another device of domestication is also at work.

Ozick and Kristeva both use Ruth's identity as a woman to soften the impact of her foreignness. Each treats Ruth as a good convert or a good immigrant, but the goodness of this convert or immigrant is a gendered goodness. For both Ozick and Kristeva, Ruth is an agent of care, a giving, maternal or daughterly woman. Both readers emphasize Ruth's love for Naomi, her devotion to her, her care for her.[47] These feminized traits subtly position Ruth as a giver and not a taker in relation to the Israelites, a support and not a threat to the regime. In short, Ozick and Kristeva domesticate Ruth's foreignness by way of her supposed femininity.[48] If Ruth can stay but the foreign Moses could not, that is because Ruth is a woman and is more available, therefore, to be absorbed into Israelite life in Bethlehem.

But Ruth is not the woman Ozick and Kristeva take her to be. She is not merely an accommodating, caring giver. She is a taker, too. Ruth's flair for taking becomes apparent once we unfasten her text from contemporary conventional expectations of feminine virtue.[49] Then we notice that all of Boaz's famous gifts to Ruth and Naomi are actually initiated by Ruth. She turns up in his field; he responds benevolently. She thanks him for his kindness, pointing out her foreignness. He offers her even more. But he does not offer her the full protection that is his to give. So she shows up in his bed and calls upon him to act on behalf of two women who cannot represent themselves in a land deal. Again, he responds positively. One can only assume that marriage was first proposed by Ruth as well.

Of all of Ruth's readers, only the feminist biblical scholar Phyllis Trible sees fully Ruth's character as a taker. Accenting Ruth's agency and initiative, Trible revalorizes the biblical figure of the grasping woman. The Bible's female takers are usually depicted as conniving, scheming, and manipulative. But, says Trible, in a patriarchal society women have to be inventive; all the more so Ruth, who is not just a woman but a foreign widow. So we must admire what just a few other commentators have noticed: Ruth's tendency repeatedly to exceed and even violate the instructions given to her by Naomi. Told by Naomi to go glean with the women, Ruth goes to Boaz's field and gleans with the men, whereupon she is welcomed by Boaz but is told again to stick with the women. Naomi tells Ruth to follow Boaz's lead in their threshing-room floor encounter. He will know what to do. But Ruth herself takes the initiative. Moreover, upon returning to Naomi, Ruth tells her that the gifts of grain with which she has once again returned from Boaz were sent to Naomi with Boaz's best wishes. But the text does not support Ruth's claim. Where most commentators see devotion and obedience, the text of the Book of Ruth repeatedly suggests invention and transgression.[50] For Trible, these departures from the conventional feminine virtues of devotion and obedience are what make Ruth an admirable heroine and an exemplary woman.[51]

Trible's rejection of the conventional assumption that women are and ought to be the giving agents of care positions her to develop a powerful and insightful reading of Ruth. But Trible's approach also highlights a problem. Trible's positively charged image of woman as taker gets its energy from the dominant identification of women as caregivers. Good female takers, no less than bad, Lillith-like takers, are judged against and thereby reinforce the same essential expectation: that women are normally nurturant and caring.[52] Her departure from that conventional expectation is what makes Trible's Ruth exceptional and heroic. But that exceptionalism also reinscribes the very standard that Trible, through Ruth, would like to upset.

In any case, it will not do to force Ruth into being either a giver or a taker, a good woman or an admirably (or not so admirably) bad one. For multiple and probably contradictory reasons, Ruth moves to Bethlehem and does what she can to claim for herself and Naomi the land, marriage, and maternity that will provide them with security. As a Moabite in Bethlehem, Ruth has no right to these things, but she claims them anyway. She acts in advance of the categories that might legitimate her actions, and so models a kind of political agency that is appropriate for those who seek to make claims in the absence of proper legal standing. It was for people such as these that Hannah Arendt developed the idea of "the right to have rights," a most basic right which she attributed to the stateless who are, as she knew, always one step (or more) away from the still largely state-secured rights that so many call simply "human."[53] What is important about the right to have rights in this context is that it invites us to distinguish the status of the immigrant as an object of charity or hospitality (Ozick rightly makes much of this, commending Boaz for his charity to Ruth, a foreigner) from an alternative status, one that does better from the vantage point of democratic theory, that positions the immigrant as a full agent empowered to make (always contestable) claims or take rights on her own behalf. Ruth never exhibits such a full agency. At best, her efforts locate her somewhere on the spectrum between full agency as a taker and the more passive object of her hosts' sometimes ambivalent magnanimity.

Kristeva's Orpahs: Cosmopolitanism without Foreignness

In *Nations without Nationalism*, Kristeva returns to Ruth, whom she sees as a daring but also accommodating border-crossing convert, to model a cosmopolitanism that Kristeva directs at French nationalists and at recent immigrants to France such as the Maghrebi denizens and citizens who "wear the Muslim scarf to school."[54] These immigrants resemble Ruth in their willingness to emigrate from their original homes, but they also resemble Orpah insofar as they remain attached to their particular home cultures.[55] They lack a Naomi to help them make what Kristeva figures as a transition from particularism to a more abstract table of values. They migrate to France but do not endorse its more universal Enlightenment ideals. And so Kristeva demands that immigrants be asked, "What motivated them (beyond economic opportunities and approximate knowledge of the language propagated by colonialism) to choose the French community with its historical memory and traditions as the welcoming lands?" With this question, Kristeva means to elicit an appreciation that is otherwise not apparent or forthcoming.

Is there nothing French that is choiceworthy and to which immigrants might feel allegiance?[56] Kristeva looks among them for evidence of any willingness to do what Ruth did: to swear allegiance to Naomi, her host, and to her god. Indeed, Kristeva's cosmopolitanism depends upon similar pledges of allegiance from French citizens and immigrants alike.[57]

The enduring attachment of many Algerian immigrants to their culture and homeland and their option since 1963 of citizenship in an independent Algeria have led many of them either to reject French citizenship or to relate to it in purely instrumental terms. In response, those on the French Right have in the last fifteen years been calling for tighter controls on immigration and demanding that citizenship be awarded only to those who relate to France affectively. Those on the French

Left resist efforts to control immigration and reject attempts to inscribe citizenship as an affective practice.[58]

Charging that the first response is too "nationalist" and the second too "world-oriented" (the Left is too ready to "sell off French national values"),[59] Kristeva carves out a middle ground between them and offers up a cosmopolitanism that is distinctively French in which the nation is still an important but not all-encompassing site of identity, centered not on *Volk* but on compact.[60] Kristeva resignifies the nation from a final site of affiliation to, in psychoanalytic terms, a *transitional object*. (The object is a device, such as a favorite blanket or stuffed animal, that empowers the child to separate from the mother[land] and eventually, in theory, anyway, move on to an independent—blanketless/postnationalist—existence.) Brilliantly cutting across the French Right-Left divide, Kristeva's cosmopolitanism is rooted and affective but attached finally to a transnational, not a national, object.

Kristeva's cosmopolitanism secures and is secured by affective relations to a series of "sets"—specifically: self, family, homeland, Europe, and mankind—in which each set operates as a transitional object for the next.[61] By locating the sets in a progressive, sequential, trajectory of transition, Kristeva avoids the issue of possible conflicts among them. She also avoids the question of a specifically French affiliation by using the abstract term "homeland" for *that* set. But her call for an identification with *Europe* positions French and Maghrebi subjects asymmetrically in relation to her cosmopolitanism.[62] And because her cosmopolitanism, as she says repeatedly, "make[s] its way through France,"[63] specifically by way of Montesquieu, it works to shore up a uniquely French identity, even while claiming to overcome or transcend it. "[T]here is no way for an identity to go beyond itself without first asserting itself in satisfactory fashion," she says.[64] But this generous recognition of the need to affirm identity before overcoming it is not extended to France's immigrant communities.

There is surely no way out of this paradox, in which cosmopolitanism must be striven for through the particular, albeit heterogeneous, (national) cultures that shape us. (Indeed, this is one way of describing the project of Chapter Four, below, which seeks to recover the nationalist myth of an immigrant America on behalf of a democratic cosmopolitanism.) But Kristeva does not explore the paradox, and she tends to leave the heterogeneity of France behind in her embrace of one particular strand of French Enlightenment thought. She is right to say we must "pursue a critique of the national tradition without selling off its assets." But her account of French cosmopolitanism ultimately protects what she sees as the nation's assets from critique and from critical engagement with others: "Let us ask, for instance, where else one might find a theory and a policy more concerned with respect for the *other*, more watchful of citizens' rights (women and foreigners included, *in spite of blunders and crimes*), more concerned with individual strangeness, in the midst of national mobility?"[65]

The limits of Kristeva's cosmopolitanism emerge again when, echoing Ozick's preference for Ruth over Orpah, Kristeva suggests that the "'abstract' advantages of a French universalism may prove to be superior to the 'concrete' benefits of a muslim scarf," implying that the scarf, unlike the nation, is essentially a fetish and is therefore unable, as such, to serve as a healthy transitional object.[66] She seems to have those who wear the scarf in mind when she says there "are mothers (as well as 'motherlands' and 'fatherlands') who prevent the creation of a transitional object; there are children who are unable to use it."[67] Kristeva sees these veiled women much as Ozick sees Orpah: tethered to their idols, their mothers and motherlands, capable of some bold mobility but ultimately incapable of proper and mature transition, they mark (what Kristeva calls) the "melancholy" of nationalism.[68]

Kristeva quite rightly sees a generative possibility in a differently conceived French *nation*.[69] Why not accord the same possibility to the Moslem scarf? In *Women and Gender in Islam*, Leila Ahmed highlights the progressive properties of veiling. Arguing that for Moslem women in contemporary Egypt the veil, worn increasingly by professional and university women, operates as a kind of transitional object, Ahmed shows how it enables upwardly mobile women to move from the familiar settings of their rural homes "to emerge socially into a sexually integrated world" that is "still an alien, uncomfortable social reality for both women and men."[70] Thus, rather than stand for an unhealthy attachment to one's culture—which is how Kristeva and other critics of veiling figure the practice—veiling, on Ahmed's account, actually enables transition and separation; it provides the distance and insulation that enable women securely to enter the public realm.[71]

Kristeva's and Ahmed's assessments of veiling mirror each other and serve as a synecdoche for broader debates about whether foreignness is good or bad for the nation. In veiling, Kristeva sees a threat of immigrant dilution of national identity, but Ahmed sees the possibility of a supportive and animating diversity; Kristeva sees backward particularism and female confinement, but Ahmed sees progress, in the form of women's entry into the public sphere; Kristeva sees fetish, but Ahmed posits a transitional object. Similarly, in contemporary France, the practice of veiling is figured simultaneously and without any sense of contradiction as both a sign of the powerlessness of Moslem women (who are controlled by their domineering fathers) and as a sign of those same women's great power (to resist the French colonial enterprise, first in Algeria and now in France).[72]

Neither one nor the other as such, practices of veiling, precariously and variously positioned somewhere between patriarchal confinement and female empowerment, harbor both the possibilities laid out by Kristeva and Ahmed (and others still).[73] But the practice's centrality to debates about immigration and foreignness raises another question, beyond that of whether veiling is good or bad for women, good or bad for the receiving regime in question: *What are we doing when we express our concerns about immigration and foreignness through the bodies of women?* This is not a new question—Fanon asked it in "The Unveiling of Algeria"—and when another commentator on veiling answers it, her response echoes Fanon's. Winifred Woodhull explains: "In the eyes of many French people, girls of Magrebian descent are generally diligent students and compliant people—in short the most assimilable element of the immigrant population; if they begin to defend their right to 'difference,' the whole project of integration seems to be jeopardized."[74]

Once again, as with Ozick's and Kristeva's figurations of Ruth, femininity (scripted as compliance) is assumed to soften foreignness. The consequences of that assumption are unmistakable. Set up as good-girl markers of the French Enlightenment project's success, Moslem women are easily cast as the foreign causes of its failure.[75] The Enlightenment project's success depends upon its ability to convert others to its values, so its failure is easily externalized, available to be blamed on unconvertible others who are now scapegoated, cast as unusually recalcitrant,

Lillith-like creatures, or immature and even "autistic" girls. This prevents anyone from asking, self-critically, whether the failure of the project of integration in this instance has anything to do with that project's particular historical articulation in this setting, or with its values or ambition or scope. And it plays into the hands of patriarchal powers by casting women as passive and weak victims of paternal powers, whether religious or familial.

Ironically, however, if Ahmed is at all right and veiling *can* function as a healthy transitional object, then Kristeva's figuring of the veil as a concreteness that must be relinquished in order to accede to the welcome abstraction of cosmopolitanism puts her in the very position of those mothers whom she criticizes, those "mothers (as well as 'motherlands' and 'fatherlands') who prevent the creation of a transitional object." The pleasing irony of this insight should not, however, blind us to the fact that the problem with Kristeva is not simply her failure to explore the transitional properties of veiling while managing nonetheless to see the transitional possibilities of the nation. Were that the case, she could simply change her position on veiling and the problem would be solved.[76] Instead, the problem with Kristeva is her failure to engage others in her deliberations about the project, goals, and instruments of a cosmopolitanism she values too much to risk by including it in the conversation as a question rather than as the answer.[77] Kristeva ends up in this awkward position because she neglects what Judith Butler calls the "difficult labor of translation," an ongoing project of political work that always also involves a critical self-interrogation and courts the risk of transformation.[78] Without a commitment to such a labor, Kristeva's cosmopolitanism already knows what it is—and what it isn't, and so it *risks* becoming another form of domination, particularly when it confronts an other that resists assimilation to it, an other that is unwilling to reperform for "us" the wonder of our conversion to world or French citizenship. This is the other that most worries Kristeva, the migrant other "whose autistic withdrawal into their originary values is not easy to deal with."[79]

When Kristeva does invite an exchange with "foreigners, [which] we all are (within ourselves and in relation to others)," she imagines it will "amplify and enrich the French idea of the nation."[80] But this imagined exchange, in which others join to complete the French idea, calls attention to the need for a different cosmopolitanism in which cosmopolitans risk their cosmopolitan (and nationalist) principles by engaging others in their particularities, while *at the same time* defending, (re)discovering and (re)articulating located universalisms such as human rights and the equal dignity of persons. There is not enough evidence of such a risk in the questions put to immigrants by Kristeva: "What does each immigrant community contribute to the lay concept of *national spirit as esprit général* reached by the French Enlightenment? Do these communities recognize that *esprit général* or not?"[81]

Mourning, Membership, Agency, and Loss: Ruth's Lessons for Politics

I return to *Ruth* by way of a psychoanalytic account of transitional objects. Transitional objects play a role both in Kristeva's account of immigration and cosmopolitanism and in Ozick's reading of the Book of Ruth, in which Naomi is in effect the transitional object that enables Ruth to make the progressive move from Moab to Israel.[82] However, a transitional object account of Ruth can also generate conclusions that are quite different from those reached by Ozick and Kristeva.

Modeling issues of separation and autonomy in terms of the child's developing independence from the mother, the object relations school of psychoanalysis emphasizes the role of transitional objects in the process of individuation.[83] Drawing on the work of D. W. Winnicott, who emphasizes the loss that attends and occasions individuation and separation, Eric Santner argues that transitional objects enable successful separation only if certain necessary conditions are met. First, the separation must not be traumatic; it must be temporary. Second, there must be a healthy environment conducive to transitional object play. And third, that play must have an intersubjective dimension; that is to say, it must be witnessed periodically by the figure whose temporary absences are being borne. If these conditions are met, the space of object play can serve as a site of healthy mourning for the loss entailed by transition. At play with the transitional object, the subject acts out her bereavement and is thereby empowered for separation and individuation (as in the "fort-da" game—a kind of peek-a-boo—described by

Freud). There is empowerment here, not just mourning: the play provides the subject not simply with a substitute (for the loss being mourned), but with a lesson in what Peter Sacks calls "the very means and *practice* of substitution." At best, the subject learns *agency* in the face of loss (perhaps even as a result of it, if the conditions are right for such a learning).[84]

If these conditions are not met, neither mourning nor empowerment will ensue. Instead, the subject will first make a fetish of the object, engaging it in a furious and hyperbolic play that signals her denial of her loss. Second, the object will ultimately lose all meaning for the subject, and she will abandon the object entirely, leaving it stranded. The evacuation of the object's meaning can result in "signification trauma," which leaves the subject stranded, silent, and speechless, outside the world of language, play, and mourning. Emphasizing all three dimensions of transitional object play—mourning, empowerment, and intersubjectivity—Santner summarizes Winnicott's view with the aphorism, "Mourning without solidarity [i.e., transitional object play in the absence of intersubjective witnessing] is the beginning of madness."[85] (Her own debts to psychoanalysis [albeit not to Winnicott] explain why Kristeva describes what she sees as immigrants' failed transition in terms of speechless autism and melancholy.)

How might this account apply to the Book of Ruth? If successful transitions are determined not by the nature of the transitional object itself but by the context in which it operates, then we must attend to the role of institutions, culture, community, and politics in projects of transition, something Kristeva does not do in her critique of immigrant particularism. Moreover, Santner's focus on mourning, empowerment, and intersubjectivity calls attention to the fact that none of these three components of successful transition is available to Ruth. Ruth's separation from Orpah (who, on my account, personifies Moab) is traumatic, not temporary. There is no healthy space for transitional object play, no intersubjective witnessing, and no possibility of proper mourning because Ruth is not given cultural, juridical, or psychological permission to mourn Orpah-Moab. Nor are we. Ruth made the right choice. Ozick and Kristeva agree on that. What could there be to mourn?

Ozick and Kristeva both seem to assume that their affirmation of the rightness of Ruth's choice (and their marginalization of Orpah) is what secures Ruth's transition from Moab. But, if Santner and Winnicott are correct, the opposite is true: Naomi's power as a transitional object for Ruth *depends upon* the proper mourning of Orpah, even upon a kind of continued (perhaps hyphenated?) relation with her (Ozick makes a move in this direction when she says we should "pause" over Orpah, but she then hurries right on past her), even upon recognizing that Orpah (Moab) is part of Ruth. We might even say that Ruth's insight into a universality (as Ozick and Kristeva would put it) is touched by a particularity with which it may be in tension but by which Ruth and her insight are nonetheless also nourished.

Indeed, contra Ozick and Kristeva, the Book of Ruth can be read as a tale of incomplete mourning and failed transition. Seen through the lens provided by Santner, Ruth's famous loyalty to Naomi now can no longer signal simply the selfless devotion of a virtuous or passionate woman, nor is it only a mark of Ruth's immigrant practicality (a possibility I myself raised earlier, along with Fewell and Gunn). What if this clinging is a symptom of Ruth's denial of her loss of Orpah-Moab, a sign of Santner's first stage in which the subject's denial of her loss leads to a frenzied attachment in which the transitional object is fetishized?

And Ruth's closing silence can no longer be taken to signal merely successful absorption.[86] Instead, what if that silence is a mark of Santner's second stage, in which the subject suffers from a "signification trauma"? In Ruth's case, the trauma is produced by the separation from Orpah-Moab and the loss of any meaningful relationship to Naomi, Ruth's transitional object. That second loss is symbolized by Naomi's adoption of Obed (in Ruth's place?) but it is foreshadowed by, among other things, Naomi's failure to introduce or even mention Ruth to the women who welcome Naomi back to Bethlehem.

These two moments in Santner's theory and in Ruth's story mark two familiar moments of immigration dynamics. One, a furious assimilationism in which all connections to the motherland are disavowed. And two, a refusal of transition and a retreat into an enclave that leaves the immigrant stranded in relation to the receiving country *and* in relation to the lost homeland. The two moments are figured developmentally by Santner and Winnicott, but immigrants and their receiving regimes may experience them simultaneously.

The binary of absorption versus enclavism is not driven by foreignness nor by individual foreigners. It is animated by our own efforts to recuperate foreignness for national projects. As we saw earlier, femininity gets similarly driven into categories of goodness or badness by the demand that it support national projects. It is the not very well hidden nationalism of Kristeva's cosmopolitanism that leads her to see newcomers to France in terms of this stern binary. She does not explicitly invoke the sense of kinship that David Miller thinks is a necessary condition of social democracy, but neither does she see foreignness itself as an occasion (and, indeed, a product) of democratic refashioning. The history of interpretative engagements with the Book of Ruth illustrates the consequences of this approach. Democracy is unexpanded and untested by the insistence that others become "us" or go back whence they came. That often punitive insistence itself plays a (never acknowledged) role in producing the very tendencies it excoriates— withdrawalism, recalcitrant particularism, separatism.[87]

We learn a great deal by treating the Book of Ruth not only as a myth of foreign-founding and immigration but also as a parable of mourning and membership. Ruth's role as mourner is signaled early in the text when Naomi, attempting to take leave of Ruth and Orpah, says: "Go, return each to your mother's house: the Lord deal kindly with you, as ye have dealt with the dead, and with me." With the dead, and with me. In that order. It is Antigone's order. First, the dead Polynices (and Jocasta) and then the living Haemon, Creon, and Ismene. It is an ordering that Creon learns from Antigone, at great cost to her and to Haemon. When Creon finally sees the light and rushes to undo his mistakes, he goes first to bury the dead Polynices and only second to save the by then already dead Antigone. In that order: "With the dead, and with me." It was a widows' household that Ruth, Naomi, and Orpah shared, a house built on death.[88]

"The homeopathic constitution and (reconstitution) of the self takes place not in a vacuum," Santner says, "but always in a particular social context."[89] Similarly, the Book of Ruth suggests that there are institutional and cultural conditions for the proper work of mourning, and it teaches the importance to a meaningful and empowered agency of intersubjective spaces, actions in concert, multiple solidarities, civic powers, and (always contested) connections to the past. Because such spaces, actions, powers, and connections are available to Naomi in Bethlehem (Boaz is her relative, the women of Bethlehem are her friends, and her connection to Moab is preserved by Ruth), Naomi is restored to plenitude and agency (symbolized by her adoptive nursing of Obed). Ruth's fate is different because Bethlehem positions her and Naomi asymmetrically in relation to their losses. Naomi's dead sons and husband can be mourned in Bethlehem, but one of Ruth's losses cannot.[90] In the margins of the women's community in Bethlehem, does Ruth mourn Orpah, the sister-in-law who stands for all Ruth left behind in Moab? Ruth's resources and context are limited because the loss of Orpah-Moab is not seen as such, and her transnational connections to Orpah-Moab (a potentially alternative site of support and power) are severed.

Like Antigone's mourning of Polynices, Ruth's mourning of Orpah is forbidden for the sake of a regime's stability and identity. Thus, Ruth's mourning—like Antigone's—is endless, melancholic. Her losses get in the way of the closure this community seeks to attain through her *and* in spite of her. Indeed, the fact that Naomi's restoration to the community is finally marked by her occupation of Ruth's position as mother to Obed suggests that the reinvigoration of this community and the stabilization of David's monarchy depend not only upon the supplement of Ruth's inspiring example but also, and at the same time, upon her marginalization. The Israelites need Ruth's foreignness to shore up their identity as a Chosen People but that identity is also deeply threatened by her foreignness (which must then be hidden or managed under the umbrella of her supposed conversion and assimilation), and there seems to be no way out of this dynamic.

The problem is not Ruth's foreignness, per se. As a foreigner she could be many things: exotic, desirable, mysterious, wise, insightful, dangerous, objective, treasured, and so on. Foreignness will signify different things depending on what work it is being made to do, depending on what goal the community is trying to achieve through the foreigner. The need to have Ruth as a supplement and simultaneously to banish her to the margins is driven by the fact that the community's goal here is not a challenged and contested democracy but rather a kinship-style national identity that needs to have its sense of Chosenness periodically shored up.

In Chapter Two, I suggested that it is important to rethink democracy in non-kinship terms, as a politics among strangers. Here, I make the converse suggestion: what if we redeployed the affective energies of kinship on behalf of a democratic politics that is more cosmopolitan than nationalist in its aspirations? Ruth's severed sororal relation to Orpah calls to mind in particular one example of such an effort: sister-cities use the model and the rhetoric of sororal relation to establish affective sites of transnational connection that bypass state apparatuses in order to pursue shared goals and establish relations of long standing. Usually founded by local civic energies and initiatives, sister-cities are not limited "to carrying out a single project," and this makes them an important complement to more temporary, issue-oriented forms of local and international solidarity that are coalitional.[91] Most important, sister-cities interrupt projects of (re)nationalization by generating practices of affective citizenship and solidarity that exceed state boundaries and sometimes even violate state foreign policy.[92] They are one site of enacted cosmopolitanism, sites of leverage in national politics, sites at which alternative (non-state-centered) forms of membership and affiliation develop.[93] Sister-cities commemorate Ruth and Orpah by enacting a sometimes forbidden sorority rather than inheriting the permitted "genetic" kind. In so doing, they contest the tendency to model state citizenship in terms of kin relations. Instead, they use "kin" relations to model extraterritorial solidarities. They disperse the sites of democratic politics beyond and within the states that would like to be democracy's privileged and exclusive centers. And they thereby reperform a kind of taking for which Ruth herself is rightly famous and should be more so. Sister-cities invite and sometimes enable people to "cross over," as did Moses—not the Moses of Freud, who was unmoved by principles of solidarity, but rather the Moses of Zora Neale Hurston, who, in her own 1930s rewrite of the Moses story, cast Moses as an Egyptian prince whose heart finally went out to the enslaved subjects of his kingdom.

Nothing is more annoying in the ordinary intercourse
of life than this irritable patriotism of the Americans.
A foreigner will gladly agree to praise much in their
country, but he would like to be allowed to criticize
something, and that he is absolutely refused.
— *Alexis de Tocqueville*

4 THE FOREIGNER AS CITIZEN

The Myth of an Immigrant America

"A hero is missing from the revolutionary literature of America," says
Louis Hartz in *The Liberal Tradition in America*. "He is the legislator,
the classical giant who almost invariably turns up at revolutionary moments to be given authority to lay the foundations of the free society"
(p. 46). Hartz may be right that the lawgiver is absent from the scene
of American founding, but the figure of the foreign-founder is not.
Again and again, the American democratic theory literature turns to
foreignness to found the regime or return it to itself. True, the vehicle
of this foreign supplement is not a lawgiver, per se. Instead, American
exceptionalists, from Tocqueville to Hartz to Walzer, treat immigrants
as the agents of founding and renewal for a regime in which member-

ship is supposed to be uniquely consent based, individualist, rational, and voluntarist rather than inherited and organic.[1] For these and many other thinkers, the future of American democracy depends not on the native born but on the recent arrival, not on someone with a past to build on but rather on someone who left his past behind. In short, exceptionalist accounts of American democracy are inextricably intertwined with the myth of an immigrant America.

The myth of an immigrant America depicts the foreigner as a supplement to the nation, an agent of national reenchantment that might rescue the regime from corruption and return it to its first principles. Those first principles may be capitalist, communal, familial, or liberal.[2] In the capitalist version of the myth, the immigrant functions to reassure workers of the possibility of upward mobility in an economy that rarely delivers on that promise, while also disciplining native-born poor, domestic minorities, and unsuccessful foreign laborers into believing that the economy fairly rewards dedication and hard work.[3]

The communitarian immigrant responds to the dissolution of family and community ties, or the prevention of community formation that results in large part from a capitalist economy's unresisted need for a mobile labor force. Periodic infusions of community by way of immigration are said to soften the alienating effects of capitalism's mobilities and of the American liberal individualism that eases their way.

Still others position immigrants as the saviors of traditional patriarchal family arrangements that have been variously attenuated by capitalist mobility and materialism, liberal individualism and feminism. The patriarchal immigrant models proper gender roles and relations for a nation that has lost its sexual bearings. New World American families depend upon Old World masculinities and femininities—family values—that need to be imported periodically from elsewhere.

Finally, liberal consent theorists look to immigrants to solve the problem that Rousseau addressed in the *Social Contract*. Recall that for Rousseau, a legitimate regime is one in which the law, which is always alien, can be made our own by our willing it. Rousseau understood that merely periodic practices such as voting do not position citizens to experience the law as their own. Hence, he argued, the law must be willed frequently, and this was possible under certain, elusive circumstances (by relatively homogeneous citizenries in small polities, and so on). Those circumstances do not exist in the mass, heterogeneous democracy of the United States. While some liberals have argued that American democracy legitimates itself through tacit consent, there is also another mechanism of legitimation at work here, one that operates through the agency of foreignness. The regime's legitimacy is shored up by way of the explicit consent of those celebrated foreigners—immigrants—who, almost daily, are sworn into citizenship in the nation's naturalization ceremonies. More Ruth than Moses (as Hartz's observation about America's lack of a heroic lawgiver would lead us to expect), the liberal consenting immigrant addresses the need of a disaffected citizenry to experience its regime as choiceworthy, to see it through the eyes of still-enchanted newcomers whose choice to come here also just happens to reenact liberalism's own cleaned-up Sinai scene: its fictive foundation in individual acts of uncoerced consent. Simultaneously, the immigrant's decision to come here is seen as living proof of the would-be universality of America's liberal democratic principles.

In all four versions, the myth of an immigrant America recuperates foreignness, en masse, for a national project. It does so by drawing on and shoring up the popular exceptionalist belief that America is a distinctively consent-based regime, based on choice, not on inheritance, on civic not ethnic ties. The exceptionalists' America is anchored by rational, voluntarist faith in a creed, not ascriptive bloodlines, individualism, not organicism, mobility, not landedness.[4] The people who live here are people who once chose to come here, and, in this, America is supposedly unique. In short, the exceptionalist account normatively privileges one particular trajectory to citizenship: from immigrant (to ethnic, as in Walzer but not in Tocqueville) to citizen.

The exceptionalist account captures something about American democracy while also missing a great deal. American democracy is founded not only on immigration but also on conquest (Native Americans) and slavery (the forced importation of African slave labor) and, in the postfounding era, on expansion (Hawaii, Alaska, Puerto Rico, etc.), annexation (French settlements in Illinois, St. Louis, and New Orleans as well as a significant Spanish-speaking population in the Southwest as a result of the war with Mexico), and more slavery. These other foundings are often obscured by the hegemonic myth of an immigrant America. In Charleston, South Carolina, for example, a tourist pamphlet announces that Sullivan Island, off the coast of the city, "might well be viewed as the Ellis Island of black Americans."[5]

In its favor, we might say that at least the myth generates an open and inclusive tolerance of diverse immigrants. But things are not so simple. In fact, the myth generates a sense of quite *anxious* dependence upon the kindness of strangers. The foreigners whose immigrations to the United States daily reinstall the regime's most beloved self-images are also looked on as threats to the regime. And this is no accident.

American political culture is marked by a play of xenophobia and xenophilia that is not simply caused by periodic power changes from nativists to inclusionists, as Michael Walzer and Rogers Smith both suggest.[6] Nor is it merely a sign of changing economic "realities," from expanding to shrinking labor needs.[7] These may be parts of the story, but there is a deeper logic at work here.

In the various versions of the myth of an immigrant America, it is— as was the case with Ruth—the immigrant's *foreignness* that positions him to reinvigorate the national democracy, and that foreignness is undecidable: our faith in a just economy, our sense of community or family, our consent-based sense of legitimacy, or our voluntarist vigor are so moribund that only a foreigner could reinvigorate them. But the dream of a national home, helped along by the symbolic foreigner, in turn animates a suspicion of immigrant foreignness at the same time. "Their" admirable hard work and boundless acquisition puts "us" out of jobs. "Their" good, reinvigorative communities also look like fragmentary ethnic enclaves. "Their" traditional family values threaten to overturn our still new and fragile gains in gender equality. "Their" voluntarist embrace of America, effective only to the extent that they come from elsewhere, works to reaffirm but also endangers "our" way of life. The foreigner who shores up and reinvigorates the regime also unsettles it at the same time. Since the presumed test of both a good and a bad foreigner is the measure of her contribution to the restoration of the nation rather than, say, to the nation's transformation or attenuation, nationalist xenophilia tends to feed and (re)produce nationalist xenophobia as its partner.

Ali Behdad is the only critic who comes close to seeing this undecidability of foreignness. He describes the "nation's mode of identification" as always "ambivalent: on the one hand, we are a nation of immigrants; on the other hand, we identify ourselves against our immigrants as we try to control them." That ambivalence is worth attending to, Behdad astutely argues, because it is a productive site for the state's development of myriad "strategies of discipline, normalization, and regulation."[8] In other words, rather than strive to undo that ambivalence—by attributing it to different parties (as Walzer does) or to different traditions (as Smith does) or to different time periods (as many historians do)—Behdad asks about the performative effects of that ambivalence. What productive energies are unleashed at its site? How does that site serve as "a space of contestation where concepts of nationality as citizenship and state as sovereignty can be re-articulated and re-affirmed"?[9]

Behdad's account and mine work these issues through different texts, and we use different analytic lenses, but we form an obvious and, I hope, productive alliance that calls for the reexamination of some staple assumptions in the study of American nationalism and democracy. However, we differ on one crucial point: when Behdad traces out American ambivalences about immigrants, he misses the pole that is, to my mind, most important. Pointing out that both pro- and anti-immigration movements in the United States are marked by an "us" and "them" mentality, he argues that even those who favor immigration tend to cast immigrants in "symbolically violent" terms.[10] He illustrates the American ambivalence regarding foreigners with the following list of "contradictory stereotypes: on the one hand, the immigrant is weak and wretched [and therefore possessed of a claim on our 'humanitarian' sentiments], and, on the other, powerful and dangerous [and therefore a threat to our nation]; on the one hand an opportunist who steals our jobs, and, on the other, a lazy parasite who abuses our social welfare funds." In sum, Behdad concludes, "these stereotypes point to the ambivalence of the nation toward its immigrants, an ambivalence marked by both knowledge and disavowal, control and defense, exclusion and amnesty, acceptance and rejection."[11]

But one stereotype is missing here: the supercitizen immigrant.[12] Neither needy nor threatening, as such, but always mirrored by and partnered with those others, the supercitizen immigrant is the object of neither American hostility nor charity but of outright adoration. The stereotypically weak immigrant and the stereotypically powerful one both elicit disavowal. But the supercitizen immigrant is an object of identification. He is the screen onto which we project our idealized selves. He works harder than we do, he values his family and community more actively than we do, and he also fulfills our liberal fantasy of membership by way of consent. Somehow, this iconic good immigrant manages to have it all—work, family, community, and a consensual relation to a largely nonconsensual democracy—even though these very goods are experienced by the rest of us as contradictory or elusive: work in late modern capitalist economies often demands hours and mobilities that are in tension with family and community commitments; meaningful consent eludes the native born for reasons I discuss below.

The immigrant as supercitizen is a staple of the exceptionalist literature and is worth attending to now because he is still very much alive as a political-cultural resource today. In recent years, with the rise of xenophobic initiatives in the United States, Americans on both the Right and the Left have sought to recover the iconic good immigrant who once helped build this nation and whose heirs might contribute to the national future. Both political theorists and activists have responded to renewed anti-immigrant sentiment by stressing the gifts that foreigners have to offer receiving regimes. But what if their xenophilia is intimately connected with the xenophobia they deplore and seek to combat? Deploying the supercitizen immigrant on behalf of a national ideal, do these xenophiles feed the fire they mean to fight?

Another perhaps useful way of exploring the potentially intimate connections between xenophobia and xenophilia might be to recast what I am calling the undecidability of foreignness in terms of the politics of friendship elucidated by Jacques Derrida. Recall Aristotle's distinction among three kinds of friendship—virtue, pleasure, and use—and Derrida's claim, contra Aristotle, that politics is not confined to the register of use but arises instead when mistakes are made among the different kinds of friendship. In Chapter Three we saw how Aristotle's three kinds of friendship correspond to three readings of Ruth's famous speech to Naomi. The same three kinds of friendship also correspond to the varieties of immigrant supplement traced here. Friendship as use is represented by the capitalist immigrant who comes here to make money. Friendship as virtue is represented by the communitarian and familial immigrants who model proper community and family devotion. And friendship as pleasure is represented by the consenting immigrant who exhibits an exemplary love for the law. The lines of demarcation are not perfectly clear; there are traces of all three kinds of friendship in each of the four supplements of foreignness mapped out here. For example, there is virtue in loving the law and pleasure in capitalist success. Nonetheless, the trichotomy works well enough to enable us to map out the patterns of misunderstanding and disappointment that generate a politics among would-be friends (and not, *pace* Behdad, between an us and a them, per se). Again and again, as we shall see throughout this chapter, from community-oriented foreigners who live in enclaves to those women who come to the United States as foreign brides, the play of xenophilia and xenophobia is accelerated or renewed when the one friend's (or nation's) expectations of a particular sort of relationship are disappointed and met instead by another. Often, this disappointment is expressed by way of the charge that the other is a taker who is just using us rather than a giver who really wants to be one of us. As we saw with Ruth, however, the "taking" foreigner actually has something very important to give to democratic theorists and citizens.

Because the myth of an immigrant America is very powerful and its effects are quite real, it is important to ask whether democracy is well or ill-served by it.[13] And are there any alternative, also normative but less nationalist and more cosmopolitan uses to which the myth of an immigrant America might be put in a counterpolitics of foreignness? These questions are particularly pressing because the success of the myth of an immigrant America in setting the thoroughly nationalist terms of the contemporary immigration debate in the United States suggests that those who look to the mere fact of heightened migration as a bellwether of a new, *post*national order are falsely confident. If left unchallenged, national imaginations (and the U.S. national imagination in particular) are creative enough and well funded enough to recuperate symbolic immigrant energies for national projects, while also often mistreating actual immigrants.

Mere facts—the mere fact of heightened migration—cannot be counted upon to do the world-building work of politics. People cross borders all the time. As we saw with Russia's Riurik and with the Israelites' Ruth, it is not the fact but the significance of those crossings, the meanings and causes on behalf of which those crossings can be pressed into service, that is the stuff of politics. Riurik was mobilized on behalf of nationalist and cosmopolitan causes alike. Similarly, Ruth was available for capture on behalf of diverse causes ranging from Ozick's ethnonationalist Judaism to Kristeva's still nationalist cosmopolitanism. American immigrants are just as variously available for capture on behalf of diverse causes, and this is what the symbolic politics of immigration is all about: the struggle and counterstruggle to define the terms of foreignness in relation to the always shifting terrain and values of national or democratic polities.

Class Mobility as American Citizenship

It is by now commonplace to hear the capitalist success of (a small minority of) immigrant and ethnic groups explained in terms of their immigrant drive (often said to be lacking in domestic minorities) and in terms of their large extended families and communities who provide cheap labor and pool their resources. What is valued here are the resources available to be sacrificed for financial success, not the affective family or community relations themselves, nor their potential to serve as sites of associational political power.[14]

The capitalist immigrant helps keep the American Dream alive, upholding popular beliefs in a meritocratic economy in good times and bad. If he can do it, starting with nothing and not knowing the language, surely anyone can. At the same time, however, the use of foreignness to supplement the national economy and discipline the domestic poor engenders resentment of foreigners for competing with the native born for scarce resources. Because the capitalist foreigner is depicted as someone who is interested only in material things, he quickly turns from someone who has something to offer us into someone who only wants to take things from us.[15] His virtuosic acquisitiveness slides easily into a less admirable, crass, and self-serving materialism. The nationalist, xenophilic deployment of the foreigner to model the American Dream does not just offset these xenophobic reactions, it itself helps to generate them.

The effects of the capitalist version of the myth of an immigrant America on American democracy are particularly unwelcome. The resources of democratic citizenship are diminished, not enhanced, by a supplement of foreignness that is made to stand for privatization, the accumulation of extreme wealth, and a complete disinterest in civic and political life. The myth undermines potential interethnic and transnational coalitions of labor, and it celebrates radical inequalities that are in deep tension with democratic citizenship. The new model minorities do not just "make it"; they become outlandishly wealthy. This version of the myth identifies citizenship with materialism, capitalist production, and consumption. The foreigners depicted here are not politically engaged. They are too busy living the American Dream.

Hence the tone of surprise governing a typical *New York Times* article reporting on the politicization of Asian Americans: "Marty Shih is the kind of person who has earned Asian Americans the widespread characterization as the model minority," writes Steven A. Holmes, perversely assigning to Mr. Shih the responsibility for the media's label. In just eighteen years, Mr. Shih, "through grit and hard work" turned the $500 with which he arrived in America into a $40 million business. "But Mr. Shih's rags-to-riches story *took an unusual path* last month when he established the Asian American Association to, among other things, campaign against legislation that would drastically reduce the levels of legal immigration, an issue that has galvanized Asian Americans like no other in recent times."

The "usual" trajectory of Asian American incorporation is commercial, not political.[16] Immigrants, especially America's model minorities, stay away from politics. But do they? Completely absent from this now conventional picture are noncitizen or new citizen political actors as diverse as the Haymarket activists (imprisoned or deported), Sacco and Vanzetti (executed), Harry Bridges (leader of the 1934 San Francisco general strike who fought deportation efforts in the courts and won),[17] Emma Goldman (expelled), Harry Wu, and a whole slew of others involved in contemporary labor, local and school politics, from undocumented workers in Southern California active in unionization politics to Cambodians agitating for decent public schooling for their children in Lowell, Massachusetts, to Chinese locals involved in "educational struggle" in San Francisco, to aliens stumping for local candidates in New York.[18]

Contemporary depictions of immigrants as concerned only with material acquisition and not with empowered democratic agency are not only misleading. Worse yet, they are often *enforced* in response to immigrants who become politicized enough to trouble this dominant normative image of quiescence. Take California's Proposition 187, for example. Given the local economy's dependence upon foreign labor, it makes little sense to think that the intended effect of that proposition was simply and merely to deter immigrants from crossing the border. Deterrence may have been part of the intended effect. But another effect is surely also counted upon: the recriminalization of the alien population and new, heightened costs of alien visibility. The result is not just to reduce illegal immigration but to quash the potential power of the undocumented as political actors, labor organizers, and community activists.[19]

Ethnic Bases of Social Democracy:
Michael Walzer's Immigrant America

Michael Walzer's communitarian version of the myth of an immigrant America is tailored to respond to the private realm withdrawalism wrongly valorized by the capitalist version of the myth. Given the success of the capitalist economy and America's liberal ideology in individuating, uprooting, and alienating most of the regime's members, Walzer argues, only newcomers can be counted upon to have and to foster the social, civic, and familial ties that social democracy presupposes. For Walzer, then, the model immigrant is not the capitalist overachiever but the family member who cares for his own and builds community institutions. The communitarian immigrant imports a form of citizenship that liberal capitalist America is always in danger of losing or consuming. Walzer's iconic immigrant reinvigorates civil society and the mediating institutions upon which social democracy depends.

In *What It Means to Be an American*, Walzer observes that "citizens are not effective one by one but only when they are bound together in states or freely associated in parties, interest groups, or social movements. And culture is not sustained by private men and women but by families, nations, and communities of faith."[20] The health and vigor of social democratic pluralism depends upon new waves of immigration because the newest hyphenates are the most zealous in their community-sustaining activities.[21] But activists get battle fatigue. Community members get distracted by private concerns and withdraw their energies from one another and from public concerns over time. The black feminist activist, Bernice Johnson Reagon, responds to these inevitabilities with the instruction to keep our eyes on the oldest activists whose commitments have somehow endured.[22] Walzer's counsel is to focus on the newest comers: "Continued large-scale immigration . . . creat[es] new groups of hyphenate Americans and encourag[es] revivalism among activists and believers in the old groups."[23]

Walzer's immigrants import the family and community ties that life in capitalist America destroys. They tend to their own and—with federal government help in the way of funding and support for continued immigration—they are empowered to build and run much-needed institutions.[24] Walzer's America is dotted by Jewish hospitals, Moslem schools, and Swedish old-age homes. If ethnic communities are allowed to deteriorate, or if they are prevented from forming (by way of enforced assimilation, lack of funds, or the elimination of immigration), then, Walzer worries, the basic institutions of American social democracy will vanish as well. For Walzer, America's immigrants and ethnics moderate the excesses of American individualism (the form of corruption that attaches to liberalism) while also refusing the fragmentation of subnationalism and separatism (the forms of corruption that attach to communitarianism).

Walzer's image of the immigrant as, effectively, a refounder of American civil society is powerful, and its worthy aim is to generate a tolerance and magnanimity toward newcomers that is all too often absent from the American political landscape. But, positioned as the bearers of a "communitarian corrective" to American liberal capitalism, Walzer's immigrant communities attract not only gratitude but also, inevitably, suspicion.[25] These much-lauded organic communities of virtue, positioned as so contributive to the national democracy, are also seen as threatening enclaves that reject American values even while living in our midst.[26] The communitarian xenophilic deployment of foreignness *on behalf of a national project* itself plays into the hands of and, indeed, helps to feed this xenophobic response.

That xenophobic response may in fact be amplified by the other gift borne by Walzer's immigrants. For Walzer, the supplement of immigrant foreignness perpetually resecures the character of American liberal democracy as thinly patriotic rather than zealously so. American national affect consists in little more than "the flag and the pledge" *because* it is a nation of immigrants, Walzer says. "However grateful they are for this new place, [immigrants] still remember the old places."[27] But what is the significance of their memory? Does Walzer mean to say that it stands in the way of immigrants' becoming nationalized to the point of zealotry? A powerful if literal illustration to the contrary is the organization by myriad ethnic groups of their members into volunteer units to fight in the Civil War: the "German 18th Regiment, the Polish Legion, the Cameron Rifle Highlanders, the Guard de La Fayette, the Netherlanders' Legion, and the [more multicultural] Garibaldi Guard, which was made up of Hungarians, French, Spaniards, and Croats, as well as Italians."[28]

Is there a singular "experience" to which Walzer can be referring when he says: "This is not Europe; we are a society of immigrants, and the experience of leaving a homeland and coming to this new place is an *almost* universal 'American' experience. It should be celebrated"?[29] Perhaps Walzer is not trying to refer to an antecedent experience so much as he is trying to generate a new one: a thinly national sense of commonality around a not yet shared but perhaps now soon to be shared sense of immigrant journey. What could be wrong with that?

One problem is that the celebration of America's "almost universal" immigrant experience does not simply limit American nationalism; it is also a vehicle of it. The myth of an immigrant America is a nationalist narrative of choiceworthiness. In the American context, the pleasure and reinvigoration of having been chosen is illustrated and produced by the *New York Times's* periodic publication of a photograph of new citizens taking the oath. That pleasure is further protected by the failure of the United States to keep any continuous official statistics on remigration or emigration.[30] And as Walzer's self-conscious "almost" indicates, the universalization of America's immigrant "experience" has effects on those minorities whose membership in the regime does not map on to the immigrant trajectory to citizenship normatively privileged by Walzer.

In particular, when landed and racial minorities "still remember the old places," the political import of their memory is quite different from the nostalgic yearnings of Walzer's immigrants. Unlike America's traditional ethnic groups, some blacks, Native Americans, and Hispanics have legitimate land-based claims. Unlike America's traditional ethnics, these groups have sometimes sought more than mere recognition. Contra Walzer, who says this never happens, these groups have at times sought secession, or even self-government.[31] It is no accident that these forms of political activism are obscured by Walzer's redeployment of the myth of an immigrant America.[32] Their demands might divide or fragment the nation-state rather than reanimate it from below. For Walzer, as for many on the Left, the nation-state must be protected from such divisive claims because it is the most likely organizing force of any social-democratic politics.

Landed and racial minorities are not the only ones whose claims are marginalized by Walzer's account, however. Also obscured from view are the many nonethnic institutions for health, education, and welfare in the United States. Especially noteworthy in the last decade or two have been such groups as Planned Parenthood, ACT UP, and the Gay Men's Health Crisis. Why aren't the rather substantial democratic energies of such groups also granted a privileged place in Walzer's immigrant-invigorated civil society? If "citizens are not effective one by one but only when they are bound together in states or freely associated in parties, interest groups, or social movements," why not include as many groups as possible, as long as those groups contribute to the furtherance of social democratic projects?

Walzer's broad commitment to a vigorous civil society suggests he does support such groups. If he does not mention them explicitly, that may be because gay, lesbian, and feminist movements highlight the formation of secondary associations not just out of new migrations (Walzer's preferred source in the U.S. case) but also (as in feminisms or gay rights movements, for example) out of *injuries* wrought by established, traditional groups.[33] Feminists, gays, and lesbians establish alternative institutional resources because their needs are not met and their ways of life are often not tolerated by the ethnic and civic communities with whom they might otherwise identify. In short, the autonomy of these extraethnic groups is itself a *symptom* of the sometime injustices of the various immigrant groups whose energies animate Walzer's civil society.

Others, more socially conservative than Walzer, share his concern about the rootlessness and mobility of late modern life, but they associate these explicitly with the loss of the very traditional family and community structures against which many feminist, gay, and lesbian groups often define themselves. For many pro-immigration conservatives, immigrants import the roles and expectations that maintain traditional, patriarchal structures. Here, new immigrants are mobilized symbolically to renormalize the native born into traditional heterosexual gender roles while "we" supposedly normalize "them" into a new national citizenship. This dynamic is powerfully illustrated in a popular fable of immigration and national renewal: the Australian film, *Strictly Ballroom*.

Foreign Brides, Family Ties, and New World Masculinity

Strictly Ballroom, a campy comic Australian fable of immigration and national renewal, tells the story of an atrophied community of ballroom dancers saved from corruption by a Spanish immigrant, Fran, who brings new life and virtue to their practices and new energy to their flamenco.[34] Initially, Fran seeks assimilation. She assiduously studies the forced steps that are the unquestioned ground upon which the community's dancers are judged. But her quest for inclusion is bound to fail. She has no connections in this corrupt community in which connections are necessary for success, and she has little to recommend her. Dancing "their" steps, she is awkward. She is also unattractive, weighed down by the thick glasses that film heroines have forever removed to reveal a stunning but somehow hitherto unsuspected beauty.

There is an opening for her, however. The powdery white, desiccated community is not only corrupt, it is also riven. One of its members, their star dancer, is a renegade who dares to depart from the community's fetishized steps. When Scott does his own thing, Fran is thrilled and impressed, but the community is aghast. From their perspective, he is too undisciplined, wild, all over the place. His dance seems to have no structure. The choice seems to be between the structure and discipline of a corrupt and unjust but orderly and established community, and a radical individualism that is irresponsible, chaotic, and nihilistic.[35] (In short, the film replays the most caricatured versions of contemporary political theory's liberal-communitarian debate.)

Scott's free dance style represents a self-seeking individualism that is symptomatic of the community's larger corruptions. Scott's mother, a disciplinary agent who consistently tries to renormalize Scott into the extant ballroom community, herself acts as a self-seeking individualist, too: she is cheating on Scott's father, having an affair with an oily man of superior standing in the dance community.

These corruptions are healed by the foreigner, Fran, and her family. Scott's individualism is tamed and structured by Fran's father, an Old World patriarch. This dark Spanish immigrant gives the couple lessons in authentic flamenco dancing.[36] (Fran's father used to dance with her mother[land], but his partner passed away.) At the same time, Fran's father teaches the youths two other lessons: his daughter learns to affirm her roots rather than deny them, and Scott learns that his dance and life choices are not exhausted by the options of the "strictly ballroom" community versus a renegade individualism. In the authentic flamenco of this immigrant community, Scott finds a Walzerian resource that provides his innovative dance (and his life) not only with the energy he craves but also with a shaping structure that distinguishes that newly energized dance from the chaotic individualism Scott's home community fears.[37]

At the final dance contest, Scott and Fran dance an energized and innovative flamenco that is not undisciplined and is capable, therefore, of finally felling the corrupt leaders of the strictly ballroom community whose lies and deceits are exposed. Scott's (Australian) individualism, now moderated and anchored by Fran's émigrée authenticity and familial bonds, refounds the dance community, rescuing it from its pallid fetishisms and restoring to it its original energy and its founding principles of elegance, honesty, creativity, and fairness.[38]

Fran functions as the communitarian/ethnic corrective of Scott's loveless individualism. But the film features a second supplementary relation as well: Fran's father, an empowered father-figure and a representative of the old patriarchal order, takes the place of Scott's father, a hopelessly henpecked, feeble, and feminized man who is utterly powerless to help his troubled son. Indeed, it often seems that Scott is more drawn to Fran's father than to Fran, that Scott values Fran because she is a way for Scott to get closer to a real father. This immigrant patriarch's foster fathering does not only benefit Scott; it also frees Scott's father from his dominating, castrating wife. The energies unleashed by these foreigners and, in particular, the example of Fran's Old World father benefit Scott's father: they make a man out of him.

In short, the supplement of foreignness works on at least two registers in *Strictly Ballroom*: through the agency of foreignness, proper virtue is restored to the social world of the ballroom while proper order is restored to the patriarchal family at Scott's house. With the proper containment of the feminine (in the form of Scott's outrageously ambitious mother), Scott's father can be a father again, and the world is made safe for the (re)emergence of an Australian masculinity from within the confines of the feminized, suburban household. The agents of all this are the foreigners who import proper masculinity and proper femininity to a place that has lost its gender bearings. That is to say, *Strictly Ballroom* replays the classical republican identifications of corruption with female ambition and male emasculation and of refounding with a return to proper gender identities and roles.[39]

But the importation of a real masculinity from elsewhere does not only save Australian masculinity. It also stands as a perpetual reminder of the inadequacy of Australian masculinity. By comparison with Fran's father, who personifies an authentic, Old World masculinity, won't Australian masculinity always be a mere copy? And yet, without Fran's father, Australian masculinity will continue to be consumed by the feminized household of suburbia. There is no way out of this quandary.

Perhaps the point is that Australian masculinity needs not just the supplement of Fran's father but also that of Fran herself, who is enough of an Old World woman to provide Scott in marriage and in dance with the sort of adoring feminine prop that proper masculinity requires. The young couple's relationship, the film implies, will be different from Scott's parents' marriage because Scott's immigrant girlfriend comes from a family that values family more than the instrumental goods and status that led Scott's mother astray. By modeling immigration politics in terms of this new relationship, the film suggests that it may be possible for immigrants and members of the receiving regime to relate to each other without politics, as two Aristotelian friends somehow positioned on a single, unambiguous (and safely heterosexual) register of friendship.

The desire for an Old World wife to prop up New World masculinity and restore the patriarchal family is evident not only in film. These days the demand is met (and fed) by companies such as Scanna International Worldwide Introductions, which "introduce" American men to foreign women. As one of their clients, David Davidson of Fairlawn, Ohio, explains: " 'There's an exodus of men leaving this country to find wives,' Davidson said. 'They're looking for women with traditional values like we had 40 years ago.[40] They're finding Russian women have those values. Family comes first for them—not work or the Mercedes or the bank account,' said Davidson who has been married and divorced four times." Of his own Russian fiancée, Davidson said, "She is the most feminine young woman that I've been in the company of. She knows how to be a lady."[41]

Davidson's confident opposition between family values and rank materialism is called into question by another American man interviewed for the same article: "In one form or another [American men] are sick and tired of the princess attitude of American women. . . . Russian women are old-fashioned. . . . Their husband and family come first." But he added that "Russian women see marriage to U.S. men as a way to improve their impoverished lives."

The existence of a foreign bride *trade* already suggests that—the protests of American men notwithstanding—these marriages are not simply romantic. Indeed, the trade highlights the nature of the institution of marriage in general as not only an institutionalized form of heterosexual intimacy but also always a site at which all sorts of goods and services are exchanged, including citizenship, legal residence status, money, companionship, and sex.[42] Moreover, the fact that diverse American, Japanese, Taiwanese, and Arabic men locate a real femininity in places as diverse as Russia, Thailand, and the Philippines suggests that none of these places is a wellspring of true femininity. What if, instead, the foreignness of the imported brides functions to produce a set of relations and inequalities that are available to be (mis)read as femininity?[43] This would account for how it is that, somehow, the purchase of a foreign bride—for $7,500 and a residency permit—is said to put the romance back into an institution that is losing its charm.

A foreign bride's perceived family priorities may be less a matter of feminine affect than a matter of necessity. Isolated from others and dependent upon her husband, the foreign bride is ignorant of local customs and languages. Her subject position mimes that of the traditional, feminine wife, but foreignness abets or trumps femininity as the real and reliable cause of a foreign bride's dependence and acceptance, her so-called family values. What is labeled "feminine" and eroticized is the foreign bride's would-be powerlessness, her confined agency and her limited alternatives. That perceived powerlessness is why the husbands, who believe that their foreign wives are feminine and unmaterialistic, are undisturbed by the knowledge that these women—who are seeking to escape poverty and limited opportunities, after all—are actually quite interested in the very thing to which they are supposed to be indifferent: their husbands' proverbial "bank account" and the size of it. What is most important is not finally whether the woman is interested in money but whether she has the power to pursue that interest by way of employment for herself or ambition on her husband's behalf.

The xenophilic embrace of foreignness to reenchant traditional family structures generates two xenophobic responses. Increasingly, the popular press has been publishing stories of foreign brides who turn out to have been using the husbands who sponsored their entry into the United States. Instead of self-sacrificing caregivers, these women are said to be untrustworthy takers. Acting as Lilliths rather than Ruths, they cheat their husbands, rob them, and leave them. More fundamentally, they wrong not only their husbands; they cheapen the institution of marriage by treating it instrumentally. An Aristotelian reading of the situation would say that it is because these wives relate to their husbands on the register of use rather than on the register of pleasure or virtue that the institution of marriage is politicized. Derrida would probably suggest, however, that it is the inevitable confusion of pleasure, virtue, and use (clearest here but attached to the institution of marriage as such) that is responsible for the politicization of marriage.

Such loveless marriages are seen as doubly dangerous (certainly more dangerous than all the other loveless marriages in the nation) because they disenchant two of the nation's most beloved institutions: the institution of marriage, which foreign brides are supposed to help prop up, as well as the institution of citizenship, which is supposedly damaged when immigrants acquire it improperly.[44] The affective health of both institutions depends upon immigrants' being attracted to them not for the sake of money or other worldly goods but rather for the sake of a love, devotion, or virtue that is seen as prior to the institutions in question and not as one of their ideological effects. To the critical question—Do these passions give legitimacy to the state (or marriage), or does the state (or marriage) itself generate and legitimate these passions?—this first xenophobic response has an emphatic if conventional answer: "First comes love, then comes. . . ."

The second xenophobic response generated by this particular xenophilia is audible in my own text. Here patriarchal immigrants are seen as threats to the rough (very rough) gender equalities that are American liberal democracy's ambiguous achievement.[45] The xenophilic deployment of foreignness on behalf of traditional family structures is particularly troublesome for social democrats because the foreign bride trade promises to resecure and revalorize female powerlessness and male power. The xenophilic deployment of foreignness to solve the problems of gender politics generates these xenophobic responses. This is what happens when foreigners are pressed into service on behalf of institutions—capitalism, community, family—that seem incapable of sustaining themselves. The deployment of foreignness as a restorative supplement itself positions foreigners also as the original cause of the very institutional illness they are supposed to be curing. Where foreign women are figured as exemplary wives who can save the institution of romantic marriage, they inevitably fail, and then they are also set up as betrayers of that and other ideals: the self-interested corrupters of increasingly devalued institutions whose downfall can now be safely attributed to the institutions' abuse at the hands of untrustworthy outsiders who never really loved us but were only out to use us all along.

Dramatizing Consent: The Universal Charms of American Democracy

The demand that foreign women bring feminine romance to American marriages is paralleled by the demand that immigrants romance America and help to reenchant another institution that many feel is in danger of losing its affective charms: the institution of citizenship. The fourth and final redeployment of the myth of an immigrant America, the liberal version, looks to immigrants to reperform the official social contract by naturalizing to citizenship. In the case of the United States, this means (re)enacting for established citizens the otherwise too abstract universalism of America's democratic constitutionalism.[46]

Immigrants not only testify to the universality of American constitutional principles, they are also the only Americans who actually *consent* explicitly to the regime. Since liberal democracies draw their legitimacy from their consent base, the failure of the native born to consent explicitly seems to pose a deep problem for liberal democracies. Some liberals solve the problem by way of tacit consent. Others, like Peter Schuck and Rogers Smith, have sought instead to provide heightened opportunities for the native born to consent explicitly.

In *Citizenship without Consent: Illegal Aliens in the Polity*, Schuck and Smith argue that native-born citizens should be offered the opportunity to self-expatriate at the age of majority.[47] Although a right of expatriation now exists, few know about it and it is not easy to exercise. Schuck and Smith favor routinizing the choice (by way of automatic mailings to native-born citizens at the age of majority) and lowering the costs (citizens might choose permanent resident status, not necessarily emigration).[48] Why make these changes? "In a polity in which actual consent is expressed symbolically only through periodic elections, these proposals can impart a new social meaning and integrity to the tacit consent that must suffice during the intervening periods."[49]

It is possible that these changes may heighten consent for the native born, and they may help relegitimate the liberal state, as Schuck and Smith say.[50] But such changes may have other effects as well. For the sake of a heightened affect and legitimacy, Schuck and Smith are willing to risk the creation of a rather substantial class of resident aliens, which is what will become of those who eschew the new invitation to consent. How will Schuck and Smith's revalorized citizenship benefit from the development of a potentially large class of persons willing to live here and consume goods and services without partaking of the rights (voting) and obligations (military service) of citizenship?[51] What will become of state citizenship when it is transformed from a supposedly universal category into a property of a self-chosen few? (This is not to say that citizenship should be preserved without change but rather to ask, genuinely, what would happen to its meaning and practice if the changes called for by Schuck and Smith were actually instituted.)

More to the point, what sort of power can we expect to come out of a mailed-in consent form? Consent by mail, an action, typically liberal, taken in private, is not likely ever to have the same affective symbolic-cultural effect as the public scene it is intended to mime: that of new citizens taking the oath of citizenship. As Sanford Levinson suggests, immigrant naturalization ceremonies function as a kind of "national liturgy."[52] With a hope and a prayer and an oath, the gap of consent is filled. Immigrant naturalization ceremonies—frequently publicized on the front pages of the nation's newspapers—testify to the fundamental consentworthiness of the regime by symbolically representing the consent that is effectively unattainable for native-born citizens of a liberal regime.

Does this mean that new citizen oath takers act as consenters by proxy, giving voice to the (supposed) silent, tacit consent of the native born? There is something odd about thinking that immigrants can fill the gap of consent when immigrants are so often infantilized (they can't speak English, they need help) and seen as desperate.[53] How could such (symbolic) persons be positioned to enact the mature, balanced, and reasonable reflection of rational consent? If the immigrant is desperate, infantile, or "too foreign," his speech act will misfire (it may look like parody to the native born). Indeed, liberals who want immigrants to help solve liberal democracies' legitimation problem are pressed by their own demands to distinguish impossibly between sincere and fraudulent speech acts, admirable immigrant idealism and rough practicality, and among virtue, pleasure, and use—is it true love or are they just using us?[54] As of April 1, 1997, elderly or mentally ill immigrants who cannot utter the words of the citizenship oath can no longer become citizens. Is it the inaccessibility of immigrant intentions that drives the last decade's obsession with the quite literal performance of the speech act of citizenship? Or is that obsession, perched on the "paradox of intention and capacity," itself a symptom of the modern liberal effort to (in Elizabeth Wingrove's words) "theorize an individualism consistent with new standards of political legitimacy: consent"?[55]

The intractability of these problems (is the naturalizing immigrant sincere or is he just out for himself?) suggests that if immigrants and their swearing-in ceremonies are doing some symbolic-cultural-political work, that work must be something other than the simple provision of consent by proxy. What else might it be?

First, these ceremonies give the abstract value of consent a material and embodied form, thus addressing a problem that Elizabeth Wingrove identifies by way of Rousseau: "that consent makes sense only in its material enactments and that it remains unintelligible when divorced from worldly—institutional, bodily—conditions."[56] As we saw with Ruth, so too here the abstract universal (the invisible god of Judaic monotheism, the universal and formal rights and powers of American constitutionalism) requires its abstractness in order to be what it is, but it also requires, paradoxically, concretization by way of particular, empirical manifestations of its power; hence Ruth's endlessly retold "conversion" story, hence the dissemination of the now iconic photo of new immigrants taking the pledge of citizenship. The American need for periodic testimony to the true universality of its principles and the choiceworthiness of its democracy is met by new immigrant foreigners. Indeed, as we saw with Ruth, the more foreign the new consenter, the more powerful the impact of her consent as testimony to the universal's universal attractiveness.[57]

At a deeper level, the rite of naturalization does not just reenact or embody consent. It reperforms the origin of the regime *as* an act of consent. The oft-disseminated spectacle of new citizens taking the oath of citizenship—a scene in which the new citizen and the state embrace each other in an act of speech—recenters the regime on its fictive foundation of voluntarist consent. Two effects are achieved thereby:

1. First, an emphatic answer is given to the question of who comes first, the law or the subject, by depicting a subject who exists as such prior to the law and is able therefore to consent to it without apparently being always already formed by it. In this regard, the iconic scene of new immigrants taking the pledge of citizenship has an ideological effect. It privileges a choosing subject as a natural subject prior to the law, and it grounds the law in a choice that is its foundation and its raison d'être.

2. Second, rites of renaturalization reenact the regime's ideologically approved origins, obscuring the nonconsensual and ascriptive bases and present-day practices of American democracy. The broadcasting (on television, in the nation's newspapers) of this verbal, visible path to citizenship remarginalizes the varied, often violent, sources of the republic (slavery, conquest, appropriations, and constitutional conventions), and it recenters the regime on a voluntarism that most citizens and residents never experience directly. The scene may even excite in some citizens a sympathetic denaturalization that enhances their sympathetic renaturalization (just as many married couples effectively renew their vows when they go to other people's weddings, reexperiencing the pleasure of the gaze of the state and the community upon marital union).

But this (symbolic) "solution" to the problem of consent generates problems of its own. It places the legitimacy of the regime (and its claimed universality as a republic or a democracy) in the hands of foreigners who may or may not close the gap of consent for "us." This is a problem because many newcomers do not satisfy the national need to be chosen—many do not seek citizenship. And those who do naturalize do not simply solve the legitimacy problem; they also inadvertently highlight it by simultaneously calling attention to the fact that most American citizens never consent to the regime. (We saw the same dynamic at work in *Strictly Ballroom*, where Australian masculinity was both refurbished and also perpetually undone by the importation of masculinity from the Old World.)

In any case, even (or especially) when immigrants do prop up the national fantasy of consentworthiness, the regime's fundamental (unacknowledged) dependence upon foreigners produces an anxiety that finds expression in a displaced anxiety about foreigners' dependence upon us (an anxiety that, of course, erases the regime's dependence upon foreignness). Thus, it comes as no surprise that in Schuck and Smith's book (and in American political culture, more generally: the book is deeply symptomatic), the good, consenting immigrant, the model of proper, consensual American citizenship, is shadowed by the bad immigrant, the illegal alien who undermines consent in two ways: He never consents to American laws, and "we" never consent to his presence on "our" territory. Schuck and Smith's illegal takes things from us and has nothing to offer in return. He takes up residence without permission; he is interested in social welfare state membership (the proverbial bank account), not citizenship (except for instrumental purposes having to do with securing access to social welfare goods); she takes services without payment (the example repeatedly invoked is that of illegals' unpaid maternity bills at Los Angeles hospitals).[58] In short, the "illegal" in Schuck and Smith's text slides from being a person defined by a juridical status that positions him as always already in violation of the (immigration) law into being a daily and wilfull lawbreaker.

The illegal's threat to consent is crystallized most vividly in *Citizenship without Consent* (a book widely touted at the 1996 Republican convention) by the American-born children of illegal aliens (hence, perhaps, the authors' [displaced] obsession with unpaid maternity bills). Schuck and Smith argue, against a century of Supreme Court decisions, that American-born children of illegals have no constitutional right to citizenship. The Fourteenth Amendment applies to people born in the "jurisdiction" of the United States. Illegal aliens, in the United States without the approval of the state or the consent of its citizens, are on American territory but not in its jurisdiction.[59] Schuck and Smith do not argue that this means that these children should *not* receive birthright citizenship. It simply means that this right is not constitutionally entrenched and that the decision about whether or not to grant birthright citizenship to the children of illegal aliens is available for democratic (popular and legislative) debate and consent.[60]

The rhetorical weight of the rest of the book, however, is on the side of excluding children of the undocumented from birthright citizenship.[61] For Schuck and Smith, the goal is to revalue American citizenship, to (re)gain control over its distribution.[62] Schuck and Smith frame the issue in terms of consent and depict the state as the nonconsenting victim of wayward migrants, but it is not at all clear that the state does *not* consent to the presence on its territory of large numbers of illegal immigrants. Illegal migration is not only combatted by the state; it is also simultaneously enabled, covertly courted, often managed, and certainly tolerated by it.[63] Established citizens profit from the subsidies that cheap migrant labor provides to their child-care costs and food prices.[64]

More to the point, the liberal xenophilic deployment of the foreigner as the truest citizen because the only truly consenting one actually feeds the xenophobic backlash against the nonconsenting immigrant—the illegal alien—to whom we supposedly do not consent and who does not consent to us.[65] If this analysis is correct, then the iconic good immigrant—the supercitizen—who upholds American liberal democracy is not accidentally or coincidentally partnered with the iconic bad immigrant who threatens to tear it down. Popular ambivalences about foreignness are not, as Rogers Smith has argued elsewhere, the product of distinct, nativist ideologies that are unconnected in any deep or significant way to American liberal democracy.[66] The co-presence in American political culture of xenophilia and xenophobia comes right out of America's fundamental liberal commitments, which map a normatively and materially privileged national citizenship onto an idealized immigrant trajectory to membership. This means that the undecidability of foreignness—the depiction of foreigners as good and bad for the nation—is partly driven by the logic of liberal, national consent, which, in the case of the United States, both produces and denies a fundamental dependence upon foreigners who are positioned symbolically so that they must and yet finally cannot fill the gaps of consent and legitimacy for us.[67] That is, nativist ideologies may shape, direct, and accelerate the xenophobia in question. But, contra Rogers Smith, it is misleading to see them as the external corrupters of an otherwise fundamentally egalitarian and tolerant liberal tradition whose only weakness is its failure to inspire in communitarian terms.[68] Indeed, as we saw in Chapter One, Smith's characterization of the problem as one of liberalism's corruption at the hands of an outside agitator itself replays the xenophobic script that Smith is out to criticize.

But xenophobia is not the only problem here. The iconic bad immigrant is also problematic because he distracts attention from democracy's real problems.[69] Schuck and Smith's deployment of the figure of the illegal exceeds their apparent intent and highlights a different, more tenacious corruption than that of "illegal aliens in the polity"—that of the withdrawal of most American citizens and residents from political life.[70] The illegal imagined by Schuck and Smith turns out to stand for the much rehearsed corruption of American citizenship from an active liberal voluntarism to a nonconsenting, passive social welfare consumerism in which good citizens—"givers"—have been replaced by self-interested maximizers and free-riders, "takers." No more than a minority of American citizens votes in American elections; fewer still involve themselves directly in politics. Schuck and Smith externalize these corruptions of American democratic citizenship and, in good Girardian style, project them onto a foreigner who can be made to leave. These Girardian scapegoats represent our best virtues and our worst vices. They become the occasion of a new social unity that Schuck and Smith hope, somehow, to achieve by way of some small policy changes, periodic mailings, constitutional reinterpretations, and better border policing. In short, Schuck and Smith's iconic foreigners, both good and bad, are problematic because they invite unfair treatment of foreigners but also because they mislead us into believing that the solution to liberal democracy's problems and the right response to heightened migrations are a politics of national retrenchment.

Taking Liberties:
Intimations of a Democratic Cosmopolitanism

> To change a story signals a dissent from social
> norms as well as narrative forms.
> — Rachel Duplessis

Tracking the varied workings of the hegemonic myth of an immigrant America helps identify sites at which it may be possible to evaluate, interrupt, and reinhabit dominant figurations of foreignness. The next step is to ask: "How might the myth of an immigrant America be redeployed as part of a counterpolitics of foreignness?"

Fundamentally, the various versions of the myth of an immigrant America all seek to renationalize the state and to position it at the center of any future democratic politics. By pressing the foreign immigrant into service on behalf of the nation and its iconic economy, community, family, and liberal individual citizen, the myth positions the immigrant as either a *giver* to or a *taker* from the nation. Indeed, the xenophilic insistence that immigrants are givers to the nation itself feeds the xenophobic anxiety that they might really be takers from it. We saw this dynamic at work in Chapter Three, as well, where it threatened to be viciously circular. I suggested that we might break the vicious circle by thinking about immigrants in relation to democracy, rather than the nation, and by thinking of "taking" as the very thing that immigrants have to give us. I reconsider those possibilities here in a bit more detail and in the somewhat different context of American democratic theory.

Does the ostensibly pejorative symbolic depiction of immigrants as "takers" have a positive dimension that democratic theorists could mobilize? In 1792, Madison said: "In Europe charters of liberty are granted by power [while] in America . . . charters of power are granted by liberty." Madison's insight is that democracy is a form of politics in which power is not received by grateful subjects but rather is taken, redistributed, reenacted, and recirculated by way of liberty, that is, by way of popular political action. Might the negative depiction of immigrants as those who take things from the nation (possibly a projection of a returning, repressed guilt for the original takings on which the regime is founded) be available for recuperation on the part of those who, like Madison, think democracy *always* involves some sort of taking?

Not all takings are performed by immigrants or foreigners, but they are all performed by subjects who are not fully included in the system of rights and privileges in which they live. The practice of taking rights and privileges rather than waiting for them to be granted by a sovereign power is, I would argue, a quintessentially democratic practice. Indeed, it is one of the practices whereby the American experiment in democracy itself began. As Alexis de Tocqueville points out in *Democracy in America*, American "settlers" began "exercising rights of sovereignty" without the prior knowledge or authorization of the "motherland." Says

Tocqueville, "The new settlers, without denying the supremacy of the homeland, did not derive from thence the source of their powers, and it was only thirty or forty years afterward, under Charles II, that a royal charter legalized their existence."[71]

Jacques Rancière, in *Dis-agreement*, offers several other examples of the same sort of practice in which new rights and standing are taken and then recognized only later (if at all). Working with Pierre-Simon Ballanche's nineteenth-century retelling of Livy's tale of the Roman plebeians' secession on Aventine Hill, Rancière notes that, contra Livy, this is a battle not about poverty and anger but about who has the status of a speaking being and about how those who are denied such a status can nonetheless make their claims or make room for themselves. Rancière puts it beautifully: "Between the language of those who have a name and the lowing of nameless beings, no situation of linguistic exchange can possibly be set up, no rules or codes of discussion." Is armed battle, then, the only recourse for the nameless class? The plebeians found another way: "They do not set up a fortified camp in the manner of the Scythian slaves. They do what would have been unthinkable for the latter: they establish another order, another partition of the perceptible, by constituting themselves not as warriors equal to other warriors but as speaking beings sharing the same properties as those who deny them these." They mime the speech acts of their would-be superiors and "through transgression, they find that they too, just like speaking beings, are endowed with speech that does not simply express want, suffering or rage, but intelligence." All of this, Rancière refers to as the "staging of a nonexistent right."[72] Rancière gives another example of the practice when he cites the case of Jeanne Déroin who, in 1849, "presents herself as a candidate for a legislative election for which she cannot run," thus staging the contradiction at the heart of the French republic which is a regime founded on both an "equality that does not recognize any difference between the sexes" and on "complementarity in laws and morals," where the latter is the proper sphere of women.[73] Yet another example, this one not in Rancière, is that of Victoria Woodhull, a nineteenth-century American feminist who, instead of campaigning to have women's right to vote added to the constitution, asserted that the right to vote was already implicit and (along with other women) simply began voting and was arrested for it.

These examples of nonimmigrant democratic takings invite a reassessment of the much-reviled figure of the bad immigrant taker. A positive valuation of the taking immigrant as a *democratic* taker anchors a fifth way of looking at the myth of an immigrant America, this one on behalf of a democratic cosmopolitanism. Here the myth is a narrative of democratic activism whose heroes are not nationals of the regime but insist, nonetheless, on exercising national citizen rights while they are here. Historically, such immigrants have banded together to take or redistribute power. Their demands were resisted, denied, misunderstood, sometimes grudgingly granted or yielded, often greeted with violence, once in a while ceded without fanfare. The people who made the demands were sometimes deported, imprisoned or executed. Others sometimes stayed, sometimes left to go elsewhere, sometimes returned to their points of origin, sometimes died. The nation was not their telos. But they were all engaged in what Rancière calls, honorifically, "political activity," a form of activity that "shifts a body from the place assigned to it or changes a place's destination. It makes visible what had no business being seen, and makes heard a discourse where once there was only place for noise; it makes heard as discourse what was once only heard as noise."[74]

The democratic aspect of this version of the myth of an immigrant America lies not in its aspiration to tell a story of ever broadening *national* inclusion, nor in its effort to expose the "lie regarding the universal" enshrined in the nation's constitution. The peculiarly democratic character of the reinhabited myth inheres in its character as a history and a continuing present of empowerment, frame shifting, and world building. We have here a story of illegitimate demands made by people with no standing to make them, a story of people so far outside the circle of who "counts" that they cannot make claims within the existing frames of claim making. They make room for themselves by staging nonexistent rights, and by way of such stagings, sometimes, new rights, powers, and visions come into being.[75]

Because the myth of an immigrant America is a narrative of demands made by outsiders, it is not just a nationalist story; it is also, potentially, a myth of denationalization. Reinhabited as a democratic rather than a nationalist narrative, the recovered myth of an immigrant America might push late modern democratic actors to pursue two conflicting aims simultaneously: (1) to insist on the inclusion of immigrants and migrants in democracy's national future, while also (2) pressing for the (symbolic and institutional) denationalization of democracy at the same time.

One way to include immigrants in democracy's national future while resisting the recuperation of immigrant energies for the state's renationalization is to expand alien suffrage. Contrary to popular belief, the history of suffrage is not one of ceaseless expansion. The United States has a long history of alien suffrage ("Finally undone by the xenophobic nationalism attending World War I"), in which democratic participation is linked not to the juridical status of citizenship but to the fact of residence.[76] At present, several cities allow noncitizen residents to vote in local, school board (Chicago and New York), or municipal (several Maryland localities, such as Takoma Park) elections.[77]

Promoting social and worker movements might help win for presently unrepresented populations a voice in institutional self-governance as well as greater autonomy in daily life. One excellent example of such an effort is the Workplace Project, an organization that provides legal representation and advice to the undocumented while also training them to advocate and organize on their own behalves, representing themselves to bosses, landlords, school administrators, and state officials. The Workplace Project extends citizenship practices to noncitizens. It includes aliens in democracy's national future while also transforming citizenship from a state-granted juridical status to a civic practice.[78] Here is an education in democratic citizenship far worthier of the name than the citizenship classes offered by the state in preparation for naturalization. As Michael Walzer says, citizenship cannot be learned "just by watching."[79]

At the same time, the denationalization of democracy must be furthered by enacting transnational ties to empower local minorities. Groups like Women Living Under Islamic Law, Amnesty International, or Greenpeace press states and hold them accountable for their treatments of persons and public goods. In the name of fair and equal treatment of all persons, such groups provide state residents with alternative, not state-originated sites of support and power.[80]

The point of this democratic cosmopolitanism is not to replace the state with an international government. The state remains an important potential and actual organizer of social welfare and justice as well as a potentially powerful ally to citizens and groups struggling to hold accountable certain powerful local and international institutions. But the state also remains the institutional source of a great deal of injustice, inequity, and violence in the lives of its citizens and residents. Thus, it is important for social democrats to find ways to offset the still too singular power of the state by multiplying the memberships and affiliations of state residents. The goal is to empower people who are among the weakest and least empowered residents of the regime because they are weak politically and vulnerable to exploitation. For example, given the U.S. government's role in creating, administering, and obscuring the problem, the situation of undocumented workers and their availability as exploitable labor can only be effectively addressed by mobilizing social and political energies to counteract the effects of the state's criminalization and denationalization of this class of persons. Of migrant laborers, Labor Secretary Ray Marshall said in 1978, "These people work scared and hard." They still do, but twenty years later farmworkers work for about 20 percent less money than when Marshall spoke out on their behalf.[81] Michael Walzer is right to say that political effectiveness depends upon people joining together in groups to act.[82] People who are scared, denationalized, and criminalized are less likely to take the risk of visibility that joining together entails.[83]

The goal of a democratic cosmopolitanism is to offset the risks and vouchsafe the benefits of state (non)membership by widening the resources and energies of an emerging international civil society to contest or support state actions in matters of transnational and local interest such as environmental, economic, military, cultural, and immigration policies. This is a *democratic* cosmopolitanism because democracy—in the sense of a commitment to local, popular empowerment, effective representation, and the generation of actions in concert across lines of difference—is its goal. Such actions are generated out of a sense of solidarity that may be located on any of a number of registers—local, national, or international. Forms of national unity may sometimes support a cosmopolitan commitment to democracy, sometimes not.[84]

Movements need myths. Activists can make up new myths, or they can take those already in existence and recycle them. The latter strategy is preferable because it takes advantage of existing cultural resources and simultaneously deprives opposing forces of the powerful narratives that would otherwise continue, uncontested, to support them in their nationalist objectives. The myth of an immigrant America can be turned from its nationalist functions to serve a democratic cosmopolitanism in which citizenship is not just a juridical status distributed (or not) by states, but a *practice* in which denizens, migrants, residents, and their allies hold states accountable for their definitions and distributions of goods, powers, rights, freedoms, privileges, and justice.

⎯⎯•◦•⎯⎯

As we saw in Chapter One, political theorists have given little serious attention to cosmopolitanism because they identify it too quickly (and wrongly) with world government. But there is also another reason for their reluctance to explore democracy's cosmopolitan impulses. Political theorists tend to figure the question of democracy's past, present, and future in terms of a debate between nationalism versus cosmopolitanism that is deeply caricatured and so abstract that it erases the long history of internationalism in politics.[85] Mirroring its predecessor debate between liberalism and communitarianism, this new set of engagements figures cosmopolitanism (*qua* individual ethic or governance) as rootless, abstract, shallow, lacking depth, meaning, and purpose, fundamentally untrustworthy. Nationalism or patriotism is figured as rooted, bounded, structured, full of trust and meaning but capable of erring on the side of zealotry.[86] The same sort of debate circulates with reference to citizenship: Is it instrumental or affective? Should it operate on the register of use or virtue? The caricature of cold cosmopolitanism versus warm nationalism (often revalued as cool, level-headed cosmopolitanism versus hot, irrational nationalism) is seductive enough that many liberals have recently given up their seemingly natural coalition with cosmopolitanism in order to forge a partnership with the nation. Liberal nationalism, the resulting hybrid, claims to be able to offer both individual liberty and group solidarity, freedom of movement, and meaningful bonds of civic and social trust. The claim has been contested, of course, by unreconstructed liberals and nationalists alike.

Rather than adjudicate these debates as they now exist, I turn to practices of democratic cosmopolitanism as a way to negotiate the divide between the binaries of cosmopolitanism versus patriotism, instrumental versus affective citizenship. A democratically activist cosmopolitanism scrambles the linkages on either side of this opposition. Such a scrambling renders visible already existing sites of sub- and international activisms and memberships that are affective, but not nationalist, rooted but not simply in culture, deep but not particularist, transnational but not simply disloyal. Some of these have already been mentioned: new social movements such as migrant workers' rights groups that operate in domestic and international arenas; professional internationalisms such as Médecins du Monde that act on, in, and among sovereign states; extranational, citizen-forged institutional linkages such as sister-cities and NGOs; gay and lesbian movements for civic equality, health care, international human rights, or queer world-buildings; human rights watch groups that in the last generation have helped to change the structures of accountability governing the behavior of would-be sovereign states; and various feminisms, many of whose members or affiliates develop affective ties to one another precisely by exposing the merely instrumental character of existing would-be affective national citizenships.[87]

In other words, rather than renationalize the state, democratic cosmopolitans seek to denationalize the state, not because they do not value affective ties and memberships but precisely because they do. They denationalize the state in order to make room for the generation of alternative sites of affect and identity against which states often guard. Just one typical example of such guardedness may suffice to make the more general point: "Canada has explicitly challenged attempts by Indians to use UN forums for indigenous peoples on the grounds that Indians are Canadian citizens."[88] Because aboriginals are citizens of Canada, the claim is that they do not need alternative or competing extranational affiliations, identities, or forums. They are already represented as citizens. However, it is precisely because they do belong to states in some way (whether as citizens, as in the case of Canada, or not) that aboriginals (and other citizens and residents as well) seek other sites of affiliation and affect. They seek to offset the power that states have over them. Hence, the resistance of states like Canada to aboriginal efforts to go into transnational coalitions. The resistance of states to their citizens' or residents' efforts to organize along extranational axes of identity suggests that the denationalization of the state from an affective to an instrumental set of institutions may be a necessary step on the road toward a more vibrant and empowered democratic politics.

This insight seems to me to be at the heart of Gayatri Spivak's ideal of a feminist internationalism that does not simply broaden the circle of already existing nationalisms. Spivak says about groups such as Women Living Under Islamic Law:

> These feminist internationalists must keep up their precarious position within a divided loyalty: being a woman and being in the nation without allowing the West to save them. Their project, menaced yet alive, takes me back to my beginning. It is in their example that I look at myself as a woman, at my history of womaning. Women can be ventriloquists but they have an immense historical potential of *not* being (allowed to remain) nationalists; of knowing, in their gendering, that nation and identity are commodities in the strictest sense: something made for exchange. And that they are the medium of that exchange.[89]

Spivak's hortatory call puts women's national citizenship on the register of use, marks it as specifically instrumental, and on that basis calls women to an internationalism that need not be itself instrumental; it is, after all, perched on a "loyalty," even if a divided one. Spivak's call is effective in part to the extent we are aware of the traffic in women, the long histories of state productions and uses of sexual difference for their own purposes: in other words, to the extent that we are aware of the state's own instrumental relation to its citizens.

But it is not enough to challenge the binary of affective nationalism versus instrumental cosmopolitanism by showing that cosmopolitanism can be affectively charged and that the nation can be related to instrumentally. This leaves in place the governing, limiting binary of affective versus instrumental citizenship and merely switches the objects of our (non)attachments—we now have an instrumental relation to the nation-state and an affective relation to the cosmopolitan. Is there a way out of this problem? What if we refigured our understanding of civic attachment as a kind of passionate ambivalence? It is partly in quest of such a refiguration that I turn in Chapter Five to consider the literary genre that gives play to such ambivalence: the genre of gothic romance.

I feel as if I'm gonna keel over at any minute and die. That is
often what it feels like if you're really doing coalition work.
Most of the time, you feel threatened to the core and if you
don't, you're not really doing no coalescing. . . . You don't go
into coalition because you just *like* it. The only reason you
would consider trying to team up with somebody who could
possibly kill you, is because that's the only way you
can figure you can stay alive.
— *Bernice Johnson Reagon*

5 THE GENRES OF DEMOCRACY

Reading foreign-founder texts like Rousseau's *Social Contract*, Freud's
Moses and Monotheism, the Book of Ruth, and the myth of an immigrant America together suggests that sometimes the (re)construction of
the national may require or depend upon the violation of the national.
Democratic law, which is said to be fully willed by the people but never
truly is, may call on an iconic foreign-founder to make sense of the felt
alienness of that law and of the ongoing mutual opacity of a people
that is supposed to develop (but rarely does) a sense of kinship and
commonality in the joint enterprise of self-government. Alternatively,
or in addition, democratic regimes implicated in violences that could
delegitimate them may risk their democratic power in order to restore
or preserve its innocence, by telling themselves stories about themselves in which a scapegoatlike foreign-founder takes the people's vio-

lences upon himself. National culture may look to have its sense of distinctive choiceworthiness refurbished periodically, and the agency of an extranational may be the best—if also most threatening—vehicle of that reassurance. Democracies, especially the American exceptionalist variety with its emphasis on individualism, liberty, and voluntarism, may need to have not just their sense of choiceworthiness but also their mediating institutions (like the family) and their ground of consent periodically recemented. Newcomers, as opposed to the native born, seem best positioned to serve—even while they also undermine—those ideological and cultural needs.

The questions are: Why, then, in all the contemporary political theoretical debates about citizenship, and even about immigration, has no one paid attention to the complex, constitutive, role of foreignness as an undecidable supplement in national democratic imaginations? Why has the foreignness of Rousseau's lawgiver gone largely unremarked? Why has Ruth been seen as only a support but not also a threat to the people she rejuvenates? Why haven't democratic theorists paid attention to the ambivalent role of the myth of an immigrant America in sustaining liberal democratic values and institutions? What is it that makes (in)visible the role of foreignness in shaping democratic imaginations? Or better, in Girardian terms, what is it that makes (in)visible the organization of pervasive, indeterminate social crises into particular, concrete, positive and negative engagements between an "us" and a "them"? One possible if partial answer to these questions has to do with the genre in which we read the texts of democratic theory.

Does Democracy Have a Genre?

Drawing on Northrup Frye's taxonomy in *Anatomy of Criticism*, Hayden White has argued that historians, contrary to their self-representation as authors of objective prose, write in modes.[1] Historians narrate events like the French Revolution as romance, comedy, tragedy, or satire, casting history itself or historical actors as heroes, villains, or buffoons. Does democratic culture or democratic theory have a mode, too?[2]

Unlike Hayden White, whose aim is to persuade historians to become more self-conscious about their writing practices, I ask this question in order to call attention to the *reading* practices of political theorists. Most democratic theorists approach the texts they interpret through the mode of romance. But they bring a particular set of genre expectations to their texts. They read democratic theory according to the genre conventions of a popular or modern romance, as a happy-ending love story. (Indeed, some explicitly invoke marriage—happy marriage—as a key metaphor for social contract or social unity.)[3] From their perspective, the problem of democratic theory is how to find the right match between a people and its law, a state and its institutions. Obstacles are met and overcome, eventually the right match is made and the newly wed couple is sent on its way to try to live happily ever after.[4]

But what genre best fits a work of political thought in which a people with a great deal in common decide to share the burdens and pleasures of a life together only to find that they have cast in their lot with a bunch of untrustworthy strangers? What genre dictates that, when their joint project founders, a mysterious foreigner will appear on the horizon to rescue these wayward people from their misfortune? What genre then trades on the reader's uncertainty as to whether that apparently rescuing foreigner is really a hero or villain? In what genre would the reader be unsurprised to find that soon the foreigner is using violence and even the penalty of death to make the local people accept his gifts to them? In what genre would the reader be right to expect this mysterious foreigner suddenly to disappear one day, never to return? These are the plot pieces of Jean-Jacques Rousseau's *On the Social Contract* (on our first reading of it) and the genre that seems to fit them best is not modern romance but *gothic* romance (also called modern gothic or female gothic).[5]

"Gothic" might also be the most parsimonious description of the reading of the Book of Ruth developed here, in contrast to other readings that are more romantic. In the gothic reading, troubling questions about Ruth's motivations and about the nature of her relations to Naomi and Boaz are allowed to disturb the reader's romantic assumptions and expectations. The Book of Ruth is thoroughly hospitable to a female gothic reading given how it plays with Ruth's foreignness as an undecidable sign of support and threat to the Israelites who welcome and fear her. But if there is one single scene that gives strongest support to a gothic treatment of the text, it is that in which a frightened Boaz awakens unable to identify the shadowy figure who has disturbed his sleep. Boaz's anxiety that the virtuous Ruth might after all really be a Moabite—even a Lillith—never goes away.[6] So, too, the myth of an immigrant America, with its perpetual play of xenophobic and xenophilic impulses, positions the native born as the anxious spouse of the mysterious, undecidably safe and/or treacherous foreigner.

In *Loving with a Vengeance*, her 1984 book on gothic and Harlequin romance, Tania Modleski explains that the (anti) hero in " 'pure Gothics' " is always undecidable, " 'a handsome magnetic suitor or husband who may or may not be a lunatic and/or murderer.' "[7] He is also often a foreigner or someone who lives in a foreign (often a Catholic) place. "In the typical [female] Gothic plot, the heroine comes to a mysterious house, perhaps as a bride, perhaps in another capacity, and either starts to mistrust her husband or else finds herself in love with a mysterious man who appears to be some kind of criminal." While Harlequin romances trace the transformation of the young heroine's feelings for the hero from fear into love, in gothics the heroine is older and "the transformation is from love into fear." In short, Harlequins are preoccupied with "getting a man" but "in Gothics the concern is with understanding the relationship and the feelings involved once the union has been formed."[8]

If we allow marriage to stand as a metaphor for the social contract, we can see how Rousseau's *Social Contract* (again, on our first reading of it) explores the community's feelings about the union it has formed. Then Rousseau's text goes on to follow this female gothic path of dangerous disenchantment. Rousseau begins with a full faith in the people and their power to will the general will. But once the union is in place, he becomes suspicious of them, as indeed they become suspicious of each other as well. Playing the coltish new wife to the people's Maxim de Winter, Rousseau begins to suspect his beloved republicans of engaging in plot and intrigue. The people's devotion to the polity may not be sincere or total, after all. Rampant mutual mistrust puts the dream of an intimate democracy at risk. The narrative shifts from a mood of comfortable identity to one of unease, suspicion, and mistrust. And then the author, like many classic gothic heroines, casts frantically about for a rescuer. At the very moment when the project of legitimation through the General Will seems least likely to succeed, Rousseau—otherwise intent upon crafting a socially unified regime—introduces a foreigner into the text. A foreign-founder (who just might be a charlatan) arrives to animate a General Will that either cannot animate itself (our first reading) or can found its polity only by way of a delegitimating violence, which it must then disavow and project onto an outsider who can be made to leave (our second reading).

Tania Modleski relies on Norman Cameron's psychosocial account of paranoia to explain the rise of female gothic romance novels. The move from love to mistrust, intimacy to fear, symbolized in gothics as an encounter with the foreign, the strange, or the ghostly, is produced by extreme isolation, itself often the product of marrying and moving away from one's family of origin (effects, therefore, likely to be found among foreign brides, which, in the gothic formula, is what all newly married women are, in some sense). These are the effects of living a life out of the reach of any public sphere, "without the corrective effects that the talk and action of others normally provide."[9]

For Cameron, the social may serve as an inoculation against the development of such anxieties into full-fledged paranoia; the social is a source of security, sanity, and reassurance. Others have written about the social's power to generate and feed paranoia, not just assuage it, a point Modleski does not consider.[10] But Modleski's use of Cameron is still suggestive insofar as it points to historical institutional changes as an occasion of genre innovation. Did gothic romances arise because women lost access to the "social"? Did changes in family structure from extended to nuclear family forms isolate individuals, especially women, in ways that were conducive to the development of paranoid conditions to which female gothics, in turn, gave vent?

A variation on this theme might take seriously the role of female gothics in working out certain ambivalences that are social and political rather than strictly familial.[11] Modleski turns to psychoanalysis to show how gothics work through the reader's ambivalence toward her parents and her anxiety about separating from them by telling a story in which the heroine finds a *real* enemy on whom to hang her discomfort—not her remote father, but her really strange or foreign husband. Echoing Freud's reading of "The Sandman," Modleski says, "Often the attempt to find an enemy and the attempt to exonerate the father are part of the same project."[12] But we might think of the anxiety about the father to which Modleski alludes as itself symptomatic, the product of an anxiety about the regime to which the subject belongs. In other words, what if the issues being worked through by way of female gothics have less to do with separation anxiety from familial parents than with an anxious need to separate oneself from democratic or national communities that implicate their members in practices and violences that the subject cannot abide and seeks to disavow?

Perhaps we ought to interpret the rise of the female gothic genre not simply or primarily as a response to changes in family structures, but rather as a response to changes in political arrangements ongoing from around the time of the publication of Rousseau's *On the Social Contract* up to the early twentieth century. Especially given the prominence of marital metaphors for citizenship, should we be surprised to find that anxieties about the identities and agendas of one's (often recently arrived) compatriots in increasingly mass democracies might find expression by way of novels that are set in the uncanny domestic terrain of the (notably, often foreign) household? Similarly, why wouldn't the democratic citizen's (especially the eighteenth and nineteenth centuries' nonvoting woman citizen's) anxieties—about the always erased and increasingly distant violences of the nation-state's birth and the remoteness of the law that is repeatedly declared to be his/her own—find expression in a genre that focuses on remote fathers and husbands and seeks to call them to account for or absolve them of possible past and hidden crimes?[13] Such historical speculations might perhaps be supported by the coincidence of timing between the development of a mass (reading) public in the nineteenth century and the nation-state building projects with which that century's democracies busied themselves.

But even if such an historical wager should fail to pay off, it could still be the case, as I would indeed argue, that contemporary democratic agendas of openness, equality, inclusion, national and extranational solidarity, and accountability are well served by the project of (re)reading democracy's romantic narratives through a female gothic lens. In other words, my aim is less to assign the correct genre identity (is it *really* gothic?) to Rousseau's *Social Contract* than it is to start an argument about what genre it, and other texts of democratic theory, should be read in (that is, regardless of what genre they were written in).[14] The issue here is the normative import of our reading practices as political theorists and as citizens and residents of democratic regimes.[15]

By rereading national and democratic myths of lawgiving, (re)founding, and national democratic renewal through a female gothic lens rather than through the lens of modern romance, we have trained our eyes on the power of foreignness as a symbolic force. We have seen how foreignness is used to figure and perhaps manage enduring problems in democratic theory. We have been made alert to the problem of the alienness of the law, and we have seen how various efforts to domesticate or conceal that alienness work to open some and close other lines of solidarity among citizens and residents, natives and foreigners.

But our gothic lenses do not only enable us to generate fuller and more textured readings of democratic theory's received texts and democracy's popular ones. We are also, as gothic readers and as fans of gothic heroines, better positioned for the responsibilities and challenges of democratic citizenship. In du Maurier's *Rebecca*, the new Mrs. De Winter desires to be "older" or simply "old" (pp. 22, 196, 299). She succeeds. In the end, her early naïveté is replaced by a mature self-assurance, testified to by a clear, calm sense of her new class identity in relation to her inferiors ("I am Mrs. De Winter now, you know") and by a newly maternal relation to her husband ("I held my arms out to him and he came to me like a child") (pp. 290, 352, 375). Smug social mobility and maternalism are not democratic virtues, it is true. But might the maturation plot typical of this genre offset the infantilizing effects of democracy's scapegoat narratives? Those scapegoat narratives grow out of the desire of some democratic peoples to preserve their innocence and abjure their power (as well as their violence) even at great cost to their own democratic agency. The new Mrs. De Winter, by contrast, seeks to lose her innocence in order to acquire power and agency.

Jane Eyre has some of the same *bildungsroman* qualities of *Rebecca*, but Jane has some valuable counters of her own to offer democratic readers. Jane's story is also one of entry into mature, independent adulthood, but some critics have argued that Jane's power depends in the end upon the enfeeblement of Rochester (oedipally handicapped, rendered lame and blind by fire). It is, however, not the case that Jane's power and independence are established by way of her marriage and in relation to Rochester. They come as a result of Jane's good fortune and hardy effort in establishing for herself some significant, unusual attachments. She adopts and is adopted by the Rivers family (uncannily strange and, indeed, as it turns out, related to her) and acquires two sisters and a brother as her own. Notably, these relations are discovered and made possible by the death of an uncle, Jane's sharing of her inheritance from him, and the departure and eventually the death of the brother. This leaves Jane, formerly an orphan, with a nuclear family that is distinctly sororal (and probably a bit too perfect: siblings without rivalry?). It is from the stage of this achievement of social place by way of something like—yet unlike—kinship that Jane marries Rochester.

This reading of *Jane Eyre* harkens back to our reading of the Book of Ruth. Ruth is also put into closer relation to Naomi by way of a fortuitous inheritance (the unredeemed land) and by way of the deaths of several male family members in Moab and in Bethlehem. But Ruth's story inverts Jane's. Ruth fails to achieve a social place, and her failure seems to be related to her inability to establish sororal relations with Orpah (Moab). And, of course, in both these stories, the newly included woman's (quasi or would-be) membership seems to depend in some deep way upon the exclusion of an other who is her double. In the Book of Ruth it is Orpah, and in *Jane Eyre* it is, as Gayatri Spivak first pointed out, Bertha Mason.[16] Similarly, in *Rebecca*, the new Mrs. De Winter takes up her new social place only after learning that her double, Maxim's first wife, was not in fact cherished by him but was instead a cruel, Lillith-like creature—sexually appetitive, disloyal, and perhaps, therefore, deserving of her husband's (unintended?) violence against her.

In short, from *Rebecca*, we could learn to counter the impulse to self-infantilize, and from *Jane Eyre*, we could learn the importance to independence of relations of solidarity and enacted sororal kinship. From these two novels in tandem, we learn again the lesson first taught by Spivak by way of Bertha Mason: that circles of solidarity and kinship are usually drawn in ways that not only include but also always exclude as one of their enabling conditions. Gothic romances do not tell us how to solve the problem of exclusion, but they do make it visible.

Gothic romances have a great deal to offer democratic readers. As we first saw in Chapter Two, and then with some variations in Chapters Three and Four, the subjects best prepared for the demands of democracy are those who exist in agonistic relation to a founder (or a father or law) whose alienness is a poorly kept secret; subjects who do not expect power to be granted to them by nice authorities (fathers or husbands) with their best interests at heart (or, if they do harbor such an expectation, they are the sort that is able to rally after an initial disappointment); subjects who know that if they want power they must take it (isn't this often the lesson of female gothics many of which are, at bottom, basically *bildungsromane*?); subjects who know that such takings are always illegitimate from the perspective of the order in place at the time (the new wife's real or paranoid fears often drive her to violate conventional expectations); subjects who know that their efforts to carve out a just and legitimate polity will always be haunted by the violences of their founding (can the marriage of the gothic heroine flourish after the intrigue, suspicion, and perhaps real violence the couple has suffered?); subjects who experience the law (the father, the husband) as a horizon of promise but also as an alien and impositional thing. In Chapters Two, Three, and Four, we did not have a name for them yet, but such subjects might best be termed *gothic subjects.*

Democracy's Romance: A Tale of Gothic Love

A democratic theorist who advocates a gothic perspective can hardly ignore Richard Rorty's recent diatribe against gothics. In *Achieving Our Country*, his most sustained argument in favor of the renationalization of the democratic state, Richard Rorty rails against the "temptation to gothicize" as a "stumbling block to effective political organization." What does he mean?

Rorty is referring to the genre of horror gothics, not female gothics, and he has in mind the trademark tendency of horror gothics to generate and explore feelings of paranoia and paralysis in the face of pervasive powers that determine human fate from places beyond the reach of human agency. "Gothic" is Rorty's metaphor for a worldview in which human agency is nugatory, hope is naive, it is useless to struggle, and the future holds no promise of change. Rorty's diatribe against gothics is intended to open up room for renewed leftist political activity in America. The irony is that his diatribe is itself written in the most conventional horror-gothic terms. Rorty casts many on the Left as foreign and dangerous to his project, missing an opportunity to make coalition with a wide range of national and international democratic actors.

In the last third of the twentieth century, Rorty says, there has been no real leftist politics at work in America. The problem is that old Left elites have been replaced by the so-called cultural Left, academics seduced by popular culture, theory, and identity politics. The new cultural elite squanders opportunities for a real politics that addresses issues of class and social justice, preferring instead to disunite America with its focus on past wrongs and difference (Vietnam, racism, sexism, anti-Semitism). Theirs is "a Gothic world in which democratic politics has become a farce" because in it human destiny is governed by a "preternatural force."[17] Too haunted by past wrongs to be able to love their patria, too haunted by amorphous powers to be able to act, the new cultural Left is unable to offer a positive vision of an American future that might motivate others to join them in a fight for justice. Unable or unwilling to dream, the cultural Left can bring about no change, for in order to "urge national political renewal . . . [y]ou have to be loyal to a dream country rather than to the one to which you wake up every morning."[18]

There are no proper names attached to these charges. (The lack is significant in someone like Rorty, who loves to throw around proper names in sometimes long, dizzying signifying chains.) That is because Rorty's cultural Left is itself a gothic monster, an amorphous, dreamless creature so caught up in a past that it has no future, a creature haunted by powers beyond its control and yet itself so powerful that it is almost single-handedly responsible for the success of the Right in the last twenty-five years, a creature so pervasive and monstrous that it takes possession of the souls of young girls, as in this scene early in *Achieving Our Country*:

> A contemporary American student may well emerge from college less convinced that her country has a future than when she entered. She may also be less inclined to think that political initiatives can create such a future. The spirit of detached spectatorship, and the inability to think of American citizenship as an opportunity for action, [all hallmarks of the "cultural Left"] may already have *entered such a student's soul.*[19]

Here Rorty casts the university as the haunted castle to which unsuspecting parents send their innocent young daughter. In the castle of the academy, the girl's soul is lost. Doomed to a state of nightmarish dreamlessness, she is—like the victims in the 1950s horror movie *Invasion of the Body Snatchers*—fated to follow but never to lead or initiate action for the rest of her life.

Rorty's nightmarish scenario takes place in the United States. In a more self-conscious and classic gothic narration, the corrupted university would be in a foreign place. But true to the horror-gothic form he decries, Rorty soon puts the people responsible for the university's corruption outside the circle of Americanness and renders them foreign to the body politic. The cultural Left is "unpatriotic," not part of mainstream America.[20] "Outside the academy, Americans still want to feel patriotic. They still want to feel part of a nation which can take control of its destiny and make itself a better place."[21] Inside the academy, behind the closed doors of the English Department, something very different is going on. If only, in place of the academy's dark gothic musings, we could have the "daylit cheerfulness" of Whitman, who, along with Dewey, gives "us all the romance, and spiritual uplift, we Americans need to go about our public business."[22]

Predictably, Rorty's horror-gothic call to romanticize rather than gothicize the nation sets in motion the very dynamics of demonization I have been tracing throughout this book.[23] As we saw in Chapters Two, Three, and Four, the insistence on total identification with an idealized object—the nation, the demos, the General Will, a Ruth, the lawgiver, the good citizen—tends to drive the subject to split the beloved object into two (the good object and the bad) and to defend the former against the now externalized threat of the latter: the nation against the foreigner; the demos against the outsider; the good, old, nation-loving Left versus the bad, new, cultural and unpatriotic Left; the General Will against the particular will; Ruth against Orpah; the kind lawgiver against the brutal tyrant; the good citizen against the bad immigrant; the giver against the taker.

Again and again, we have seen how the politics of foreignness are driven by failed efforts to insist on the unity of the nation or the demos and to insure that the supplement of foreignness only supports regimes that are, however, always also unsettled by it. One result of this insistence is the loss of opportunities to pass one of democracy's strictest tests, the challenge to work and live and share not just with people with whom we have a great deal in common but also with those with whom we just happen to be bound up; that is, in Bernice Johnson Reagon's phrasing, the challenge to work and live and share "with somebody who could possibly kill you . . . because that's the only way you can figure you can stay alive."[24]

Rather than return home to the nation and love it (or its idealization) fully and completely, democratic actors could move their fellows into democratic action along multiple registers: subnational, antinational, transnational, and national. At the same time, they would do well to nurture some ambivalence regarding their principles, their leaders, and their neighbors and to put that ambivalence to good political use, relying on the gothic lenses whose aid to vision I have been advocating in this chapter. These lenses come from female gothics, not horror gothics. What they provide us with is not a sense of paralyzing paranoia in the face of monstrous forces beyond our control, nor a clear distinction between the forces of good and evil, but a healthy caution to be wary of authorities and powers that seek to govern us, claiming to know what is in our best interests. From female gothics, we get a valuable exhortation to take matters into our own hands.[25]

The best female gothic heroines are takers. They take it upon themselves to leave their suitors or to discover the truth about their husbands, who may or may not be out to get them. Whatever they discover—it doesn't matter what, really—the exercise of detection teaches them agency, and they become less vulnerable to their husbands (good or bad) because they have learned their powers. Gothic heroines never take total control of their lives. They are *gothic* heroines, after all, and so they usually remain vulnerable: they end up with a man who still might be a murderer, or they uncover only some but not all the secrets that haunt them. Female gothics teach us not only the powers but also the limits of self-conscious agency. Democratic actors should find both lessons valuable.

Similarly, we, as readers of female gothics, can make our own, sometimes limited, discoveries.[26] We can discover that the devices used by gothics to heighten our sense of uncanniness—devices such as foreignness—are devices that work on us every day and that we, as democratic agents, do not just have to yield to them. Instead, we have some power to explore, unmask, detect, and even expose them. Often in gothics, it turns out that it is not the apparently scary foreigner but the nice man next door, meek and mild, who is the real murderer. In real life, gothic readers know, we don't get such neat resolutions. The nice guy and the scary one are often the same person. The president who introduces vast new social welfare programs is the same one who escalates the war in Vietnam. Or better, since there need not be a tight or necessary link between those two of Lyndon Johnson's legacies, the iconic supercitizen foreigner who reenchants the nation can only do that for us because he is foreign in the same way as that other foreigner, the one who might be a Lillith, the one who is here illegally and seeks to take our wealth, pleasure, and politics away from us. These two can be foreign in the same way because their foreignness does not come from them, it comes from or through us.

Nationalists like Richard Rorty and Rogers Smith find it difficult to find a public place for the ambivalence that female gothics deepen and explore. Philosophical ruminations on such things may, Rorty says, "be useful to some of us in our quest for private perfection," but they can only do damage to a worthwhile politics.[27] Similarly, Smith, whose goal is also to reawaken contemporary citizens to politics (albeit to a liberal rather than a social-democratic politics such as that envisioned by Rorty), himself offers clear-cut distinctions between good and evil, not gothic ambiguity or undecidability. Proposing a national history for committed, nationalist citizens, Smith explains that such a history should be "understood to include serious struggles among people, movements, principles, and causes with different aims and interests— struggles in which the actors a particular citizen decides to regard as the 'good guys' may not always, perhaps even not often, win."[28]

But why tether the passion that politics requires to the nation? As we have seen throughout, passion, involvement, and identification are daily called into action on behalf of many extra- and subnational affiliations and memberships and causes. Moreover, even if we do tether such passions to the nation, why then split the nation's history into a battle between bad guys and good (distinct and separable as the "traditions" they represent), as if these are not usually found combined, inextricably, in a single person, ideal, or movement? The need for passion, involvement, and identification in politics does not require us to move in these directions. Even if, along with Smith and Rorty, we believe that we must romance the nation, the question still remains: Should ours be a Harlequin or a gothic romance?[29]

Smith and Rorty are right that passion, involvement, and identification are necessary to a vibrant (and redistributive) democratic politics. They provide an important corrective to my own reactive tendency toward mere instrumentalism as an antidote to the nationalisms I reject. Recall that in my first reading of Ruth, I cast Ruth as a merely practical émigrée who related to the Israelites solely on the register of friendship as use. Then, motivated by Derrida's interpretation of Aristotle, I moved instead to think of Ruth as undecidably perched on all three registers of friendship—virtue, pleasure, and use. In Chapter Four, however, I suggested that "the denationalization of the state from an affective to an instrumental set of institutions may be a necessary step on the road toward a more vibrant and democratic politics." As I noted there, that apparent embrace of instrumentalism requires modification, too, for it risks merely relocating the binary of instrumental versus passionate attachment (our relation to the nation-state is now instrumental, and the international is now the real location of passionate attachment) rather than breaking out of that binary. Can we move beyond that statement, beyond Spivak (whose hortatory call, quoted at the end of Chapter Four above, put women's national citizenship on the register of use) and beyond Reagon, who imbues coalition politics with urgent passion ("do it everyday you get up and find yourself alive") but also seems to slide toward instrumentalism when she says that we work together only because we have to ("because that's the only way you can figure you can stay alive" [368])?

I have been trying throughout this book to pluralize our sense of the *objects* of our attachments, but as we have just seen, this can leave the binary of instrumentalism versus passionate attachment still in place. What if we pluralized passion itself? Gothic readers knows all about passion, but they understand it differently from their romantic counterparts. Gothic readers know that we may passionately support certain heroes (or principles or institutions) in political life while also knowing that we ought not take our eyes off them for fear of what they might do to us if we did. They know that one can be passionately attached to something—a nation, a people, a principle—and be deeply and justifiably (and even therefore!) afraid of it at the same time. As we have seen, again and again, it is the refusal of this ambivalence regarding democratic law (the foreigner as founder), the nation (the foreigner as immigrant), and national or liberal democracy (the foreigner as citizen) that drives the troubling politics of foreignness traced here.[30] What if, instead, democratic subjects related ambivalently, gothically, and, yes, passionately, to their leaders, their nations, their state institutions, and all their sites of belonging?[31]

An example of such a relation is provided by James Baldwin, who, in *Notes of a Native Son*, resists the temptations of mere instrumentalisms like Reagon's for the sake of a more fully gothic romantic (neither merely instrumental nor conventionally patriotic) account of black-white relations in America.

> In every aspect of his being, [the American Negro] betrays the memory of the auction block and the impact of the happy ending. In White Americans he finds reflected—repeated, as it were, in a higher key—his tensions, his terrors, his tenderness. . . . Now he is bone of their bone, flesh of their flesh; they have loved and hated and obsessed and feared each other and his blood is in their soil. Therefore he cannot deny them, nor can they ever be divorced (pp. 122–123).

Like the more conventionally romantic interpreters of American democracy, Baldwin uses marital and familial metaphors to describe relations among the polity's members but, in his hands, these are not in the service of a happy-ending romance nor on behalf of a simple sense of national belonging. What he provides instead is a sense of the terror of belonging, the hope and betrayal that come with the inextricable intertwining of people in one another's lives across lines of difference and power. What he captures and distills and animates is the impossibility of being dispassionate and merely instrumental in relation to institutions and structures that govern and shape us as thoroughly as our national and state institutions do.

Exhorting citizens to return to the nation and relate to it or to its good guys in unambivalent terms is not the way to (re)inaugurate a vital and magnanimous democratic politics, though it may serve the rather different cause of nationalism or patriotism. Instead, we need a politics that acknowledges our passionate ambivalences and engages them by pluralizing our attachments so that the nation-state is just one of several sites of always ambivalent attachment rather than the sole and central site of simple romantic love.[32] The democratic cosmopolitanism that results from such efforts may not escape the paradoxes and conundra of which the symbolic politics of foreignness are symptomatic, but it might relieve some of the pressures that intensify those paradoxes. Perhaps it might even stop us from rescripting those paradoxes into political problematics that usually end up pitting "us" against "them."

Notes

Chapter One
Natives and Foreigners

1. Plato, *Laws*, 705a; Aristotle, *Politics* 1272b15.

2. Arthur Schlesinger sees assimilation as necessary to the maintenance of American liberal institutions (*The Disuniting of America*). David Miller worries that foreignness—insofar as it attenuates the viability of national membership—puts social democracy at risk: social democracy requires a unity of community and purpose (*On Nationality*). See also Lind, *The Next American Nation*, and Brimelow, *Alien Nation*, for arguments in favor of limiting immigration in order to increase social democracy or preserve existing identities and ways of life. On multiculturalism, see Tully, *Strange Multiplicity*; Kymlicka, *Multicultural Citizenship*; and Carens, *Culture, Citizenship, and Community*.

3. This is the case both in Kymlicka's *Multicultural Citizenship* and in Tully's *Strange Multiplicity*, two books that are otherwise quite different. Kymlicka's liberal principles are expanded but not really tested by their encounters with otherness. Tully's book is more interested in exploring the transformative consequences of engagements with otherness.

4. Holston and Appadurai, "Cities and Citizenship," p. 188.

5. Chambers, *Migrancy, Culture, Identity*, p. 30.

6. As is suggested by Laclau and Mouffe's theorization of the "constitutive outside," in *Hegemony and Socialist Strategy*. In its role as "constitutive outside," the other gives definition to an identity by marking what it is not. Interestingly, given my view that the "constitutive outside" lacks a sufficiently positive content, Laclau has since gone on to theorize another site of (supposed) contentlessness in the form of the (supposedly) "empty signifier." See his *Emancipations* and Linda Zerilli's review, "This Universalism Which Is Not One."

Tina Loo and Carolyn Strange provide an unusually dense and layered example of communal and national (re)constitution by way of contrast with foreignness in "The Travelling Show Menace."

7. Although these other contributions, novelty, cultural breadth, and depth, are also part of the picture, Parekh is right to say, in the spirit of John Stuart Mill's experimentalism, that "new ways of life also bring with them new talents, skills, sensitivities, ways of looking at things, different kinds of imagination, new psychological and moral resources, new sources of spiritual energy and give their receiving society a cultural breadth and depth" (Parekh, "Three Theories of Immigration," p. 108). Portes and Rumbaut also emphasize the reenergizing effect of immigrants on America in *Immigrant America*. This gift of foreigners is not restricted to states like the U.S. that see themselves as immigrant regimes, as Parekh's Millian argument about immigrants' effects on Britain suggests. Similarly, although we hear a great deal in the popular press about the failure of immigrants and their children to acquire or master English, we also get the following, lovely insight from Hugh Kenner (himself a Canadian immigrant to the U.S.), writing about Joseph Conrad: "Though his spoken English is reported to have been often impenetrable, his fiction abounds in local brilliances no native speaker would have thought of, like 'He was densely distressed' " (Kenner, "Between Two Worlds," p. 14).

8. The answer to this rhetorical question may well be "yes." As Thomas Pangle points out with reference to Plato's *Laws* (a dialogue, set in Crete, in which the main character, an Athenian, is a foreigner): "A political philosopher who wishes to bring about fundamental changes is more likely to succeed if he appears to be not merely an old conservative, but a 'foreigner' in some sense, whose circumstances compel him to defend the ways of 'his people' against the implicit and explicit criticisms of his 'hosts' (the persons he wishes to change or to be the agents of change). Only thus can he openly introduce and defend

alien ways and yet appear to be neither a traitor nor a man without loyalty" (Pangle, "Interpretive Essay," p. 396).

9. This use of foreignness appears in Mill's assessment of Chinese culture: remarking on the great wisdom of the Chinese, their excellence in educating community members, and their success at putting the best educated into power, Mill worries that the Chinese "have become stationary, have remained so for thousands of years." How to improve and get themselves back on the road of progress which they themselves initially charted so well? "If they are ever to be improved," Mill says, "it must be by foreigners" (Mill, "On Individuality," p. 67).

10. All of these explanations are considered by Jean Carbonnier, who also notes with curiosity the foreign-founder phenomenon, in his "A beau mentir qui vient de loin ou le mythe du legislateur étranger."

11. I am indebted to Henry Bienen for making this objection and for pressing me, therefore, to think through the ideas in the next few paragraphs.

12. Zenkovsky, *Medieval Russia's Epics, Chronicles and Tales*, pp. 49–50. See also Riasanovsky, *A History of Russia*, p. 24.

13. According to Wachtel, drawing on Anatole Mazour, " 'The founding of [the] Norman school dates back to the first half of the 18th century, traced largely to a group of German scholars' that included 'Bayer, Müller, Schlozer, and others.' [As Pritsak points out, Müller's lecture drew on an article of Bayer that had been published thirteen years earlier, in 1736 (p. 3).] Historians of Russian descent, including Tatishchev and Lomonosov in the 18th century, rejected this theory, primarily because of 'its tendency to consider the Slavs only a backward people, but as incapable of governing themselves.' " According to Pritsak, it was Lomonosov's testimony before the committee investigating Müller that was most devastating to his cause (p. 4). See Wachtel, *An Obsession with History*, p. 26, and Pritsak, *The Origin of Rus'*, pp. 3–5.

14. Wachtel, *An Obsession with History*, pp. 42–43 and passim. I am indebted to Andrew Wachtel for his help in figuring out the Slavic sources.

15. See Wachtel's very interesting discussion of Catherine's identification with Riurik as a foreign-born ruler but more importantly as a literary object (Wachtel, *An Obsession with History*, pp. 26ff).

16. Said Solovyev: "Try to think of Russian history from the exclusive national point of view. Even if the Scandinavian origin of our state could somehow be explained away, it cannot be denied that the introduction of Christianity into Russia by the Greeks at once brought our nation into the sphere of the supernational life of the world" (Solovyev, *The Justification of the Good*, p. 428).

17. Pritsak, *The Origin of Rus'*, pp. 6–7.

18. This argument recirculates points made by Wittgenstein in his critique of James Frazer's treatment of the Fire-festivals in *The Golden Bough*. Frazer argued that Fire-festivals, in which effigies are burned or in which there is a pretense of throwing a victim into a fire, "may naturally be interpreted as traces of an older custom of actually burning human beings on these occasions." Witt-

genstein countered that Frazer's search for an origin to explain the power of a contemporary practice missed the point. "But why should it not really be (partly, anyway) just the *thought* (of the festival's sacrificial origin) that makes the impression on me? Aren't ideas frightening? . . . Hasn't the thought something terrible?" The meaning of our stories and practices is related not to a privileged referent that causes them in some way but to all kinds of evidence, "including such evidence as does not seem directly connected with them from the thought of man and his past, from the strangeness of what I see and what I have seen and heard in myself and others."

Of course, Wittgenstein being Wittgenstein, the argument does not stop here. Not only do those who ask after the meaning of an event have to take account of infinite possible sources; they also have to direct their attention away from sources as such and toward the conduct of the event itself in its daily practice. Meaning, as Wittgenstein said famously in the *Philosophical Investigations*, is in use. In Frank Cioffi's summary: "Preoccupation with the origins of the Fire-festivals is mistaken, not because it is impertinent to 'the inner character of the ritual' but because it is impertinent to the impressions [the ritual] engenders." And later: "That men should pretend to burn men gets its 'depth' from our prior knowledge that men have burned men, not from our conviction that in this particular ritual men were once burned" (Cioffi, *Wittgenstein on Freud and Frazer*, pp. 90–91).

René Girard is also vulnerable to the criticism Wittgenstein levels at Frazer. In *Violence and the Sacred*, Girard treats all ritual violence as a way of working through (in modified form) an original violence: "The community is both attracted and repelled by its own origins. It feels the constant need to reexperience them, albeit in veiled and transfigured form . . . [T]he ritualistic imagination . . . allows violence a certain amount of free play *as in the original instance*, but not too much" (p. 99; emphasis in original). Wittgenstein's point is that we need not think of the "original instance" as an actually existing event or referent that explains or causes the later ritual. Instead, the "original instance" may be thought of as itself the *product* of the ritual that itself projects an original as its (sometimes unconscious) cause. This is one reason for my own insistence, throughout this book, that the politics of founding is always the politics of (re)-founding.

19. Regarding my use of the term "regime" above, I should note that throughout this book, I use the term in the Straussian and Foucaultian senses, which connote not just government institutions but the widest array of political, cultural, and ethical practices, ways of life, powers, and knowledges that make up the world of citizenship.

20. Consider another example: in and of itself, unlodged in any symbolic context, the fact that many Americans came from elsewhere could mean many different things. In Canada, as in the United States, the vast majority of the population is descended from immigrants, and yet Canadians have not histori-

cally taken an "immigration experience" to be essential to their identity. Canada has no Statue of Liberty. Immigrants are officially welcomed these days but they have not historically been idealized. In the Canadian context, the *facts* of immigration simply do not bear the same symbolic meaning as in the United States. Why not?

An explanation is suggested by Gerard Noiriel's analysis of the United States and France. Noiriel argues that, contrary to conventional understandings, France is actually an immigrant country: "Approximately 20 percent of people born in France have at least one parent or grandparent of immigrant origin. If we take great-grandparents into account and include the foreign population born outside French territory, we reach a total of nearly one-third of the total population." And yet, no one thinks of France as a nation of immigrants, and the figure of the immigrant in France does not possess the same idealized symbolic import that it has in the United States. (This is not to say that it lacks symbolic import, however. On immigration politics in France, see my discussion in Chapter Three.) According to Noiriel, the difference between France and the U.S. is not simply that one has few immigrants and the other has a great many. The difference is the way in which each regime mobilizes and shapes the facts of immigration at the symbolic level. In the United States, that mobilization is part of a *myth of origins*; in France it is not: "In all countries, the nation-state's constitution is accompanied by a certain number of 'myths of origin' designed to reinforce the cohesion of a population which has divided itself into antagonistic groups. In countries where immigration played a decisive role in the initial populating, the theme of 'immigrants' often occupies an important place in the constitution of the 'myth of origins.' " In France, "Mass immigration only began in the 19th century," well after the republican founding, "at a time when the structures of the French State had already been in place for quite some time" (Noiriel, "Immigration: Amnesia and Memory," pp. 368–371). Thus, where the United States turned Ellis Island into a national icon, France razed the point of disembarkation used by immigrants in the nineteenth century.

But did immigration in fact play "a decisive role in the initial populating" of the United States? Is that the fact that explains the later symbolization? Although it is true that the original U.S. inhabitants came from elsewhere, one could well argue that they thought of themselves not as immigrants but as Puritans, and that therein lies an alternative myth of origins for the United States in which it is not the original travels and travails of the newcomers that made for what ultimately became their supposedly quintessentially American character but rather their common mission, religion, and purpose. (Indeed, American immigration policy reflected this self-understanding on and off—mostly on—until 1965, a fact largely approved by Peter Brimelow in his *Alien Nation*.) In short, notwithstanding the facts of its origins, even the American self-understanding as a nation of immigrants is at least underdetermined and is as in need of explanation as the nonimmigrant-centered self-understanding of countries with sub-stantial immigrant populations like France and Canada.

21. As this list shows, both high and popular culture feature stories of for-eign-founding. Some of these stories are true, as may be the case with the story of Russia's foreign-founder, and others are mythic. Still others, like *Shane* or Clint Eastwood's spaghetti Westerns, are merely stories, but they recirculate a foreign-founder script that precedes them and whose power exceeds (but is also bolstered by) their particular iteration of the script. Indeed, that is surely part of what motivates the retelling. Repeated stories, from *The Wizard of Oz* to the *Social Contract*, interest me because they frame (and are symptomatic of) our expectations and assumptions about our own powers. The power of such stories is most visible when we see them operating as cultural shorthands. For example, a management company posted the following advertisement on a billboard en route to Chicago's O'Hare airport: picturing a pair of ruby slippers and some emerald green towers, the copy read, "If M-B [the management com-pany], managed Emerald City, she would have stayed." The ad can allude suc-cessfully to Dorothy without naming or depicting her because the iconography of the ruby slippers operates as a fairly universal symbol in our culture.

22. Kant famously argued that the Jewish people were a people of the sub-lime, incapable of relating to the beautiful. Only Europeans could apprehend both, and only the German people could find the right balance between the two (Kant, *Observations on the Feeling of the Beautiful and Sublime*). My reading of Ruth as a beautiful reinhabitation of the Mosaic sublime may be a way of devel-oping an alternative to that reading of the Jews, though I do not pursue that thought in this book. (In his forthcoming book, *On the Psychotheology of Every-day Life*, Eric Santner argues that Franz Rosenzweig was also trying to find a way to liberate the Jewish people from this prejudice.)

23. As I suggested above: those who rely on mere population movements, increasing in proportion and tempo in late modernity, to produce a postnational politics wrongly rely on a mere fact to do the work of politics. If new and increased population movements are going to bring about a postnational poli-tics, that will be because proponents of a postnational politics win a(n) (ongo-ing) contest over the symbolic significance of such population movements. In the absence of popular participation in that contest, nation-states will exercise their uncontested right of persuasive definition, and these "foreigners" will be assimilated into the traditional, nation-centered and nation-centering paradigm of immigration. The United States, with its (re)founding myth of immigration, is particularly well positioned to do this.

24. Thus, against the feminist critic of social contract theory, Carole Pateman, Rogers Smith argues that although she "provides undeniable evidence that lib-eral writers endorsed conventional beliefs in natural sexual inequality," she does not succeed in showing that the problem lay with their liberalism per se. According to Smith, Pateman's evidence suggests not that liberalism is itself a

patriarchal ideology, but "that theorists like Locke" were themselves wedded to multiple, sometimes conflicting traditions and simply "did not really reconcile their inherited patriarchal beliefs with the implications of their more novel, distinctively liberal arguments." In line with his own multiple-traditions thesis, Smith contends that liberalism and patriarchy are "two intertwined but relatively autonomous systems of ideas and practices that . . . many Americans [like their great influence, Locke] have often inconsistently endorsed" (Smith, *Civic Ideals*, p. 29).

Smith tries to make the point again in response to Uday Mehta's claim that Lockean liberalism, in spite of its universal and " 'inclusionary character' has 'spawned practices' involving 'the political marginalization of various people.' " But here Smith makes an important concession: Mehta is right, he says, to connect these marginalizations to liberalism itself. There is no disputing Mehta's observation that the universality of Lockean liberalism refers to the universal *potential* of all humans to be rational. Equal political rights were to be awarded only to those who realized their potential, and this usually meant that women, children, workers, foreigners, and others were excluded. Says Smith: "Such liberal arguments have played a role in America's history of hierarchical citizenship laws." But ascriptive arguments have played a larger role, he insists, and in failing to address these, Mehta "reinforces conventional views that the liberal sources matter far more" (Smith, *Civic Ideals*, p. 517n.48, citing Mehta's "Liberal Strategies of Exclusion" and *The Anxiety of Freedom*). Here at least (by contrast with Smith's critique of Pateman), the issue is whether liberal sources of exclusion matter "more" or less, by contrast with elsewhere in *Civic Ideals*, where the question seems to be whether they matter at all. If they matter at all, which is all I am in a position to claim in this book (the question of whether they matter more or less than other ideologies is not my question, nor indeed was it Mehta's), then they and their shortcomings are surely worthy of attention.

25. Smith, *Civic Ideals*, p. 505. Smith notes that readers of articles published prior to his book's appearance had accused him of "wrongly exonerating liberal values and institutions from any share in promoting unjust inequalities." In response, he points out that he himself argues that "liberalizing and democratizing changes have often created the conditions for the resurgence of inegalitarian ideologies and institutions" (Smith, *Civic Ideals*, p. 5). That is, the main problem is still those contending, multiple traditions. Liberalism's fault is its creation of an opening for them by producing changes and dislocations in the name of overly universal ideals, such that those displaced by the changes cannot identify with the end goals. Those citizens become bitter and ripe for (re)-capture by ascriptive traditions. (See also Smith, *Civic Ideals*, pp. 474–500).

26. Or, more precisely, the democratic body politic, with its zealous passions and ascriptive traditions, is rendered foreign to the liberal egalitarian project, which is forced to secure its own relevance by way of an elitist disavowal of the actual people it claims to champion.

27. No less than was Frazer's search for the real referent of the Fire-festivals.

28. Smith's argument is, in any case, tautological. He defines liberal values as egalitarian (which is the question, not the answer), and then everywhere he finds egalitarianism he claims to have found liberalism and only liberalism, and he never finds liberalism anywhere else. This means that in spite of its apparently historical character, Smith's argument is effectively a logical (or illogical) one, notwithstanding its social science trappings. (He presents his reading as a hypothesis that he is testing in the lab of history in which the civic ideologies offered by "the Tocquevillian and multiple traditions accounts [are] independent variables and the citizenship laws" of each era are "dependent variables" [Smith, *Civic Ideals*, p. 8]). The point is worth noting since in a 1995 article Smith casts Michael Rogin, an earlier and much different sort of critic of American "political demonology," as making unhistorical claims about the "logic of liberalism" when Rogin's arguments are, in fact, more relentlessly historical (but not, it is true, social scientific) and for the most part eschew ideal types of the sort upon which Smith relies (Smith, response to "Beyond Tocqueville, Please!" by Jacqueline Stevens).

29. Or, as Jean Carbonnier puts it in regard to law: "La xenophilie juridique serait-elle donc, quoique moins consciente, aussi naturelle que son contraire, la nationalisme du droit?" ("Could one say that the xenophilia of the law, albeit in a less conscious manner, is as natural as its contrary, the nationalism of the law?") (Carbonnier, "A beau mentir qui vient de loin ou le mythe du législateur étranger (1)," pp. 228–229). For the more nationalist assumptions regarding democracy, see Beiner, *Theorizing Citizenship*; Smith, *Civic Ideals*; and Miller, *On Nationality*.

30. See, for example, Beiner, *Theorizing Citizenship*, and Smith, *Civic Ideals*.

31. This is another respect in which I differ from Smith, whose analysis is in the service of the problem of governance, not politics qua civic action. It is from the perspective of governance that he issues a call, at the beginning and end of his book, for a new national myth: political leadership requires "a population to lead that imagines itself to be a 'people'" (Smith, *Civic Ideals*, p. 6). And again: "Political elites must find ways to persuade the people they aspire to govern that they are a 'people' if effective governance is to be achieved" (p. 9). And again: "Because the imperative to constitute a people that feels itself to be a people is politically necessary, it is also a weighty though certainly not absolute moral imperative" (p. 474).

I move away from this focus on the problem of governance to an alternative emphasis on the problem of political action, from a focus on the state and its needs to a focus on democracy and its needs (which may be quite different from and may even conflict with those of the state). Therefore, the assumed "necessity" of national identity and affect to democratic politics is very much in question in this book.

32. Thus, contra Beiner, Smith (*Civic Ideals*, p. 9), and others, who treat cosmopolitanism as aiming to *replace* states with an international government, states remain important potential and actual organizers of social justice as well as potentially useful allies against powerful international institutions that can be difficult to hold accountable. But cosmopolitan politics offers another register at which to hold states and other institutions accountable for their actions in the world.

33. Rousseau, *Discourse on the Origin of Inequality*, p. 160; emphasis added.

Chapter Two
The Foreigner as Founder

1. Salman Rushdie points out the repeated grayness (Rushdie, *The Wizard of Oz*, p. 16) and also notes that the home-yearning phrase—"There's no place like home" (in Rushdie's estimation, "the least convincing idea of the film")—that now functions as a synecdoche for the film was not itself part of the book upon which the film is based (pp. 14–16). "There's no place like home" was a Hollywood addition, intended (futilely, given the phrase's fundamental undecidability [see p. xiii above]) to bring comfort and closure to what is otherwise, in Rushdie's estimation, fundamentally an open-ended fable of emigration and adventurism: "At the heart of *The Wizard of Oz* is a great tension between . . . the human dream of *leaving* [and] its countervailing dream of roots," but, when Dorothy sings "Over the Rainbow," "can anyone doubt which message is the stronger?" That song, says Rushdie, "is, or ought to be, the anthem of all the world's migrants, all those who go in search of a place where 'the dreams that you dare to dream really do come true.' It is a celebration of Escape, a grand paen to the Uprooted Self [strikingly, initials that stand as well for the United States, land of the Uprooted Self], a hymn—*the* hymn—to Elsewhere" (p. 23).

2. Salman Rushdie captures, with an émigré's eye, the film's depictions of the many rites and rituals whereby people try to secure the safety of their homes against the vagaries of nature, contingency, injustice, inequality, and power politics. In the opening scenes of the film, for example, Dorothy's Auntie Em and Uncle Henry are too busy to pay attention to their distressed niece. They are, as they say impatiently, "trying to count." Counting eggs they have collected, they are literally—given the coming tornado—counting their chickens before they've hatched. They rely on their counting to impart a certain safety and reliability to their windswept and politically tumultuous world. (Home, as Marina Warner points out, is always the fragile product of "men's and women's labour together" [Warner, *Managing Monsters*, p. 112]).

This ritual of addition is supported by the film's geometry. Rushdie notes that the "world of Kansas . . . is shaped into 'home' by the film's use of simple uncomplicated shapes (triangles, circles, parallel lines); none of your citified complexity here. Throughout *The Wizard of Oz*, home and safety are represented by such geometrical simplicity, whereas danger and evil are invariably twisty, irregular, misshapen." Think of the hunchbacked wicked witch of the West by contrast with the perfect-postured good witch, Glinda. And recall that the aunt's and uncle's mundane defenses are undone by a *twister* (Rushdie, *The Wizard of Oz*, pp. 21–23).

3. Adventurous, yes, but also, as Rushdie points out, rather "meek," especially by contrast with the Wizard, who is also an immigrant: "These two immigrants have adopted opposite strategies of survival in a new and strange land. Dorothy has been unfailingly polite, careful, courteously 'small and meek,' whereas the Wizard has been fire and smoke, bravado and bombast, and has hustled his way to the top, floated there, so to speak, on a cloud of his own hot air" (Rushdie, *The Wizard of Oz*, p. 54). These two immigrant strategies—points on a spectrum that ranges from submission to the host culture over to the immigrant demand that the host culture meet him on his own terms—are often gendered feminine and masculine, respectively. We will revisit them in Chapter Three by way of a different immigrant tale, the biblical Book of Ruth.

4. In Baum's book, the story ends differently: Dorothy's three companions are assigned different sections of Oz to rule over. Nonetheless, Henry M. Littlefield reads even Baum's *Oz* as a populist parable in which the cowardly lion represents William Jennings Bryan. (Littlefield, "The Wizard of Oz: Parable on Populism").

5. Dorothy does not leave because she *wants* to avoid dominating the peoples of Oz. She leaves simply because she wants to go home. In so doing, however, she unwittingly acts out a foreign-founder script in which foreigners reenchant the regimes they visit without overstaying their welcome.

6. Actually, as Rushdie points out, Dorothy's fantasy is to be *more* powerful than the grown-ups she knows. Her Auntie Em and Uncle Henry are weak, unable to protect Dorothy and Toto from Miss Gulch, and this leads to Dorothy's departure. Later, when she is "confronted by the weakness of the Wizard of Oz, she doesn't run away, but goes into battle, first against the Witch, and then against the Wizard himself. The Wizard's ineffectuality is one of the film's many symmetries, rhyming with the feebleness of Dorothy's folk; *but Dorothy's difference of reaction is the point*" (Rushdie, *The Wizard of Oz*, pp. 10–11).

7. Is it odd to treat such disparate texts as the *Wizard of Oz* and the Hebrew Bible as if they had some sort of relation to each other? Both high and low culture contribute to contemporary democracies' cultural unconscious. As I myself write about Dorothy en route to writing about Moses, I am reminded of my own deep association of the *Wizard of Oz* and Moses. When I was a child, *The Wizard of Oz* was broadcast on television every spring, right around the same time as Passover, the holiday that memorializes Moses' founding of the Israelites as a people of the law. As I write this, Moses is ascending (or descending?) to

an even larger cultural iconicity, however, by way of the first animated film to be produced by Dreamworks: *Prince of Egypt.*

8. Freud argues that there were in fact two leaders named Moses: the first, an Egyptian prince, was murdered by his people; the second introduced Jehovah to the Israelites in the desert.

9. Miller, *On Nationality*, pp. 94–95 and passim. Others whose work proceeds from such neo-Rousseauvian assumptions are Michael Walzer (*What It Means to Be an American*) and Michael Sandel (*Democracy's Discontents*).

10. That is, there is a tension in Rousseau between a formal conception of the General Will, where the General Will is whatever the people will under ideal circumstances (small territory and population, regular assembly meetings, relative material equality, etc.), and a more substantive conception of the General Will, where the General Will is whatever is really and truly in the public interest, regardless of whether the people will it or not. On this latter view of the General Will, one can never fully entrust power to the people except, paradoxically, at the risk of the General Will's corruption.

11. Rousseau does not just rely on rules or laws to solve the problem. As Steven Johnston points out, the General Will is supported by a host of practices, beliefs, festivals, and rituals that operate, deniably, below the official registers of the General Will (*Encountering Tragedy: Rousseau and the Project of Democratic Order*). On Rousseau's reliance on "woman" and (hetero)sexuality to contain the social order, see Zerilli, *Signifying Woman*; and Wingrove, *Rousseau's Republican Romance.*

12. I discuss the *aporia* of founding in detail in "Declarations of Independence: Arendt and Derrida on the Problem of Founding a Republic."

13. Rousseau, *On the Social Contract*, Book II, Chapter 7. See also Aristotle, *Politics*, Book II, 1274a23–1274b25.

14. Thomas Pangle argues that Rousseau's references to Geneva are an instance of using foreignness as an agent of change, given that Rousseau, himself Swiss, was addressing French society in this text. In this, Pangle notes, Rousseau was preceded by Plato, who, as we saw in Chapter One, also exhibits some appreciation of the usefulness of foreignness as an agent of change ("Interpretive Essay," p. 396).

15. Beyond Rousseau's signal reference to prior foreign-founders, the possibility that Rousseau's lawgiver is a foreigner is also supported by Rousseau's insistence that the legislator, "[h]e who frames the laws," cannot be a member of the sovereign body (Book II, Chapter 7). Since the sovereign body is the entire people in Rousseau's *Social Contract*, this means that the legislator cannot be a member of the people for whom he proposes legislation. He must come from elsewhere.

Further evidence for this reading of the legislator as a foreigner is provided by the fact that the issue of translation comes up in this context—his language "cannot be understood by the masses." True, Rousseau himself attributes the need for translation not to the founder's foreignness, per se, but to his "overly general perspective," his focus on " overly distant objects" and the abstractness of his ideas, which "are impossible to translate into the language of the populace" (Book II, Chapter 7). Nonetheless, the language of translation suggests that a linguistic difference is also operating here or at least that the difference between the abstract and the particular is being metaphorized in terms of the foreign and the familiar. Similarly in Freud, as Patchen Markell reminds me, the harshness of the Mosaic founding of monotheism is attributed not solely to Moses' foreignness, but also and perhaps even primarily to the abstractness of Mosaic monotheism, which demands a painful instinctual renunciation. But the point is surely not to have to choose between abstractness or foreignness as the real cause of the Rousseauvian lawgiver's opacity or of the Israelite resistance to Freud's Moses. One could focus on the abstractness of the law as the real issue and treat foreignness or alienness as a mere metaphor for that abstractness. Or one could, as I do here, *take that metaphorization seriously* and ask after the goals and consequences of figuring the law (abstract or otherwise) or the lawgiver as foreign. Why is foreignness enlisted as a vehicle or device of the abstract law's domestication? And what politics of foreignness follows from that?

16. Hence the reliance of Italian city-states on foreigners to serve in the office of *podesta*, a magistracy. "Justice was the province of the official known as the Podesta, who was invariably the citizen of another place, since Italian cities were so torn with feuds that they could not rely on a local citizen to give impartial justice" (Mark Girouard, *Cities and People: A Social and Architectural History*, p. 53). Weber, too, makes note of the podesta and then goes on to discuss the use of foreigners as both adjudicators and legislators: the former is "summoned from outside the group, not for the purpose of creating a new social order, but to provide a detached, impartial arbitrator, especially for cases in which the adversaries are of the same social status. On the other hand, the legislators were generally, though not always, called to their office when social tensions [*between* classes] were in evidence" (Weber, *Sociology of Religion*, p. 49).

Hannah Arendt also makes note of the practice, not in Italian city-states, but in ancient Greek ones, of relying on foreigners to be lawgivers. She offers an entirely different explanation: "The Greeks, in distinction from all later developments, did not count legislating as among the political activities. In their opinion, the lawmaker was like the builder of the city wall, someone who had to do and finish his work before political activity could begin. He therefore was treated like any other craftsman [like a migrant worker?] and could be called from abroad and commissioned without having to be a citizen, whereas the right to *politeusthai*, to engage in the numerous activities which eventually went on in the *polis*, was entirely restricted to citizens. To them, the laws, like the wall, around the city, were not results of action but products of making. Before men began to act, a definite space had to be secured and a structure built where all subsequent actions could take place, the space being the public realm of the *polis* and its structure the law; legislator and architect belonged in the same category. But these tangible entities themselves were not the content of politics (not Athens, but the Athenians were the *polis*) and they did not command the same loyalty we know from the Roman type of patriotism" (Arendt, *The Human Condition*, p. 195).

Jean Carbonnier would probably call Arendt's a rationalist explanation of the foreign-founder phenomenon. He is more interested in making symbolic sense of it and so draws, in his own analysis, on features such as those I listed above (Carbonnier, "A beau mentir qui vient de loin ou le mythe du legislateur étranger (1)"). Were Arendt interested in giving a symbolic reading, she might see how a foreign-founder is positioned to solve what she sees as the insoluble problem of (secular) founding: that the "we" has no authority to do what it sets out to achieve. (On this problem in Arendt, see my "Declarations of Independence: Arendt and Derrida on the Problem of Founding a Republic.")

17. Hence Machiavelli's observation that the best founders are foundlings, people whose origins are mysterious. Machiavelli was not so sure that foreigners made good founders, however. Of the two origin stories of Rome, he preferred the foundling version, represented by Remus and Romulus, to the foreign-founder version, represented by Aeneid (Machiavelli, *Discourses* I.1). In Rome, both myths of founding coexisted. But it was the Aeneid version that was influential in America at the time of the founding. (Thanks to Sacvan Bercovitch on this last point.)

18. Keenan, *The Democratic Question*, p. 17.

19. For my purposes here, it is not important to distinguish strangers from foreigners. The point is simply to note the recurring theme of (re)founders who come from elsewhere to save hapless citizens for democracy. In connection with this, see Lauren Berlant's brilliant analysis of the "infantilization of citizenship" in the United States in *The Queen of America Goes to Washington City*.

20. "Within the parable of the western, the hero is a man with sure moral bearings who plays the role of enforcer only in the absence of law enforcement," says Kiku Adatto in *Picture Perfect*, p. 129.

21. Derrida, *Politics of Friendship*, p. 173.

22. Of course, his reliance on a foreign-founder could be Rousseau's way of highlighting the virtual impossibility of real democracy in the modern world. Such a reading of Rousseau would be buttressed by attending to the list of other necessary conditions for democracy given by Rousseau, including small size of population, territory, and relative isolation, all of which, Rousseau knew, were extremely unlikely in the modern world and have only become more unlikely since the time of his writing.

23. Lincoln, "The Perpetuation of Our Political Institutions," p. 18.

24. Bloom, "Interpretive Essay," p. 4.

25. George Washington exhibited the discipline necessary to secure such a timely departure. Or better, the ideal of the citizen-farmer that influenced Washington's decision not to seek a third term in office may have counterbalanced the ambition that such an office tends to generate (Wills, *Cincinnatus*).

26. Crossette, "And You Thought the Age of Viceroys Was Over," p. 3.

27. Geoffrey Bennington, one of the few to note the foreignness of Rousseau's founder, also notes the founder's "radical undecidability," but Bennington makes no connection between the founder's undecidability and his foreignness. Instead, Bennington says the lawgiver is undecidable because it is impossible to know for sure whether the lawgiver is authentic or a charlatan. Neither signs nor durability of the institutions founded (Rousseau's two criteria) can help a people faced "with a possible legislator," says Bennington, because signs are ambiguous and the people cannot assess durability in advance. "Legislator and charlatan thus remain radically undecidable" (Bennington, *Legislations*, p. 222). Rousseau concedes the unreliability of signs, but, contra Bennington, Rousseau himself treats durability as a reliable, corrective criterion: " 'Vain wonders [miracles, signs] form a transient bond, but only wisdom makes it durable' " (quoted in Bennington, *Legislations*, p. 220). While Bennington is right to say that durability cannot be assessed ahead of time, it is also the case that it cannot happen that a people should be in the position of deciding ahead of time about the authenticity of the legislator prior to the legislator's formation of them into a people. The issue of the lawgiver's authenticity is post hoc, an issue for the judgment of posterity (as Hannah Arendt might put it), not for deliberations of a group deciding by whom it should be founded. That never happens. That such a judgment, when made post hoc, can be wrongly made— "a durable state may always be a mere simulacrum of a good one" (p. 222)—is part of the structure of judgment itself and not a sign of a *radical* undecidability that has anything in particular to do with Rousseau, lawgiving, or democracy (as Bennington shows he knows when he later says "any event of thought . . . involves this undecidability" [p. 222]). Samuel Weber also makes note of the foreignness of Rousseau's lawgiver, but he does not pause to analyze it at length (Weber, "In the Name of the Law").

28. Rousseau also admired Lycurgus and Numa (*Government of Poland*, Chapter II, "The Spirit of Ancient Institutions"). I learn from Jan Assmann that this treatment of Moses as a lawgiver or founder is decidedly un-Jewish: "It is not a particularly Jewish project to make Moses the creator of the Jewish nation," and, notably, it is this Moses, "the lawgiver and political creator, who needs his Egyptian education" (Assmann, *Moses, the Egyptian*, p. 165).

29. Freud, *Moses and Monotheism*, p. 38. Rousseau echoes Moses' protest to God that he cannot lead the Israelites because he has a heavy tongue and will not be understood: Rousseau's legislator has a problem because his language "cannot be understood by the masses." It seems that one thing these foreign-founders have in common is that they are precisely not "great communicators."

30. That Moses' foreignness fitted him for his task of liberating the Israelites is suggested in *Acts* 7:22: "And Moses was learned in all the wisdom of the Egyptians, and was mighty in words and deeds" (quoted in Assmann, *Moses, the Eyptian*, p. 149).

31. Most responses to Freud's text focus on his claim that Moses was an Egyptian, often using it as a way to explore Freud's relation to Judaism, rather than treating Freud, as I do, as a contributor to an independent genre of foreign-founder scripts. For example, Jonathan Boyarin suggests that Freud, in this text about a father-killing, actually enacts a parricide of his own, killing off the inconveniently Jewish Moses in order to replace him with a more acceptably assimilative (in the context of 1930s Vienna) Egyptian version. If the non-Jewishness of one's name signals a non-Jewish identity, as Freud argued regarding Moses, then, Boyarin points out, not only Moses' Jewishness, but also Sigmund's, is conveniently undone.

Barbara Johnson also sees Freud's Egyptianization of Moses as a self-erasure but, contra Boyarin, she insists the erasure is paradoxically affirmative: "For Freud, the nature of his Jewishness was to be *sous rature*, under erasure. And yet that erasure was somehow *itself* the very erasure of Jewishness" (Johnson, "Moses and Intertextuality," p. 21). This paradox probably provides too neat a 'solution' to Freud's difficult relation to Judaism. (If the very act of denying his Jewishness is Freud's way of affirming it, what would one have to do really to deny it? Or is "the essence of Jewishness" precisely the impossibility of [non] identification? In that case, however, what could one possibly do to affirm it? And [why] is this paradox the essence of *Jewish* identity and not of *every* form of [non]identification?) But Johnson considers another possibility as well. Freud's rewriting of Moses, she argues, marks Freud's refusal "to confine the notion of difference within a logic of identity." Describing "participation in a people as an experience of *self-difference*" (p. 23), Freud's text (which was published in German in 1935 and in English in 1937) is, in effect, Johnson suggests, a secret letter to Hitler, one that challenges the identitarian premises of Nazi anti-Semitism.

Contra Johnson, Jan Assmann argues that Freud aims to identify the real reasons for—rather than the unreal objects of—anti-Semitism. Freud's Egyptian Moses does not challenge anti-Semitism simply by showing that the supposedly unitary object of anti-Semitism, the "Jew," does not in fact exist because identity is riven all the way down. Instead, on Assmann's account, Freud uses the foreign Moses to locate the source of anti-Semitism's hatred in (in Assmann's words) the " 'hostility' inherent in monotheism as a religion of the father. Not the Jew but monotheism had created this undying hatred. By making Moses an Egyptian, [Freud] deemed himself able to shift the sources of negativity and intolerance out of Judaism and back to Egypt and to show that the defining fundamentals of Jewish monotheism and mentality came from outside of it" (Assmann, *Moses the Egyptian*, p. 167). In short, the "struggle against the Mosaic distinction could" be anti-Semitic, but it could "also assume the character of a fight against anti-Semitism." That it could be the latter is evidenced, on Assmann's account, by the fact that "the most outspoken destroyer of the Mosaic distinction was a Jew: Sigmund Freud" (*Moses the Egyptian*, p. 5). I think Assmann is right about the undecidability of the struggle against Mosaic distinction, but he is clearly quite wrong to assume that if a Jew propounded the argument, that is—all by itself—evidence that the argument is not anti-Jewish.

32. The exposure myths help to manage not only class difference but also the problem of foreignness: "Thus Cyrus is for the Medes an alien conqueror; by way of the exposure myth he becomes the grandson of their king" (Freud, *Moses and Monotheism*, p. 11).

33. Why does the Moses story reverse the usual chronology? "Whereas in all other cases the hero rises above his humble beginnings as his life progresses, the heroic life of the man Moses began by descending from his eminence to the level of the children of Israel" (Freud, *Moses and Monotheism*, p. 13).

34. This is an *assumption* on Rousseau's part. He does not study Moses. He simply infers Moses' authenticity as a judicious lawgiver from his success in founding a people capable of such sheer durability. That is, as I argued above contra Bennington, the judgment of the lawgiver's authenticity is post hoc.

35. Rousseau admires Moses for using "countless prohibitions" and practices to make the Jews unable to be absorbed by other peoples, to preserve their distinctiveness, to make them "outsiders forever." So it is funny to note that circumcision, the very practice that was touted as marking the Israelite difference, might actually have made the Israelites more like their foreign masters than unlike them, and would certainly have provoked in the Israelites not just a sense of distinctness but also an uncanny memory of their former foreign masters.

36. Indeed, there is an oddly (for Freud) identitarian premise doing unacknowledged work here. Freud repeatedly suggests some sort of connection between the violence with which Moses founded the Israelites and the impositional quality of Mosaic law as *foreign* law. The implication, that if a code of norms is your own its transmission is less impositional, is contradicted by Freud in *Civilization and Its Discontents*, where the transmission of norms (there the transmission is cross-generational rather than cross-cultural) is traumatic as such.

37. The foreign-founders of Rousseau and Freud *both* find it necessary to use violence to form their followers into a people, but the violence of Freud's founder is more explicit, more extreme, more colorfully described, and more centrally related to the process of founding. Quoting from the Bible, Freud says Moses "directed the Exodus 'by strength of hand'" (Freud, *Moses and Monotheism*, p. 32). Freud goes on to report (with Machiavelli hovering in the background) that "Moses, trained in Ikhnaton's school, employed the same methods as the king; he gave commands and forced his religion on the people" (p. 57).

In those times, Freud notes in a footnote, "any other form of influence would scarcely have been possible." Exodus reports "a series of grave revolts" against Moses while the people were "wandering in the wilderness." All of these "were suppressed with savage chastisement" (p. 58). In his reading of Rousseau, Johnston emphasizes the violence of Rousseauvian democracy's (re)founding (*Encountering Tragedy*).

38. Joan Copjec distinguishes between the slain primal father who is the principle of *jouissance* and the ideal father, represented by the son who, by way of his "eviction of excess pleasure [the slain father]," is formed "as an ideal father, 'mild and provident' in the words of de Tocqueville, kinder and gentler; in the words of George Bush's speechwriter, Peggy Noonan. He is the place to which all our questions are addressed, the place of knowledge; he is therefore often imagined under the traits of the educator (take, for example, Noonan's ideal: America's new 'educational President'). The ideal father installs a badly needed certainty in the place of the devastating uncertainty, the crisis of legitimation, that follows in the wake of the primal father's murder" (Copjec, "The Unvermögender Other," p. 36). Rousseau's lawgiver, who educates the people into the law, is like the ideal father. As we shall see soon, however, he can also be read as the primal (soon to be slain) father.

39. In other words, don't we here have a version of the paradox of founding? As with the father, so with the lawgiver: if it is up to the lawgiver in his wisdom to decide that the time is right for him to leave, then doesn't that mean that the people are not yet ready to be left? Were they ready to be self-governing, they would know the time was right and they would take it upon themselves to send the lawgiver packing (or, as in Freud's version, they would kill him). But Rousseau does not envision the lawgiver's departure that way. The paradox exemplifies Rousseau's tendency both to trust and mistrust the demos at the same time, a tendency that makes itself felt throughout the *Social Contract*.

40. And, as Bill Connolly reminds me, the boy also calls out: "Mother wants you. . . ."

41. Freud, *Totem and Taboo* cite, summarized in *Moses and Monotheism*, pp. 102–103.

42. Freud mentions the idea of screen memories in passing in *Moses and Monotheism*, albeit not with reference to the departure of the lawgiver (p. 93). It is interesting to note that where Rousseau's lawgiver's fantastically timely departure is what makes his law stick (and this accords with the traditional interpretation of the biblical Moses' timely death before entering the Promised Land), in Freud it is precisely the absence of such a timely gift that leads to the murder of the father, and it is that murder, and its haunting aftereffects, that gives his law its lasting quality.

43. Again, we are revisited by the paradox of founding.

44. But he does ask about the consequences of Moses' foreignness for later Christians and Jews. On this point, see Assmann, *Moses the Egyptian*. See

also Connolly, "Freud, Moses, and Secularism," and Connolly, *Brains, Techniques, and Time: The Ethics of Nonlinear Politics.*

45. Freud explains why Moses' foreignness was concealed, but he never asks why it was *poorly* concealed: the concealment was motivated by a desire "to glorify the new God and deny his foreignness" (Freud, *Moses and Monotheism*, p. 85). But why did the Israelites not conceal their secret better? The question recalls Yerushalmi's engagement with Freud: Yerushalmi says, contra Freud, that if the Israelites had murdered Moses, they would not have concealed it, since they are presented throughout the Hebrew Bible as extremely recalcitrant, and the murder would fit with that picture. If the Israelites were really interested in concealing the foreignness of Moses, and their supposed murder of him, they had the power to do so, and they would have also then concealed what they chose instead explicitly to reveal: the fractious nature of the relationship between this founder and his people, who constantly challenged his authority and violated his rules (Yerushalmi, *Freud's Moses*). But, as Jacques Derrida argues, with and against Yerushalmi, why not assume that the Israelites could have both concealed their murder of Moses and confessed it at the same time? After all, what event vanishes with*out* a trace? I suppose I am saying the analogous thing with reference to Moses' foreignness, which is only more obviously both concealed and disclosed at the same time (Derrida, *Archive Fever*).

46. Indeed, as Linda Zerilli points out, Rousseau's insistence on the need for self-identity ultimately drives his intense hostility to all forms of difference (Zerilli, *Signifying Woman.*) For a reading of Rousseau that focuses on his emphasis on self-identity, see Derrida, *Grammatology.*

47. I have in mind here Rawls and Habermas and their various devotees.

48. Rousseau, too, uses xenophobia as a way to generate social unanimity, not in the *Social Contract*, but in *The Government of Poland*. In the *Social Contract*, Rousseau does note that a certain unitariness becomes characteristic of the body politic "in regard to the foreigner"; that is, when the polity operates in relation to other polities, "it becomes a simple being, an individual" (Book I, Chapter 7). Notably, in Girard, the social unanimity sought includes the agreement of the scapegoat himself: "What is required is their [the scapegoats'] enthusiastic agreement with the decision to destroy them" (Girard, *Job*, p. 116).

49. Girard, *Violence and the Sacred*, p. 12. In *Job*, Girard also mentions orphans (p. 78). When Girard explains that kings are sometimes scapegoats because they are liminal, he assimilates kings to a larger category that includes foreigners, children, mad people, and so on (Girard, *Violence and the Sacred*, p. 12). (See also his reading of Job as a king figure.) In so doing, he offers some insight into the role of that which is figured as liminal in propping up the ordinary, but he also misses an opportunity to ask whether there is any particular, specific connection between *kings* and scapegoating, such as that explored here by way of the idea of the alienness of the law. This is the flip side of the error made by Geoffrey Bennington who, because he always already knows

that the law is alien, treats the alienness of the lawgiver solely as a symptom of that other alienness and never asks what other connections may tie together foreignness and founding, or foreignness and democracy in particular (Bennington, *Legislations*). Moreover, since the law may be alien in *any* regime, Bennington's analysis begs the question we are trying to answer here: Is there a specific connection between *democracy* and foreignness?

50. The neatness of Girard's theory leaves him unable to give an adequate account of what *causes* sacrificial crises: Where do they come from? If they work so well, why do they need to be periodically repeated? Why should we assume that sacrificial rituals never exceed the economy to which Girard has assigned them? It seems that Girard overestimates the power, effectiveness, and ubiquity of scapegoating or ritual killing. (By p. 251, even foreign war is "merely another form of sacrificial violence" [*Violence and the Sacred*]). For an implicit critique of Girard, especially on the count of ubiquity, see Giorgio Agamben's analysis of the Roman law category of bare life or *homo sacer*, a form of life that is identified by law as available to be killed but not ritually or sacrificially (Agamben, *Homo Sacer*).

51. On the need of Job's friends to turn his bad luck into something deserved and meaningful rather than random or contingent, see Connolly, *The Augustinian Imperative*. Girard discusses this in some detail too, generating a nice reading of *Antigone* in relation to *Job* (Girard, *Job*, Chapter Sixteen).

52. Of course, the identification of Moses as foreign and his subsequent murder could be a way of cleansing other taints too, such as those explored above: the alienness of the law that the people nonetheless proclaim as their own, and/or the mutual opacity of a people who like to style themselves as kin. No matter what we identify as the troublesome taint, the solution could still be the scapegoating of Moses as foreign, and any one of these could still be a Girardian reading insofar as each treats Moses as a scapegoat whose "foreignness" (contra Rousseau, Freud, and Girard) is a symbolic device or *fiction* that works—as part of a (re)founding event—to *solve* a social crisis.

53. By attributing this view to many theorists of democracy, I mean to distance myself from it. As I argue elsewhere, the effort to distinguish qualitatively between the extraordinary and the ordinary, or between the politics of founding and the politics of maintenance, suggests misleadingly that these are opposite and separate phenomena, when instead they are deeply supportive of each other (Honig, *Political Theory and the Displacement of Politics*, Chapter Four). It is in order to keep in mind the relationship between the two and to mark their similarity that I talk, throughout this book, about the politics of (re)founding and not just the politics of founding. The latter refers to an origin story; the former marks the role of that origin story (retold in myriad ways) in the daily reconstitution of citizenship.

54. Lincoln, "The Perpetuation of Our Political Institutions," p. 21.

55. Yet another reading of *Shane* suggests itself if, recalling that the story is told from the perspective of the young boy, we read it together with another story of expelled violence told from a boy's perspective: E.T.A. Hoffman's "The Sandman," interpreted by Freud in "The Uncanny." Freud argues that in "The Sandman," the boy addresses his fear of his father's horrifying power (in Freud's terms, his "castration anxiety") by splitting his father into two distinct figures, one (in Eric Santner's gloss) "nurturing and caring, the other demonic and castrating" (Santner, *My Own Private Germany*, pp. 68–69). Analogously, we might say that the boy's father in *Shane* (rather than the community as a whole) does the violence that their (re)founding calls for; but the boy, frightened by his father's power, then invents a departing figure onto whom he can safely project his father's violence, leaving himself a domesticated father figure, one who is nurturant and safe, if also a bit weak.

As Eric Santner points out, Freud argues that the splitting of the father-imago is "largely the product of the son's delusional elaboration of an inevitable and universal ambivalence *vis-à-vis* the father." But the American psychoanalyst William Niederland argues that there is (in the Schreber case, anyway) a " '*nucleus of truth*' in the son's paranoid productions" and it is possible to trace many of those delusions back "to the father's *actual handling* of his son during childhood." Either way, whether the occasion of the splitting is produced or found, splitting is a strategy that allows the subject to save the object and preserve the ability to identify with it. See Santner, *My Own Private Germany*, Chapter Two, esp. pp. 64–70. See also Freud, "The Uncanny," p. 232n.1.

56. Girard offers a moving analysis of the need for the scapegoat to cooperate in his own scapegoating (Girard, *Job*, Chapter Sixteen). The analysis here could be usefully read in tandem with Berlin's condemnation of positive liberty in "Two Concepts of Liberty." Both Berlin and Girard condemn the insistence that the victim participate in his own punishment and, in effect, will it; but Girard, in my view, offers a better analysis (but not approval) of the social needs served by that insistence.

57. In *Political Theory and Modernity*, Connolly argues that the General Will cannot generate itself, and he recurs to Rousseau's *Geneva Manuscript* for firm evidence of this. Geoffrey Bennington takes the same dim view of the General Will's chances of success (*Legislations*, *Dudding*) as, indeed, did I earlier in this chapter. I mean now not to replace the earlier reading with the later one, but to add this later interpretation to the earlier one as a second possibility.

58. Saccamano, "Rhetoric, Consensus, and the Law in Rousseau's *Contrat Social*," p. 731.

59. In short, read this way, Rousseau's public myth of origins seeks to achieve the effects sought by Rogers Smith in his: the displacement of domestic violence onto a separable, external, and disavowable other.

60. This illegitimacy is symbolized by the murder of the founder in Freud.

61. "In the final analysis, then, the judicial system and the institution of sacrifice share the same function [i.e., to stem the cycle of vengeance], but the judicial system is infinitely more effective" (Girard, *Violence and the Sacred*, p. 23). Cf. "we owe our good fortune to one of our social institutions above all: our judicial system which serves to deflect the menace of vengeance" (Girard, *Violence and the Sacred*, p. 15).

62. See Jacqueline Stevens's *Reproducing the State* for an effective account of how the family and kinship are not models for the state but its products, or, better, both.

Chapter Three
The Foreigner as Immigrant

1. See the genealogy of Jesus in Matt. 1:1–17.
2. Deut. 23:4.
3. Ruth 1:8.
4. Ruth 1:15.
5. Ruth 1:16–17.
6. Ruth 1:20.
7. There is some debate about the details of this scene: Is the next of kin being asked to redeem the land through purchase or to redeem Ruth through marriage? For a summary of the debate and the single best reading of the scene, see Fewell and Gunn, *Compromising Redemption*.
8. In recent years, there has been a veritable explosion of commentary on the Book of Ruth (Kates and Reimer, eds., *Reading Ruth*; Brenner, ed., *A Feminist Companion to Ruth*; and Brenner, ed., *Ruth and Esther*). Ozick's and Kristeva's readings, in which Ruth's migration to Bethlehem is motivated either by her conversion to Judaic monotheism or by her love for Naomi, largely typify the main approaches (Ozick, "Ruth"; Kristeva, *Strangers to Ourselves*). Most recently, commentators have begun to write about Ruth from a Moabite or subaltern sort of perspective. See especially Donaldson, "The Sign of Orpah"; Dube, "The Unpublished Letters of Orpah to Ruth"; McKinlay, "A Son Is Born to Naomi"; and Brenner, "Ruth as a Foreign Worker."
9. Some doubt that the Book of Ruth can be a resource for an analysis of immigration politics because the text tells the story of a single migrant, while the contemporary issue is concerned with hordes of people. My own view is that the text's success at dramatizing enduring issues of immigration politics is due partly to its use of the device of personification. Moreover, the story of Ruth has established connections to immigration politics that precede my analysis and Kristeva's. Marjorie Garber recalls playing Ruth in the late 1940s in the U.S. in a series of fund-raisers sponsored by Hadassah to help Jewish refugees make their way to Palestine after the war. Interestingly, given Kristeva's use of the

head scarf to mark the recalcitrance of Moslem immigrants, Garber, as Ruth, wore a head scarf to mark her character's European, refugee identity (Garber, conversation with author, Cambridge, Mass., 1996).

10. Deuteronomy 34:5. Buber makes special note of Moses' burial place: "Yahweh buried him, Moses, in the valley of the land of Moab, near Beth Pe'or" (Buber, "Exodus 19–27," p. 45).

11. As we saw in Chapter One, these elements of the Book of Ruth become apparent when we read Ruth as a foreign-founder (i.e., in relation to Moses) and not as a convert, per se. Reading Ruth as a convert is the traditional reading, which invites comparison with Abraham, a comparison made by both Ozick and Kristeva, as we see below (n. 48).

12. Toni Morrison calls particularly sharp attention to the exclusionary dimension of the (re)founding effect of American immigration in relation to American blacks (Morrison, "On the Backs of Blacks").

13. Some rabbinical commentators suggest that the Moabites practiced human sacrifice. Much is made of this in the 1950s Hollywood film version of the Book of Ruth in which Ruth is a priestess of the cult that delivers young girls to be consumed by the fires of the idol, Chemosh. The charge is not supported by historical evidence, however. A. H. Van Zyl argues that this was not common practice in Moab. In general, animals were sacrificed. King Mesha did sacrifice his eldest son to the Moabite god, Chemosh, but that was under extraordinary circumstances and not part of an ordinary practice (Van Zyl, *The Moabites*, p. 201). The emphasis in Judaic texts on Moabite human sacrifice is symptomatic of the figuring of the Moabites, in opposition to the Israelites, as a people lacking respect for proper boundaries and distinctions.

14. Ozick, "Ruth," p. 221.

15. Jack M. Sasson notes this device of personification elsewhere in the Book of Ruth: "A didactic device frequently resorted to by Biblical writers is to limit the spectrum of choice to two alternatives, only one of which will prove to be correct. An obvious method of putting such a concept in effect is the creation of two brothers, only one of whom will ultimately fare well. Mahlon marries Ruth—he will live on" (through the posterity of Obed). Other biblical examples noted by Sasson are Cain and Abel, Jacob and Esau, Ishmael and Isaac—all male (Sasson, *Ruth: A New Translation*, pp. 16–17). Why does Sasson not include Ruth and Orpah in his list? Perhaps because of his Proppian assumption that Orpah is a merely marginal character, not central to the tale and not worthy, therefore, of further interpretive attention.

16. Hence the *necessity* of the link between inclusion and exclusion, contra Michael Walzer, who says he is "inclined to reject the *metaphysical* belief that all inclusion necessarily entails exclusion." I agree with Walzer in hestitating to endorse the general "metaphysical" claim. One merit of this reading of the Book of Ruth, however, is that it illustrates the claim in a particular but also more generalizable context: that of immigration. See Walzer, *What It Means to Be an*

American, pp. 44–45n.30. Another merit of this reading of the Book of Ruth is that it provides an example of an other who is both necessary to and forbidden by the community she supplements and disturbs, in which there is a deep and necessary relationship between that other's forbiddenness and necessity insofar as both stem from the *same* feature—in this instance, Ruth's foreignness. This makes Ruth a superior example to Oedipus, on whom Girard relies in theorizing the doubleness of the other (Girard, *Violence and the Sacred*). That doubleness is weak in Oedipus's case. His necessity to Thebes stems from his wisdom as a ruler, while his forbiddenness stems from his incest (and maybe from his hubris). The relation between these two is contingent, not necessary: in principle, Oedipus could have been a wise king (necessary to the order) without also being a product of incest and a committer of parricide (forbidden by the order). The contingent coincidence of these two characteristics indicates that Sophocles and his audience were exploring the connections between necessity and forbiddenness through Oedipus, but that they had not conceived of these connections in the most truly tragic terms.

Antigone does better at figuring the combination of necessity and forbiddenness to the order that requires and bans her (though Girard takes little notice of her). Here the connections are tighter than in the case of Oedipus: Antigone's necessity to the order (her exemplary fidelity to the rites of burial and the gods of the underworld) is connected to her forbiddenness as a child of incest (which marks her as death identified insofar as she ought, as it were, never to have been born, hence her name). But even here, the coincidence of necessity and forbiddenness is not quite as tight as in the case of Ruth, whose story is not, however, usually treated as tragic. In principle, one could have fidelity to the gods of the underworld (necessary) without being an incest (forbidden). But for Ruth, it is her foreignness and conversion/immigration that make her necessary to the order (as loyalty-swearing foreigner) and dangerous to it (as foreigner). And you cannot have one without the other.

17. Ozick, "Ruth," pp. 227–228.

18. Ibid., pp. 219–220.

19. Ibid., p. 221.

20. Ibid., p. 224.

21. Ibid., p. 222.

22. Ibid., p. 220.

23. Ibid., p. 221.

24. Ibid., p. 224.

25. Ibid., p. 227.

26. See Katrina Larkin, (*Ruth and Esther*) who says that Ruth's declaration to Naomi "blunt[s] the issue of Ruth's foreignness" (quoted by McKinlay, who expressly disagrees with Larkin on this point in McKinlay, "A Son Is Born to Naomi," p. 152).

27. Ozick, "Ruth," p. 223.

28. In psychoanalytic terms, Orpah's (over)attachment to her mother(land)—represented by the phrase her "mother's house" (an unusual locution for the Bible)—prevents her, as it did Antigone (who clung to Polynices, the displaced site of her longing for her mother, Jocasta), from entering the (paternal or monotheistic) Law, the realm of the Symbolic (as Luce Irigaray argues in *Speculum of the Other Woman*). Irigaray, moved by a sensibility more tragic than Ozick's, finds a subterranean location for Antigone, who eternally unsettles the dominant order. Ozick pauses to reflect on Orpah, but she does not look to Orpah as a source of eternal dissonance or (in Irigaray's appropriation of Hegel's term) irony.

29. Ruth 1:22, 2:2, 2:6, 2:21, 4:5, 4:9.

30. One commentator argues that this is because childbirth was never Ruth's desire but, rather, Naomi's all along (Reimer, "Her Mother's House," p. 105).

31. Holst-Warhaft, *Dangerous Voices*, p. 211n.54, citing Herodotus, *Histories*, 6.6.138.

32. Another possible reading, however, this one suggested to me by Harry Fleischman from San Francisco, might position Naomi as more corrupt than Ruth. Naomi, like Elimelech, left Bethlehem in a time of famine and returned only when the famine was over. This self-interested behavior suggests that she is morally compromised and that, perhaps, Ruth's foreignness effectively works to distract us from that. Naomi's morally compromised character might even foreshadow that of the line of kings that will follow, always flirting with material concerns and distracted from the one true god.

33. Ozick, "Ruth," pp. 229–230. And yet the Hebrew term used here for "feet" is a pun for genitals. Ozick's claim echoes Hegel's that the brother-sister relation, of which he takes Polynices and Antigone to be exemplars, is unerotic. As Jacques Derrida points out, the claim is astonishing given the incestuous origins of this pair: "Antigone's parents are not some parents among others" (Derrida, *Glas*, p. 165).

34. Sasson, *Ruth: A New Translation*, p. 78.

35. Ozick, "Ruth," p. 225.

36. Contra Ozick, Orpah's course was courageous, too. The difficulties of such a return are occluded by Ozick, who comments on the unusualness of Orpah's exogamy but then assumes that Orpah's life in Moab will be unproblematic: "Soon she will marry a Moabite husband and have a Moabite child" (Ozick, "Ruth," p. 224). Fewell and Gunn have a better grasp of the situation: "What are Ruth's opportunities in Moab? Who would want to marry a barren widow, much less one that had been living with a foreigner? And would she be known as the 'Israelite-lover,' the one too good for her own people? . . . In the end, we might ask, what takes more courage, the staying or the leaving?" (Fewell and Gunn, *Compromising Redemption*, pp. 97–98). Cf. Kaplan, "The Noah Syndrome," p. 167.

37. As Derrida points out, Aristotle knows that the borders among these kinds of friendship are porous and cannot be fully policed (p. 205). "Aristotle never gives up analysing the ruses that enable one friendship to be smuggled into another, the law of the useful into that of pleasure, one or the other into virtue's mask" (Derrida, *Politics of Friendship*, p. 105).

38. Rancière, *Dis-agreement*, p. 30.

39. Saccamano has in mind in particular the lawgiver's impersonation of a prophet in order to achieve this effect. (Saccamano, "Rhetoric, Consensus and the Law in Rousseau's *Contrat social*," p. 745).

40. Of course, as we saw in Chapter Two, the founder's foreignness remains a problem even if he leaves, since the law or institutions or norms whereby he (re)founded the people are associated with him and his foreignness.

41. Lacocque, *The Feminine Unconventional*, pp. 86, 91, 107–108, passim. The historical evidence on the dating of the Book of Ruth is not decisive. Lacocque's conclusion depends finally on his assumption that a Moabite ancestor could only damage David, an assumption which, as we shall see momentarily, is questionable.

42. One might well add to this the observation that the order-constituting exchange in this text is that of a male—Obed—who is passed from one woman, Ruth, to another, Naomi. On the other hand, one could just as well say that Ruth is passed from Mahlon to Boaz by way of Naomi.

43. Kristeva, *Strangers*, pp. 75–76.

44. Ibid., p. 74. Indeed, contra Kristeva, we may see David's heroic triumph over Goliath as a way of ridding himself of the taint of Moabite foreignness. Goliath, according to rabbinical commentators, is Orpah's grandson. By killing him, David may have done more than simply kill a giant in order to prove his manhood (a traditional folktale device). This test of David may have done double duty. By killing his Moabite cousin, David not only defended his people from attack and entered into manhood, he also proved his loyalty to the Israelites in opposition to Moab. Thus, he gives us Ruth without Orpah.

45. Ibid., p. 75.

46. Ruth's foreignness may also do something else: as Moses' double, Ruth may be a figure whereby Moses' lingering foreignness is dealt with. I.e., how could his repressed foreignness be a problem for the Israelites when they can take on board someone as foreign as this Moabite?

47. Kristeva, *Strangers*, p. 71; and Ozick, "Ruth," p. 226. By contrast, Gail Twersky Reimer argues that "Ruth had no desire for children and no interest in maternity." However, Reimer rightly notes, this has not prevented most commentators from reading Ruth in terms of a "single model of woman's relationship to motherhood" (Reimer, "Her Mother's House," p. 105).

48. But Ruth's gender—more to the point, Ozick's gendering of Ruth—also positions Ruth, on Ozick's account, as second to Judaism's founding father, Abraham. "Abraham—the first Hebrew to catch insight—caught it as genius

does, autonomously, out of the blue, without any inculcating traditions." Ruth, by contrast, is brought to that vision by living among Hebrews, learning their ways, and loving them. Could she have been a second Abraham? Ozick asks. We can never know for sure, for the "story as it is given is perforce inflexible, not amenable to experiment. We cannot have Ruth without Naomi; nor would we welcome the loss of such loving-kindness." But given what we do know, Ozick says, "Ruth may not count as a second Abraham because her tale is enfolded in a way Abraham's is not: she has had her saturation in Abraham's seed." His is the active agency; she is the passive recipient, "inculcation cannot be expunged: there it is" (Ozick, "Ruth," p. 378). (This difficulty of assessing the significance of a choice made under the influence of socialization comes up again in Chapter Four in relation to the issue of consent on the part of citizens born into the regime to which they are then asked to consent.)

Ruth's birth into monotheism is second to Abraham's, in Ozick's estimation, because his was an autogenetic birth while hers was enabled by a mother. This fantasy of a birth uncontaminated by a mother permeates Ozick's text. It is, in psychoanalytic terms, a masculine fantasy of invulnerability, self-sufficiency, and autonomy which, in its elimination of the mother from the moment of birth, also elides the primal scene and thereby tries to avoid entirely the question of sexual difference and of sexuality itself. It is worth recalling here Ozick's insistence that there is nothing erotic about the threshing-room floor scene.

Notably, Kristeva makes the opposite assessment of the same pairing, arguing that Ruth is superior to Abraham because she, the foreigner, "did it on her own initiative," by contrast with Abraham, who "left his father's house in answer to a call from god." To his credit, Abraham responded positively, but Ruth sought out the Israelites and their god all on her own. That is why, according to Kristeva, Boaz says Ruth deserves "perfect recompense" for her virtue. He means to suggest that she is more meritorious than even Abraham (Kristeva, *Strangers*, p. 73).

49. It is worth noting that Ruth's takings are all from Boaz or mediated by him. Ruth does not take up space in Bethlehem's public sphere. When the time comes for the legal wrangling over land ownership and inheritance issues, Boaz represents Ruth. She does not represent herself. She seems to accept that the law is not her sphere or that its workings are less available to be interrupted by her takings. This may be another reason why this foreign-founder can stay. She may be a taker who skirts established customs and violates gender norms, but she yields before the law.

50. The point is noted in the most detail by Fewell and Gunn, *Compromising Redemption*, but also by Bal, *Anti-Covenant*; Pardes, *Countertraditions in the Bible*; and Newsom and Ringe, eds., the *Women's Bible Commentary*. Notably, this last source finds *fault* with Ruth for her active seduction of Boaz and for her other daring innovations.

51. Trible, *God and the Rhetoric of Sexuality*. In the end, however, Ruth gives birth to Obed and is folded into the Israelite order, according to Trible. Trible mourns this outcome and Ozick celebrates it. Regardless of how we value it, however, the outcome presses us to ask: Was it Ruth's gender that enabled her absorption?

52. The general category of demons that included Lilliths was comprised of figures who "were thought to share one thing in common: an inability to achieve destinies commonly attributed to members of their respective sex" (Sasson, *Ruth: A New Translation*, p. 76, relies here on S. Lakenbacher, "Note sur l'ardat-lili," esp. pp. 148–158). For example, the *lamastu*, "constantly frustrated in her ability to produce children," was a woman who could not be domesticated as a mother. "Enraged, this creature roamed far and wide, ready to attack and harm unsuspecting children and women in labor." In addition, the *lilu, lilit/ ardat, lili* represented "individuals who were never able to consummate their marriages. Crazed with unquenched desires, these creatures sought to mate with humans of their opposite sex . . . to ruin marriages, and lure prospective mates into their own madness." A version of these boundary- and role-defying women was present in the ancient Semitic world as Lillith, whose name may link up etymologically with *layla*, meaning night.

53. Arendt, *Origins of Totalitarianism*. One could think of the "right to have rights" as the political-theoretical ground for the model of political agency as taking that I develop throughout this book. That is, the right to have rights could be seen as an authorizing ground for the claims made by those without proper standing to make them. (I think that's what Arendt was thinking of when she developed this idea.) But I don't pursue this point further because in general I think such authorizing grounds tend to follow, post hoc, from the making of new claims rather than grounding them in advance.

54. Kristeva, *Nations without Nationalism*, p. 36.

55. Kristeva, *Strangers*, p. 194.

56. Kristeva, *Nations*, p. 60.

57. Ibid., p. 63.

58. See Brubaker, *Citizenship and Nationhood in France and Germany*, pp. 138–164; and Hollifield, *Immigrants, Markets, and States*, Chapters Six and Seven.

59. Kristeva, *Nations*, p. 37.

60. Ibid., p. 40.

61. Ibid., p. 41. But why not reverse the chronology? Affective relations to the state may well be what undergirds and secures the ties of family (rather than the other way around). Jacqueline Stevens poses this question pointedly in *Reproducing the State*. Similarly, Micheline Ishay troubles another point on the chronology when she suggests that cosmopolitanism or internationalism is historically and conceptually prior to nationalism (Ishay, *Internationalism and Its Betrayal*).

62. See Moruzzi, "A Problem with Headscarves," p. 665.

63. Kristeva, *Nations*, p. 38.

64. Ibid., p. 59.

65. Ibid., pp. 46–47; my emphasis.

66. Ibid., p. 47. Kristeva does note the tenuousness of the distinction between fetish and transitional object, though, when she concedes that the transitional object is "any child's indispensable fetish" (ibid., p. 41).

67. Ibid., pp. 41–42.

68. Ibid., p. 43.

69. Ibid., p. 47.

70. Ahmed, *Women and Gender in Islam*, pp. 223–224. Ahmed studies veiling in Egypt, not France, but her argument was echoed by France's Federation of Councils of Parents of Pupils in Public Schools (FCPE), which opposed the expulsion of over seventy girls who wore head scarves to their schools in Lille and the Paris region: these expulsions carry with them "the immense inconvenience of confining these young girls to within their family circle and of limiting any possibility of emancipation" (*Migration News Sheet*, p. 2).

71. Ahmed explains: "[T]he fact that wearing it signals the wearer's adherence to an Islamic moral and sexual code has the paradoxical effect, as some women have attested, of allowing them to strike up friendships with men . . . without the fear that they will be dubbed immoral or their reputations damaged" (Ahmed, *Women and Gender in Islam*, p. 224).

72. The contradiction is not unique to French treatments of veiling. As Marnia Lazreg points out, scholars everywhere treat Moslem women "either as embodiments of Islam, or as helpless victims forced to live by its tenets" (Lazreg, *The Eloquence of Silence*, p. 14).

73. The complexity of the situation is implied, if not explicitly theorized by Winifred Woodhull, who speculates about what would be the effects of a French ban on the *hijeb*: "Will their parents simply take them out of school, with the result that they may marry sooner and have fewer professional opportunities than they might have had otherwise? Will the parents keep their daughters in school but be more steadfast in their refusal to allow them to participate in physical education and sex education classes, to go on class trips, or go to the movies with friends? Or will the ban have the opposite effect, reinforcing the legitimacy of the French school system so that the girls may continue their studies, participate fully in the curriculum, and so on?" (Woodhull, *Transfigurations of the Maghreb*, pp. 48–49).

74. See Fanon, *A Dying Colonialism*; and Woodhull, *Transfigurations*, p. 48.

75. Indeed, Kristeva subjects women to special scrutiny because she relies on the figure of the good mother to figure her cosmopolitanism. There are those whose maternalism preserves cultural difference in a nationalist way, she says, and theirs is "a certain conformist 'maternalism' " which "lies dormant in every

one of us and can turn women into the accomplices of fundamentalisms and mystical nationalisms as they were of the Nazi mirage" (Kristeva, *Nations*, p. 34). And there are those whose maternalism ushers into existence new cosmopolitan "living spaces" that are neither too nationalist nor too world-oriented. Why frame these two options in terms of maternalism? Because women have the luck and the responsibility of being boundary-subjects . . . more dramatically so than men are," and this positions women to be the mothers of a not yet born "polyvalent community" (Kristeva, *Nations*, p. 35). Gayatri Spivak also positions women (but not qua mothers) in exceptional relation to cosmopolitanism. See p. 106 above.

76. Thanks to Pratap Mehta on this point.

77. Here there is an important difference between Kristeva and Ahmed. While Ahmed ultimately champions just one dimension of veiling and assesses it in terms of its potential contribution to a feminist metropolitanism that she herself values, she first stops to explore the heterogeneous meanings of the scarf for some of the Moslem women who wear it. Moreover, her feminist metropolitanism seems to be shaped by what she finds. The engagement works two ways. Kristeva, by contrast, already knows the significance of veiling, has no questions to ask of those who practice it, and has, apparently, nothing to learn from them. As I point out above, this suggests that the veil is less of a fetish for its Moslem wearers than for Kristeva herself. Indeed, on one account, a fetish precisely "stands for an absent articulating context" (Rogoff, "From Ruins to Debris," p. 241).

78. Butler, "Kantians in Every Culture?" p. 18.

79. Kristeva, *Nations*, p. 11.

80. Ibid., p. 47.

81. Ibid., p. 60; emphasis in original.

82. Ozick, "Ruth," pp. 227–228. Ruth's famous speech to Naomi is interpreted by many as, effectively, a list of the transitional objects by way of which Ruth makes her passage: going where Naomi goes, living where she lives, Ruth will come to know her people and then finally her god. Kristeva approves of this transitional passage, while Ozick (as we saw earlier) sees it as inferior to Abraham's less-mediated route to monotheism.

The cultural-symbolic connections among nationalism, immigration, psychoanalysis, and transitional objects were on display when the *New York Times Book Review* used a flag-stuffed baby bottle to illustrate its review of Michael Lind's *The Next American Nation*.

83. I borrow from one version of this account, but I distance myself from psychoanalysis's reliance on the model of an original maternal relation. Separation and transition are issues not just for children or immigrants but for all of us throughout our lifetimes. I also seek to avoid the progressive trajectory of developmental accounts. That trajectory infantilizes the immigrants whose transitions are part of what is at issue here, and it works to affirm Western receiving

regimes' perceptions of sending regimes as a "past that the West has already lived out" and can be left behind without loss (Visvanathan, "From the Annals of the Laboratory State," p. 41). Kristeva's and Ozick's progressive accounts tend to feed these prejudices, too.

84. Santner, *Stranded Objects*, pp. 19–26; and Peter Sacks, *The English Elegy*, p. 8. Santner is working with Winnicott, *Playing and Reality*; and Freud, "Beyond the Pleasure Principle."

85. Santner, *Stranded Objects*, pp. 26–27.

86. Ozick and Trible both see Ruth's silence as a sign that this extraordinary woman has been successfully absorbed into the ordinary structure of the regime. Ozick approves of this; Trible, with her emphasis on the patriarchal dimensions of the order in question, sees this as a tragic ending (Ozick, "Ruth"; Trible, *God and the Rhetoric of Sexuality*).

87. Moreover, the identification of such tendencies with outsiders absolves contemporary democracies from having to face the fact that enclavism is characteristic these days less of immigrants and ethnics (most of whom still become absorbed by the third generation, according to Portes and Rumbaut [*Immigrant America*]), than of the wealthy, who show a marked propensity to withdraw from public goods and services.

88. Patricia Karlin-Neumann notes the character of the Book of Ruth as a mourning narrative, but she identifies Naomi as the mourner and Ruth as the servant who brings her back to life. Karlin-Neumann never attends to Ruth's character as a mourner who is left bereft. As in Ozick and Kristeva, Ruth is treated as an other who has a service to grant the order (Karlin-Neumann, "The Journey toward Life").

89. Santner, *Stranded Objects*, p. 24.

90. True, the rabbis say that Naomi's losses are in some sense not regrettable: the deaths of Elimelech and his sons are deserved because they abandoned the community in a time of need. But these men are, nonetheless, members, indeed once-respected members, of this group.

91. Zelinsky, "The Twinning of the World," p. 1. This is not to suggest that the relations established under the umbrella of sorority are in any way not politicized. The following is one example of the impact sister cityhood can have and the kind of politics that can be generated by such ties. In late 1988, the Lion's Club International of Taipei donated 10,000 Chinese language books to the Monterey Park, California, public library intending the gift to "reinforce the closeness they felt with their sister-city which many [had] begun to call 'Little Taipei' " Mayor Barry Hatch saw in this gift an assault on American values and fought to refuse it; however, he ultimately lost out to a coalition of local civic groups and Chinese-American community leaders (Crawford, *Language Loyalties*, pp. 1–3).

92. Chilsen and Rampton, *Friends in Deed*.

93. Of course, as with any cultural resource, this one, too, is subject to inflation, as I was reminded recently when I spotted in Chicago's O'Hare Airport a string of banners declaring Chicago the sister-city of scores of other cities in every region of the world.

Chapter Four
The Foreigner as Citizen

1. I do not discuss Tocqueville in detail here, but see Volume One, Chapter Two, and later pp. 280–281ff of *Democracy in America* for his views on how immigration and especially "the double movement of immigration" (p. 281) are fundamental to the shape, character, and success of the unique phenomenon of American democracy.

2. Sowell, *Migrations and Cultures*; Walzer, *What It Means to Be an American*; and Schuck and Smith, *Citizenship without Consent*.

3. The American Dream performs similar functions, as Jennifer Hochschild points out in *Facing Up to the American Dream*. My argument here is analogous in some ways to Hochschild's. She and I are both trying to find progressive possibilities in apparently conservative myths, rather than reject those myths outright.

4. Sacvan Bercovitch redeploys the exceptionalist interpretation of American identity even while subjecting it to greater critical scrutiny than is customary among exceptionalists: "Of all symbols of identity, only *America* has united nationality and universality, civic and spiritual selfhood, secular and redemptive history, the country's past and paradise to be, in a single synthetic ideal" (Bercovitch, *The American Jeremiad*, p. 176). My aim in this chapter is not to assay the historical success of this nationalist project, but to attend to some of its political and cultural *costs*.

5. The phrase is taken from Peter H. Wood, *Black Majority: Negroes in Colonial South Carolina*, p. xiv, itself cited in Rosen, *A Short History of Charleston*, p. 63. Thanks to Paul Pierson for calling the South Carolina quote to my attention and to Michaele Ferguson for tracking it down. See also Daniels, *Coming to America*, p. 54: "The slave trade was one of the major means of bringing *immigrants* to the New World in general and to the United States in particular" (emphasis added). Thanks to Kunal M. Parker for calling my attention to Daniels's work. For a thoughtful analysis of how the politics of race were mapped, historically, as an immigration politics by towns seeking to refuse financial responsibility for destitute former slaves, see Parker, "Making Blacks Foreigners" (paper on file with author).

6. See Walzer, *What It Means to Be an American*, and Rogers Smith, "Beyond Tocqueville, Myrdal and Hartz: The Multiple Traditions Thesis in America."

7. The economistic explanation is also judged to be limited by Ali Behdad, whose work on immigration politics I discuss below. "The conventional liberal wisdom about the public reaction to immigration is, 'When things are going well and there's a shortage of labor, people either look the other way or are actively supportive of bringing cheaper labor into the United States. But when jobs are tight, and the cost of supporting people goes up, then we suddenly redo the calculus' " (political scientist Bruce Cain, quoted in Brownstein and Simon, "Hospitality Turns into Hostility," p. A6). Behdad argues that "such an economic view of anti-immigration consensus . . . fails to address the role of immigration as both a necessary mechanism of social control in the formation of the state apparatus and an essential cultural contribution to the formation of national identity" (Behdad, "Nationalism and Immigration to the United States," p. 155).

8. Behdad, "Nationalism and Immigration to the United States," p. 175.

9. Ibid., pp. 165–166.

10. Ibid., p. 166. Although Behdad thinks I miss the most important pole, too: "The different functions of the immigrant, I would add, are the effect of an ambivalent mode of national identity in the United States, which simultaneously acknowledges the nation's immigrant formation and disavows it. When I say an ambivalent mode of national identity, I have in mind not only the general split between hospitality and hostility, xenophilia and xenophobia, that Honig convincingly discusses in her article, but also the particular ways in which the competing myths of American identity themselves are ambivalently articulated. As I will show in the cases of Crevecoeur's valorization of immigrant America (xenophilia) and the Know-Nothings in the mid-nineteenth century (xenophobia), every discourse of immigration espouses opposite notions of what constitutes an American identity. Forgetting in each instance allows for an ideologically divided response to the question of "Who is an American?" The idyllic and heterogeneous America presented in Crevecoeur, for example, is also revealed as a racially segregated community that excludes both Native Americans and enslaved Africans. Similarly, the reactionary attitude of Know-Nothings toward immigrants is also a progressive response to the industrialists' exploitative uses of immigrants" (Behdad, *Forgetful Nation*).

11. Behdad, *Forgetful Nation*.

12. Actually, more than one stereotype is missing here. Also absent is the leftist internationalist foreigner by way of whom public passions were inflamed during the trial of Sacco and Vanzetti as well as during the McCarthy era.

13. On the reality of the myth's effects, see Waters, *Ethnic Options*.

14. See, for example, Winnick, "America's 'Model Minority.' " Schlesinger, too, makes stereotypical note of the strong family relations of Jews and Asians, remarking the power of those relations as a resource for individuals (*The Dis-*

uniting of America). A recent, less stereotypical and more sustainedly empirical effort in this direction is Sowell, *Migrations and Cultures.*

Celebrants of model minorities highlight the ways in which extended families (and their cheap labor) are necessary for capitalist success, but they say nothing about how capitalist economies also attenuate such ties. Symptomatic was a front-page *New York Times* story (Dobrzynski, "For More and More Job Seekers, an Aging Parent Is a Big Factor.") on the increasing reluctance of middle-income labor to move for employment, given their desire to remain close to aging parents. In the second paragraph, the language of the story switches. The phenomenon is now called a "problem," and the perspective adopted for the rest of the report is that of the companies who have to deal with this resistance. The same story could, of course, have been written (also problematically) in a celebratory way with a headline such as: "The return of family ties."

15. For a psychoanalytic account of the foreigner as someone who only wants to take "our thing," see Zizak, *Tarrying with the Negative*, pp. 201ff.

16. Holmes, "Anti-Immigrant Mood Moves Asians to Organize," p. A1; emphasis added. An example of the more usual story about immigrants is "Hospitality Is Their Business," an account of Indian-American involvement in the hotel industry (popularized in the film *Mississippi Masala*). The role of these immigrants as supplements to the American Dream is made quite clear by Joel Kotkin, quoted in the *New York Times* story as follows: "These Indians are modern Horatio Algers. They're willing to start in marginal and sometimes risky areas that native-born Americans are not interested in going into, and working [*sic*] incredibly hard hours" ("Hospitality Is Their Business," pp. D1 and D9). Success is here measured by the move in one to two generations from hands-on labor to office management and serious wealth.

The story does not note a small irony: these immigrants are in the *hospitality* business at a time when the country is particularly inhospitable toward immigrants. Nor does it make much of one complication of the Horatio Alger comparison: some of these immigrants seem to have arrived with rather substantial reserves of capital. Mr. Patel, who "attributes the Indians' success to 'the way we were brought up' "—(whole families put their shoulder to the wheel and community members lend each other money without interest or collateral)—immigrated after "a 20-year career with Barclays Bank in Kenya" (D9).

17. The U.S. Supreme Court opinion claimed to have seldom seen "such a concentrated and relentless campaign to deport an individual" (Bernstein, "Harry Bridges: Marxist Founder of West's Longshoremen Union").

18. On undocumented worker involvement in unionization activities, see the cases of construction workers in Rothstein, "Immigration Dilemmas," and mattress manufacturing workers in Delgado, *New Immigrants, Old Unions*. On workplace activism earlier in the century, see Greene, *The Slavic Community on Strike*, and Laslett, "Labor Party, Labor Lobbying, or Direct Action?" On school politics in Lowell, Massachusetts, see Perez-Bustillo, "What Happens

When English-Only Comes to Town?" On Chinese political involvements, see Victor Low, *The Unimpressible Race*. On current alien political activism, see "Foreign Legions: Lots of Noncitizens Feel Right at Home in U.S. Political Races," *Wall Street Journal*.

19. On this point, and others related to the arguments developed here, see Shapiro, *Cinematic Political Thought*.

20. Walzer, *What It Means to Be an American*, p. 11.

21. Walzer provides no empirical evidence for this. But the claim fits well with Irving Howe's account of Jewish immigrants of an earlier generation in New York (*The World of Our Fathers*) as well as with Ronald Takaki's account of Chinese and Japanese immigrants on the American West Coast (*In a Different Mirror*).

22. Reagon, "Coalition Politics: Turning the Century."

23. Walzer, *What It Means to Be an American*, p. 48. See Holmes, "Anti-Immigrant Mood Moves Asians to Organize": "They want relatives to join them from overseas. They want their culture replenished with new arrivals" (p. A11).

24. Walzer, *What It Means to Be an American*, p. 66. Cf. p. 18.

25. Walzer develops the idea of a "communitarian corrective" in "The Communitarian Critique of Liberalism."

26. Arthur Schlesinger gives voice to the fragmentation concern (*The Disuniting of America*). Others, like Randolph Bourne, see the fragmentary potential of immigrants and ethnics but differ from Schlesinger in their evaluation of that potential. Rather than decry fragmentation as a threat to citizenship, Bourne celebrates it as a healthy check on American nationalism ("Trans-National America"). In so doing, Bourne effectively shares in Lacocque's assessment of Ruth.

Although I am relying on two different figures to give voice to it, I nonetheless continue to insist—as I did with Ruth—that we see this play of xenophilia and xenophobia as a national ambivalence, rather than as a difference of opinion between two discrete parties. This will continue to be the case in the sections that follow, as well, in which we shall see again and again how two supposedly opposing, xenophilic and xenophobic, assessments not only mirror each other but also both feed the nationalism that is a necessary condition of their respective opponent's position.

27. Walzer, *What It Means to Be an American* p. 24.

28. Binder and Reimers, *All the Nations under Heaven*, p. 52.

29. Walzer, *What It Means to Be an American*, p. 17; emphasis added. On the supposed contrast to Europe, see Gerard Noiriel on France's true character as an immigrant nation ("Immigration: Amnesia and Memory"). In a later book, Walzer acknowledges that France is "Europe's leading immigrant society," but, he points out, it is different from the U.S. in that it is not friendly to immigrants as such and demands their rapid assimilation (Walzer, *On Toleration*, pp. 37ff).

30. Estimates are that 195,000 U.S. residents emigrate annually. See Labovitz, "Immigration—Just the Facts." Regarding the first decades of this century: "Intelligent estimates of how many foreigners returned to their native countries range from a high of nearly 90 percent for the Balkan peoples to a low of 5 percent for the Jews. We do know that in the period between 1908 and 1914, immigration officials recorded 6,703,357 arrivals and 2,063,767 departures. During these years, more than half the Hungarians, Italians, Croatians, and Slovenes returned to Europe. For the most part returnees included a high percentage of single men" who migrated back and forth, seasonally, until the 1920s quota system was put in place (Dinnerstein and Reimers, *Ethnic Americans*, pp. 46–47).

31. On the black independence movement in Oklahoma, see Littlefield, *The Chickasaw Freedmen*.

32. Walzer does invite these other groups to become part of his immigrant America. One need not have entered the United States as an immigrant in order to imagine one's citizenship along an immigrant trajectory. Walzer asks whether his citizenship model "can successfully be extended to the racial minorities now asserting their own group claims." Noting recent adaptive moves by (some) black Americans to be called African Americans, Walzer approves of the move. But he is not sure they will succeed. He worries that racism may get in the way and drive some groups to seek out the "anti-pluralist alternatives of corporate division and state-sponsored unification" (*What It Means to Be an American*, p. 76). Walzer never asks whether his normative privileging of the immigrant-ethnic-citizen trajectory to membership, and the invitation to adapt to it, may itself obscure particular claims, injustices, and bases of organization for specific groups.

33. For an analysis of new group formations out of injuries wrought by the old, see Connolly, *The Ethos of Pluralization*.

34. *Strictly Ballroom*, directed by Baz Luhrmann (1992), is an Australian film, but it was very popular with U.S. audiences. Its story of heteronormative national renewal is not unique to Australia. As Peter Weir's *Green Card* illustrates, the coupling of romance and immigration themes on behalf of the nation travels well from Australia to the United States. There are several American immigration movies that would illustrate the same basic themes: *Big Night* is among the best. And since this chapter is focussed on American immigration politics, it would have been less risky to offer a reading of one of them. I chose *Strictly Ballroom*, nonetheless, precisely because it is not usually seen as an immigration movie. Thus, in addition to deepening our understanding of the relation between the politics of foreignness and the politics of gender, reading this film in terms of its politics of foreignness is defamiliarizing and helps to show how the politics of foreignness is often at work in places where we least expect it. I am indebted to Samuel Fleishacker for first suggesting to me that *Strictly Ballroom* might be

relevant to my argument (though I think he thought the movie would serve my purposes less well than it does).

35. Interestingly, Scott, the individualistic renegade, is also a bearer of the community's standards. When he takes Fran as his partner, he begins by teaching her the basic steps upon which the community insists. Later, for the sake of a dance competition which Fran, a "nobody," obviously cannot win, he allows himself to be partnered with a pale blond insider who knows how to dance properly. In the end, however, he returns to Fran.

36. These immigrants are subtly depicted as good immigrants by contrast with the stereotypical Spaniard pictured in the background taking perpetual siestas with a bottle of alcohol nearby.

37. Walzer himself uses dance to illustrate a similarly acceptable hybridity. In Gene Kelly's *An American in Paris*, Walzer finds a delightful fusion of Irish and American (African-American, to be precise) that is a synecdoche for the other admirable social, civic, and cultural fusions he admires.

38. In effect, the film illustrates Louis Hartz's thesis about fragmented societies in the new world. The Australian dance community is like a Hartzian fragment. Separated from its organic origins and frozen in time, it is incapable of either innovation or restoration. The Old World, by contrast, is capable of innovation because it has dynamism, conflict, and multiplicity within it. See Hartz, *The Founding of New Societies*.

39. Although, given Machiavelli's account of (male) *virtù* as the ability to be like (the female) *fortuna*, there is always some essential gender confusion at the base of republican politics. On *virago*, see my *Political Theory*, chap. 1.

40. On the American fantasy of the traditional family, see Coontz, *The Way We Never Were*.

41. "More U.S. Men Look for Love Overseas," *Columbus Dispatch*, p. 2C. See also Villapando, "The Business of Selling Mail-Order Brides."

42. It is no accident that the term "foreign bride" has already floated over to the financial pages, where it operates as a metaphor for international merger: "A merger flurry in the Swedish banking sector continued on Tuesday and analysts forecast more reshuffling at home before banks cast their eyes oversees for foreign brides" ("Swedish Bank Merger Flurry Seen Continuing," *Reuter European Business Report*).

43. The restoration of proper masculinity by way of the importation of truly feminine foreign brides is not exclusively practiced by American men. In Japan, Thai brides are a "sought-after commodity" for reasons that echo those given by the American men quoted here ("Here Come the Brides," *Newsday*, p. B04). And the same trend has been noted in Taiwan, where the government has recently set quotas "designed to slow the influx of foreign brides and boost the marriage prospects of Taiwanese women" ("Crackdown on Importing Foreign Brides," *Chicago Tribune*, p. 2). Business is flourishing as well in Saudi Arabia and elsewhere.

44. This intersection of the institutions of marriage and citizenship is significant. Concerns about both came together in a March 17, 1997, Letter to the Editor in the *New York Times*. The author responded to the recent spate of marriages between immigrants and American citizens (reported by the paper as part of an effort by foreigners to acquire residency) by calling attention to the "irony" of the fact that Americans allow this abuse of marriage for instrumental purposes while continuing to deny marriage to those who really value it, gay couples in love. Two critics who examine this intersection are Michael Warner, *The Trouble with Normal*, and Lauren Berlant, "Face of America".

45. Susan Okin makes this argument without apparent ambivalence in *Is Multiculturalism Bad for Feminism?* See also my response to Okin, published in the same volume, "My Culture Made Me Do It."

46. As Kant was well aware, the universal cannot survive in the absence of particular enactments of its law. Hence Kant's repeated, transgressive use in the *Groundwork of the Metaphysics of Morals* of particular examples to represent the moral law on whose unrepresentability he was otherwise insistent.

47. Schuck and Smith, *Citizenship without Consent*, p. 130.

48. Ibid., pp. 123–124.

49. Ibid., pp. 131–132.

50. Although it is beyond me why we should seek further to legitimate an institution whose legitimacy ought properly always to be in question.

51. These are the sort of people, "passport holders," that Benedict Anderson worries about in "Exodus."

52. Levinson, *Constitutional Faith*, p. 99.

53. Schuck and Smith, *Citizenship without Consent*, p. 109.

54. That is, new immigrants need to be taking on citizenship for the *right* reasons. In short, what we have here is an uneasy dependence of the performative (consent) on the constative (the right reasons). On the final unsustainability of Austin's distinction between these two, see Derrida's critical appreciation of Austin in "Signature, Event, Context." For my own extended reading of Derrida and Austin on this topic, see Honig, *Political Theory and the Displacement of Politics*, Chapter Four.

55. Wingrove, *Rousseau's Republican Romance*, p. 23. As Wingrove rightly points out, the "perceived tension between structure and act—between determining conditions and undetermined choice—is not an epistemological crisis of social theory that arises in the wake of Marx and Freud." Instead, as in her quoted passage above, it is a result of liberal efforts to theorize an individualism capable of performing the consent that liberal legitimation requires. Wingrove's book came out just as I was putting the finishing touches on mine. I find her theorization of "consensual nonconsensuality" in Rousseau to be quite valuable for thinking about consent more generally, and wish I had had access to it earlier, so as to have been able to engage this work in more detail. As my own reading of Rousseau would suggest, however, the idea that the desires for

freedom and domination are twinned (and not just connected, contra Wingrove, who in some moods, suggests that what consensual nonconsensuality comes down to is simply the fact that "the freedom [democratic politics] makes possible requires domination" [p. 23]) is worth pursuing not just through Rousseau's substantial writings on heterosexual romance (as Wingrove does). It is also worth pursuing through his figuration of the law as the both loved and feared paternal and alien figure of the lawgiver in *The Social Contract*, the text to which Wingrove pays the least sustained attention in her own reading of Rousseau. I will pursue further that twinning of love and fear in the next chapter by way of an analysis of the gothic genre. It is perhaps no surprise that Wingrove also reads Rousseau with some sensitivity to genre—not to gothic, however, but to the related genre of romance.

56. Wingrove, *Rousseau's Republican Romance*, p. 22.

57. French republicanism was founded with a similar turn to foreignness to testify to the power of France's would-be universal principles. The national legislative assembly approved granting the title of French citizen to Joseph Priestley, Thomas Paine, Jeremy Bentham, William Wilberforce, Thomas Clarkson, James MacKintosh, David Williams, George Washington, Alexander Hamilton, James Madison, and Kosciuszko, among others on August 26, 1792. (For the discussion, see *Archives parlementaires*, August 24 and 26, 1792.) This was in recognition of their writing or actions on behalf of "la liberté, de la humanité, et des bonnes moeurs." An interesting historical analysis of the xenophilic and xenophobic moments of the Revolution is provided by Virginie Giraudon, who says: "For the first time in French history, an integration status was granted in the name of the universality of ideas to those who had done the most for humanity." But later, "the need for proselytism was replaced after 1792 by the necessity to survive against foreign threats." Giraudon reports the shift from xenophilia to xenophobia but does not ask after the possible logic of their interrelation (Giraudon, "Cosmopolitanism and National Priority," p. 593).

58. Here the undocumented immigrant is clearly gendered feminine *in connection* to her character as a "taker." This figure is reminiscent of the conventional, conniving woman—often depicted in the Hebrew Bible—who takes what is not hers. As we saw in Chapter Three, it was against this devaluation of feminine taking that Phyllis Trible developed the figure of the admirably good and heroic female taker (Trible, *God and the Rhetoric of Sexuality*).

59. Schuck and Smith, *Citizenship without Consent*, p. 122.

60. By stressing the right of the existing community of citizens to "consent" to newcomers, Schuck and Smith perversely turn Lockean consent from a device designed to limit state power into a device for its enhancement. (A similar move is made by Levinson and by Walzer, though at least their way of making the point does not press into service the device of consent. Levinson: "A 'double choosing' is involved: An immigrant's choice to 'adopt' an American identity is coupled with that immigrant's need to be chosen by the United States itself as

a suitable member of the political community" (Levinson, *Constitutional Faith*, p. 97). Cf. Walzer, *Spheres of Justice*, pp. 31, 39.

61. It should be noted, though, that Schuck and Smith also say that "children (and perhaps their parents as well) may have legitimate moral or humanitarian claims upon American society" (*Citizenship without Consent*, pp. 98, 100, and passim) apart from whether they have a claim to citizenship. "It is enough for present purposes to affirm that the Constitution need not and should not be woodenly interpreted either to guarantee their children citizenship or to cast them into outer darkness" (p. 100).

62. Schuck and Smith, *Citizenship without Consent*, p. 107. One measure of the devaluation of citizenship is Supreme Court decisions such as *Graham vs. Richardson*, which insists that social welfare benefits cannot be restricted to legal residents. In a later article, Schuck is more resigned to the "devaluation of citizenship." He rightly situates this development in the context of increased international integration and migration, and he thinks, four years after *Citizenship without Consent*, that recent changes in national citizenship are "probably irreversible." But he is unwilling to let citizenship go: "It provides a focus of political allegiance and emotional energy on a scale capable of satisfying deep human longings for solidarity, symbolic identification and community. Such a focus may be especially important in a liberal ethos whose centrifugal, cosmopolitan aspirations for global principles and universal human rights must somehow be balanced against the more parochial imperatives of organizing societies dominated by more limited commitments to family, locality, region, and nation" (Schuck, "Membership in the Liberal Polity," pp. 64–65).

Schuck is right that the nation-state sometimes balances the drives toward globalization and localization. But the contrary is also true. The nation state is often a *vehicle* of both globalization and localization as well, as was clear in the United States's move to found NAFTA and in ongoing efforts to localize the administration of social services. Moreover, it is also the case that global and local affiliations are not necessarily disempowering or undemocratic. They can provide helpful, democratizing checks against the coercive powers of the nation-state. It is therefore important to think about the ways in which the emotional "human" satisfactions of citizenship can be appropriated for nonnational entities. Thus, I agree with the last line of Schuck's 1989 essay but take it as one of my *starting* points: "Today's conception of citizenship may not be adequate to meet tomorrow's needs" (p. 65).

63. Calavita, *Inside the State*, p. 167 and passim.

64. This is a practice of which Michael Walzer was rightly critical in "Membership," Chapter Two of *Spheres of Justice*.

65. It should be noted, however, that consent and voluntarism are not obviously nor necessarily enhanced by moving away from *jus soli*. Such a move makes citizenship (contrary to the authors' stated intentions) more ascriptive, not less so; it becomes a status that is more obviously inherited (or not) from

one's parents. Moreover, the practice of *jus soli* is no less consensual than other mechanisms (tolerated by the authors) that accord children citizenship and nationality at birth.

66. See Rogers Smith, "Beyond Tocqueville, Myrdal and Hartz." Here and in his recent book, *Civic Ideals*, Smith positions himself as a critic of American exceptionalism so it might seem strange that I put him in the company of figures like Tocqueville, Myrdal, and Hartz when he wrote in opposition to them. As we saw in Chapter One, however, Smith's liberalism is an exceptionalist's liberalism, unhaunted by doubts, otherness, or violences that touch it at its core. Smith departs from the more usual exceptionalists in his insistence that such a pure liberalism has not found itself fully at home in the United States—not yet.

67. That is to say, I am hazarding a strong, logical claim, by contrast with Michael Rogin, who is wrongly charged by Rogers Smith with making claims about the logic of liberalism. Rogin's rather substantial arguments about America's history of exclusion and genocide are historical, not logical. See Smith's response to Jacqueline Stevens, "Beyond Tocqueville, Please!" and Rogin, *Ronald Reagan, the Movie*.

68. Rogers Smith, "Beyond Tocqueville, Myrdal and Hartz" and *Civic Ideals*.

69. No less than all the attention paid to John Huang and other "foreign" or hyphenated lobbyists and contributors distracted attention from the real problems of money in American politics. The Center for Responsive Politics did a study of foreign money in 1996. Using some very generous definitions (e.g., U.S. firms that are subsidiaries of foreign companies), the Center found that these organizations contributed (hard and soft) a total of $12.6 million to federal candidates. A conservative estimate of the total cost of federal elections is $1.2 billion ($200 million in soft, $200 million in public, $800 million in hard money [Congressional races]). So, foreign money is no more and probably less than 1 percent—if that (Daly, "Global Connections"). I am indebted to Steve Ansolabehere for these figures and estimates.

70. The authors unwittingly call attention to this deeper problem when they say that they are seeking to complement the "actual consent [that] is expressed symbolically only through periodic elections" in America. Concerned only about the periodicity of election-based consent, they do not mention the fact that no more than a minority of American citizens vote in American elections.

This unself-conscious projection of the corruptions of American citizenship onto illegal aliens is paralleled by Michael Walzer's more self-conscious metaphorization of withdrawn American citizens as "psychological resident aliens." But Walzer's metaphor also misleads. Just as the metaphor of illegality slides from status to behavior in Schuck and Smith, so in Walzer, a juridical status assigned by the state (resident alien) slides into a political attitude imputed to the person (political withdrawalism). But there is no evidence to support the identification of resident alien status with political uninvolvement, at least not with any level of uninvolvement worthy of remark. Nor is there any evidence for the converse: that naturalizing immigrants are prone to political involvement (Walzer, "Political Alienation and Military Service," pp. 99–100, 112–113. Cited by Levinson, *Constitutional Faith*).

71. Tocqueville, *Democracy in America*, pp. 40–41.

72. Rancière, *Dis-agreement*, pp. 24–25.

73. Ibid., p. 41.

74. Ibid., p. 30.

75. The word "counts" and the phrase quoted above are both from Rancière. Rancière recasts class struggle in terms of those who—from Plato forward—"count" and the uncounted.

76. Raskin, "Legal Aliens, Local Citizens," p. 1397.

77. It should be noted, however, that residency can be a restrictive rather than a permissive requirement. Long Island uses stringent proof of residency requirements to keep immigrants out of public schools (Carvajal, "Immigrants Fight Residency Rules Blocking Children in L.I. Schools"). In a way, the move to residency harkens back to the legal practice in the eastern United States of treating settlement, not citizenship, as the decisive category of inclusion. However, settlement was hardly a benign category, no more than residence is now. On the legal use of the category of settlement to make blacks into "foreigners," see Parker, "Making Blacks Foreigners."

78. Another example of an organization devoted to immigrant worker empowerment is Choices, a domestic worker cooperative in the San Francisco Bay Area (Salzinger, "A Maid by Any Other Name"). Other examples include Asian Immigrant Women's Advocates and UNITE. The L.A. Committee for the Protection of the Foreign Born may be seen as an ancestor of these and other groups seeking alien empowerment and rights protection.

79. Walzer, *What It Means to Be an American*, p. 33.

80. Such groups are not usually state originated but they sometimes are, and perhaps they ought to be state supported. See Lester Salomon's discussion of NGOs and other third-sector associations: "Finally, perhaps the most decisive determinant of third sector growth will be the relationship that nonprofit organizations can forge with government. The task for third sector organizations is to find a *modus vivendi* with government that provides sufficient legal and financial support while preserving a meaningful degree of independence and autonomy" (Salomon, "The Rise of the Nonprofit Sector," p. 122). I would add only that in the event of such cohabitations, the third sector would do well to relate to its new partner—government—gothically rather than romantically, that is to say, with healthy measures of caution, skepticism, and ambivalence. In Chapter Five I outline in a bit more detail what would be entailed by such a Gothic perspective.

81. Calavita, *Inside the State*, p. 167, citing Ray Marshall, "Economic Factors Influencing the International Migration of Workers," p. 169. See also "U.S. Surveys Find Farm Worker Pay Down for 20 Years," *New York Times*.

82. Empowering aliens to act as citizens, even when they lack that juridical status (which is the goal of the democratic cosmopolitanism advocated here) attenuates the lines between aliens and citizens, and this is something Schuck and Smith are out to resist. They disapprove of Supreme Court decisions like *Plyler*, which award social benefits and rights to noncitizens. Oddly, such developments are seen by Schuck and Smith as symptoms of a more communitarian judiciary (one would have thought "cosmopolitan" to be a better adjective). That "communitarian judiciary," they argue, "increasingly compels government to consent by imposing obligations toward aliens that it has not voluntarily undertaken [but isn't this what courts *do*? Compel governments to provide services or respect rights in ways that they do not voluntarily undertake?]; sometimes, as in *Graham*, courts override the legislature's explicit refusal to consent" (Schuck and Smith, *Citizenship without Consent*, p. 109).

83. Of course, people often find themselves involved in political activity that is risky and even dangerous. This is because political involvement often does not happen as a matter of rational calculation based on incentives. As in my gloss on Hannah Arendt, calculation just produces a cycle of willing and nilling that would be endless were it not for the fact that "political action comes to us, it involves us in ways that are not deliberate, willful or intended." Political action "happens to the as yet unready and not quite willing (because still also nilling) subject in the private realm" and thrusts the subject into the risky visibility of the public sphere. See my "Toward an Agonistic Feminism," pp. 223–224.

84. As Randolph Bourne put it in his 1916 essay, "The Jew and Trans-National America": "We want no national unity that is not based on democratic and socialized and international goals" (p. 126). As opposed to the reverse order, which is the more commonly accepted view now: that democracy needs to be based on national unity.

Like Kristeva, Bourne sees the foreign immigrant as having a fragmenting effect, but he welcomes that effect because it staves off the further development of an American nationalism that is not conducive to the social-democratic and international goals on behalf of which Bourne was advocating. Bourne makes his position quite clear in another essay, "Trans-National America."

85. On internationalism and cosmopolitanism in politics, see Bruce Robbins's introduction to *Cosmopolitics* and also his *Feeling Global*. My own small forays onto the terrain of cosmopolitanism are informed and motivated by these texts and by conversations with their author.

86. The caricature appears in Beiner, *Theorizing Citizenship*.

87. We could call all of these "rooted cosmopolitanisms"—the name given to another hybrid meant to overcome the opposition between nationalism and cosmopolitanism. Something by that name is championed by thinkers as different from each other as Julia Kristeva and David Hollinger. Kristeva's and Hollinger's ideals are not identical but, their differences notwithstanding, these two

share a commitment to a cosmopolitanism that depends upon the renationalization of the state.

88. Carens, *Culture, Citizenship, and Community*, p. 187. Carens rightly notes that "this is an important issue for aboriginal people," but he seems to think that access to international forums is mostly a matter of gaining "recognition and respect on the world stage as distinct cultural communities and political actors" rather than (also and perhaps most important) being a matter of generating a social movement politics that is a source of leverage for native peoples involved in negotiations on myriad issues with would-be sovereign states. In the end, Carens, too, calls for the renationalization of the state, though unlike some nationalists, he sees no conflict between such a renationalization and forms of citizenship that are differentiated rather than unitary. It is, he acknowledges, paradoxical (but true) that the best way to heighten affect for the nation among minorities and immigrants is often to permit them greater freedom in self-governance and special rights and exemptions. In this, Carens differs from more unitary nationalists such as Richard Rorty and Rogers Smith, whom I discuss in Chapter Five.

89. Spivak, "Acting Bits/Identity Talk," p. 803.

Chapter Five
The Genres of Democracy

1. Frye, *Anatomy of Criticism*; White, *Metahistory*. I follow White in acknowledging the problematic but still useful nature of Frye's taxonomy (p. 8n.6). Stephen Greenblatt makes a similar argument about the genred nature of legal writing with regard to the Ken Starr report ("A Story Told with Evil Intent").

2. The question is particularly worth asking at this point in time, when (in the aftermath of Alasdair MacIntyre's *After Virtue*) recourse to narrative as a "solution" to political theoretical problems has become a virtual mainstay of contemporary theorizing. Recourse to narrative, however, begs the question of what *kind* of narrative, what mode, and what genre of narration? Without answers to these questions, it is not possible to assess what sort of work is being done (or should be done) by narrative as such.

3. Sanford Levinson has argued in favor of analogizing marriage and social contract in *Constitutional Faith*. The analogy is also drawn in the Hebrew Bible (Levinson draws on this example), where God is said to have taken the Israelites as his bride on Mount Sinai, the scene of the social contract.

4. Some democratic theorists look instead to the tragic mode to organize and inform their reflections on democracy. William Connolly, for example, uses a tragic perspective on political thought precisely to dethrone the dominant, ro-

mantic approaches (though he would not put it in these literary terms). See his tragedy-sensitive readings of Nietzsche, Rousseau, and Hegel in *Political Theory and Modernity*. See also Steven Johnston's treatment of Rousseau as a tragic thinker in *Encountering Tragedy*. In a different effort to break the spell of political theory's romantic assumptions, John Seery turns to irony in *Political Returns*. Irony is recommended by Richard Rorty as appropriate for private individuals in *Irony, Contingency, Solidarity*. For citizens, however, Rorty recommends romance (in *Achieving Our Country* and *Philosophy and Social Hope*), as we shall see below.

5. "Modern gothic" is Joanna Russ's name for the genre, "female gothic" is the term used by Tania Modleski. Russ explains: these modern gothics "bear no resemblance to the literary definition of 'Gothic.' They are not related to the works of Monk Lewis or Mrs. Radcliffe, whose real descendants are known today as Horror Stories. The modern Gothics resemble, instead, a crossbreed of *Jane Eyre* and Daphne Du Maurier's *Rebecca* and most of them advertise themselves as 'in the Du Maurier tradition,' 'in the Gothic tradition of *Rebecca*,' and so on" (Russ, "Somebody Is Trying to Kill Me," p. 666). Tania Modleski (*Loving with a Vengeance*) is less extreme on this score. She sees female gothics as in the tradition of Lewis and Radcliffe.

It should be noted that when I say that gothic romance is the genre that fits Rousseau's *Social Contract* "best," I mean both to remark on the fit and on its imperfection, as in—best, but still not perfectly. In Russ's account of the genre, for example, the heroine is always passive. Not so, however, if we take Du Maurier's *Rebecca* as exemplary (which Russ does not, in spite of her awareness of its importance in advertising Modern Gothic novels). In place of passivity, Rebecca has a *bildungsroman* quality—the heroine overcomes obstacles, faces her fears, and enters maturity—which Modleski, contra Russ, identifies as central to female Harlequins and gothics (Modleski, *Loving with a Vengeance*, pp. 20, 52). In democratic theory's received texts, the figure who occupies the place of the gothic heroine is often "the people," whose maturity is their reward for grappling with the alienness of the law, though sometimes it is (also) the author who feels betrayed by "the people," who are easily corrupted. Either way, the figure is not passive.

6. That same scene is, of course, available to be read as a simple love story (Ozick) or as comedy (as in Sasson's reading).

7. Modleski, *Loving with a Vengeance*, p. 61, quoting from Russ, "Somebody Is Trying to Kill Me," p. 667, herself quoting an ex-editor of Ace Books.

8. Modleski, *Loving with a Vengeance*, pp. 59–61. This distinction does not apply to all female gothics, of course. In *Jane Eyre*, Charlotte Brontë's female gothic, which antedates the gothics Modleski is looking at, the heroine goes through the transformation that Modleski identifies as Harlequin: from fear to love.

9. Cameron, quoted in Modleski, *Loving with a Vengeance*, p. 62. The same sorts of explanations about overisolation are often given nowadays to account for interest in the paranormal and belief in extraterrestrials, those other aliens.

Modleski's deployment of Cameron also fits well with the observation made by an ex-editor of Gothic romance novels: "The basic appeal is to women who marry guys and then begin to discover their husbands are strangers . . . so there's a simultaneous attraction/repulsion, love/fear going on." The editor is quoted by Russ ("Somebody Is Trying to Kill Me," p. 667) and then quoted again by Modleski (*Loving with a Vengeance*, p. 39). A dynamic of attraction and repulsion is also how Kant describes the practice of respect for persons. See my discussion of Kant in *Political Theory and the Displacement of Politics*, Chapter Two.

10. Hannah Arendt's analysis in *Rahel Varnhagen* of a Jewish parvenu's maddeningly impossible efforts to achieve social status and belonging are particularly instructive here. For discussions of this theme in Arendt, see Morris Kaplan, "Refiguring the Jewish Question," and Pitkin, *Attack of the Blob*. On the social as a cause of paranoia, see also Eric Santner, *My Own Private Germany: Daniel Paul Schreber's Secret History of Modernity*.

11. Modleski also toys with sociopolitical explanations, but, unlike me, she tends to assume that the thing being explained or worked through is always in some way a women's issue. For example, what she calls the "gaslight" genre (developed in the 1940s) "may be seen to reflect women's fears about losing their unprecedented freedoms," achieved in the absence of so many men during the war years (*Loving with a Vengeance*, p. 21).

12. Modleski, *Loving with a Vengeance*, p. 75. In the end, the turn to psychoanalysis is necessary, Modleski insists, because, contra Joanna Russ, "romantic disillusionment and feelings of social isolation in the newly married woman [are] not sufficient to explain the particular kinds of fantasies encountered in female Gothics" (p. 65).

13. These speculations require that we suspend the common assumption that female gothics are, as such, only by, about, and for women. They also require us to ignore Russ's dating of the genre. She locates its origins in the 1950s, but she is talking not just about a conventional genre but about a particular paperback publishing phenomenon, represented in her text by Ace Books. The genre precedes the phenomenon, as Russ herself makes clear, when she alludes to female gothics as "in the tradition of" *Jane Eyre* and *Rebecca* ("Somebody Is Trying to Kill Me," p. 666).

14. Thus, for example, even if Robert Burstein were right that American democracy developed along with a popular self-stylization of Americans as a uniquely sentimental people, the fact that America is (if it is), in Burstein's title, a "sentimental democracy" would not mean that citizens and residents of the United States cannot or ought not relate to that regime's institutions and prac-

tices gothically rather than sentimentally or romantically *(Sentimental Democracy: The Evolution of America's Romantic Self-Image)*.

15. Connections between the gothic form and democratic political culture have been noted by others, but they tend to focus on horror gothics, not on female gothics. Horror gothics were the first or the most popular—even mass—genre in the nineteenth century. They are in that sense said to be "democratic" and are for that reason often looked down upon by highbrow literary critics: "Associated with the sensational, the formulaic, and the popular, the gothic is seen to lack seriousness of purpose and connection to actual experience" (Goddu, *Gothic America*, p. 187, n. 15). Cf. Botting, *Gothic*, and Martin and Savoy, eds., *American Gothic*). But see also Punter on how the supposed massness of gothic's circulation is much overestimated (Punter, *The Literature of Terror*, p. 22).

Toni Morrison posits a different connection between horror Gothics and *American* democracy in particular. This genre of haunting is America's national literary genre, she says, because America has always been haunted by the unjust and unacknowledged racist origins it has struggled, unsuccessfully, to bury (Morrison, *Playing in the Dark*). Teresa Goddu takes up this suggestion and explores it in detail in *Gothic America*. Like me, Goddu rereads as gothic (though, again, not as *female* gothic) certain texts that are usually read as romantic or, in her case, sentimental. However, in her reading of Crèvecoeur's *Letters of an American Farmer*, for example, the gothic moments identified by Goddu are all connected to heretofore unnoted or suppressed passages in the text that have to do with figures who are black. Indeed, throughout, Goddu's gothic reading of America is identified with the scenes of America's racial horrors (mostly slavery but also, in Chapter Three, Indian removal). The uses of the horror gothic form to accent the seamy underside of American democracy are welcome insofar as they help to expose injustices that many would rather forget than confront. But such uses manage to leave democracy as such untouched by the very monsters and ghosts that gothics seek to awaken. If the gothic is safely connected to the horrors of slavery, it leaves room for the main narrations of American democracy to continue, relatively undisturbed, in the genre of simple romance. The echo to Rogers Smith's *Civic Ideals* (which I discussed in Chapter One) is unmistakable: indeed, we might say that Goddu implicitly and unwittingly replays Smith's "multiple traditions thesis" as a "multiple genres thesis."

Sure enough, Goddu makes a point of connecting American gothics and marginality: not only are *American* gothics often cast as mere copies in relation to the real British genre (a move for which Goddu criticizes Eugenia DeLamotte [p. 162, n.3]). American *gothics* are also marginalized in relation to "real" or serious literature. For Goddu, this double marginality of America's gothics may signal the genre's fittedness for its role, which is to give expression to the horrors at the margins of American democracy.

Contra Goddu and even Morrison, however, the real issue, in my view, is the need to locate the sources of democracy's hauntings in democracy itself, and not just in its attendant, possibly contingent injustices and repressions. That is, the point is to ask about the operations of the gothic in daily life rather than simply reinscribe sentimental romance as citizenship's dominant daily genre while acknowledging that this romance is occasionally interrupted by perversions that are gothic in character. It should be noted, however, that one could maintain the identification of gothics with slavery, but still achieve this demarginalization by arguing for the centrality of slavery to democracy (Morrison and Goddu don't make this case. Orlando Patterson argues for the centrality of slavery to democracy in *Freedom*).

Ronald Paulson hazards a different connection between gothics and democracy, but the effect is also a remarginalization of the genre and the insights it might harbor. Paulson traces the historical evolution of horror gothics and argues that they arise in response to the horrors of France's democratic revolution (Paulson, *Representations of Revolution*). Thus, the connection established is not between gothics and democracy in its quotidian character—Paulson is not looking at the role of the revolution in democracy's daily life—but rather, as in Burke, at the relation between exceptional revolutionary horror and the literary horror (Burke's "sublime") in which gothics trade. By contrast, I am asking after possible conceptual connections between quotidian gothics—so-called female gothics—and democracy (and democratic theory) in its everydayness.

From my perspective, Julia Stern does better than critics such as Goddu and Paulson in her gothic reading of Wilson's *Our Nig*. Arguing that those who have until now read the novel as "exclusively sentimental" ("Excavating Genre in *Our Nig*," p. 447) miss its point, Stern shows how Wilson uses horror gothic devices to show the inadequacy of the private sphere (Stowe's sentimental kitchen) as a resource for empowerment. According to Stern, Wilson shows, contra Stowe, how the kitchen can be not just hearth but also hell, and, in so doing, Stern argues, Wilson effectively insists on the importance of a public sphere for political action. Stern's critique seems to be right on the mark, but it may desentimentalize the iconic scene of kitchen domesticity while leaving uninterrogated (or does Wilson leave it uninterrogated?) a certain sentimentality that clings to the public sphere.

Finally, Joan Copjec also hazards a connection between gothics and democracy in a promissory footnote on which, to my knowledge, she has not yet delivered: regarding her essay, "The *Unvermögender* Other," she says: "This paper is an introduction to a much longer study of the contributions of detective and Gothic fiction to" modern democracy, which Copjec understands in Lefortian terms, "not simply as a form of government but more radically as a 'mutation of the symbolic order' " (Copjec, "The *Unvermögender* Other," p. 41, n. 6).

16. Spivak, *A Critique of Postcolonial Reason: Toward a History of the Vanishing Present*. I should note that the two female gothics on which I am drawing

here—*Rebecca* and *Jane Eyre*—do feature undecidable male (anti)heroes, but these are not figured as foreign, per se. I trust the points about the genre's contributions to democratic theory (points that are not, after all, specific to the politics of foreignness) can be made, nonetheless, by way of these two female gothic novels.

17. Rorty, *Achieving Our Country*, pp. 94–95.

18. Ibid., p. 101 and passim.

19. Ibid., pp. 10–11; emphasis added.

20. The charge is completely unsubtle in Rorty's op. ed. in the *New York Times* headlined, "The Unpatriotic Academy." The piece is republished in *Philosophy and Social Hope*.

21. Rorty, *Philosophy and Social Hope*, p. 99. There is hope for the cultural Left, however, if they kick their theory "habit" and make an effort (as if some have not done so already) to make coalition with labor in America. Rorty's depiction of the cultural Left as both a power beyond its own control and as capable of self-help in the face of a bad habit reiterates what Mark Edmundson describes as two sides of the same coin: contemporary victims of gothic terror turn out to be terrorized by others who are themselves victims, whether of prior abuse or addiction (Edmundson, *Nightmare on Main Street*, p. 57).

22. Rorty, *Philosophy and Social Hope*, pp. 95, 97.

23. Edmundson would be unsurprised by this mimesis: with reference to contemporary social critics, he says: "In each case, an analytic method that might have as its object a critique of gothic culture, with all of its facile pessimism, un-self-consciously reproduces gothic assumptions" (Edmundson, *Nightmare on Main Street*, pp. 42–43). Does Rorty's fall into gothicism in the midst of trying to critique it prove Edmundson's general thesis that ours is a thoroughly gothicized culture? It might. But it might also simply show how the insistent will to romance always awakens a gothic response.

24. Johnson, "Coalition Politics: Turning the Century," pp. 356–357. For a detailed reading of this essay, see my "Difference, Dilemmas, and the Politics of Home."

25. "A deep ambivalence about authority lies near the heart of our culture of the Gothic," notes Edmundson (*Nightmare on Main Street*, p. 21). That ambivalence was an admirable feature of early gothic writers, like Monk Lewis, who "were, in the main, progressives," says Edmundson (p. 63). But contemporary gothics lack the "enriching ambivalence of Monk Lewis' mode" (p. 21). Edmundson may or may not be right about the decline of the gothic genre from a complex to an overly simple form. Even if he is right about the decline, however, that would not make moot the question posed here, which is whether *some* sort of gothic lens (female, not horror) would be useful to would-be democratic citizens.

26. Modleski is less optimistic than I am regarding the capacities of gothic readers to move beyond the confines of gothic narrative: female gothics play

with paranoid feelings, and they may "not employ, as elaborately as 'high' art the psychological and formal devices for distancing and transforming the anxieties and wishes of the readers" (Modleski, *Loving with a Vengeance*, p. 31). Mark Edmundson faults horror gothics for the same reason; hence, his harsh judgment of the genre and his closing wish for new creative artists who might "take Gothic pessimism as a starting point and come up with visions that, while affirmative, never forget the authentic darkness that Gothic art discloses" (*Nightmare on Main Street*, p. 179). It is notable, however, that Edmundson, unlike Rorty, does not jettison the genre altogether in favor of its opposite: romance. Instead, Edmundson hopes for better future practitioners of the genre.

27. Rorty, *Achieving Our Country*, p. 96.

28. Rogers Smith, *Civic Ideals*, p. 499.

29. Rorty takes advantage of the ambiguity of the term "Romance," sometimes using it in Frye's sense, suggesting a mode in which Romantic heroic individuals transcend death, and at other times using it in the sense of female or Harlequin romance, suggesting a happy-ending love story, in particular with one's country. The former is dominant in "Religious Faith, Intellectual Responsibility and Romance" in *Philosophy and Social Hope*, the latter in *Achieving Our Country*. In *Achieving Our Country*, Rorty sometimes refers to Emerson in ways that seem to connote Romantic individualism, but Rorty quickly puts the term to use on behalf of national romance or patriotism (*Achieving Our Country*, p. 97 and passim).

30. Rousseau knew this. He saw the germ of this idea in Machiavelli, whose *The Prince* Rousseau read not as a manual to guide princes but rather as a warning to republican peoples: "He professed to teach kings; but it was the people he really taught." On Rousseau's account, Machiavelli made it clear that a people that allowed itself to love their king had best be on guard, because although "the power which comes from a people's love is no doubt the greatest . . . it is precarious and conditional and princes will never rest content with it." Beloved kings will turn into tyrants at a moment's notice (the romance will turn gothic) because kings prefer the certainty of subjection to the vicissitudes of love. And the people who love them had best know this (*Social Contract*, Book III, Chapter 6).

31. The ambivalence recommended seems to share something with Rogers Smith's closing caution in *Civic Ideals*. In the last two pages of that long book, Smith briefly chastens the patriotism he had until then been stoking, perhaps so that it will not be mistaken for blind (illiberal) nationalism: the challenge for citizens now is that "their patriotism must be at once profound and qualified, recognized as something both necessary and dangerous and thus as an allegiance that is deepest when it harbours searching doubts. . . . Americans should in fact accept that a time may come when the United States itself, like preceding human political creations, is less rather than more useful as a way of constituting a political community that can engage people's loyalties and serve their finest

aspirations. But they should give support and guidance to their country so long as it seems the best hope available to them for leading free and meaningful lives, and for allowing others to do so as well" (pp. 505–506). It is noteworthy that the object of potential ambivalence here in Smith is the nation alone and not the liberal tradition or principles that Smith is out to cleanse and defend and that we, in Chapter Four, saw as themselves part of the impetus for the paired xenophobia and xenophilia in American political culture. But, in any case, how much weight should be given to such a sentiment, arrived at so late in the day, when it is preceded by numerous references (in opposition to abstract "liberal democratic precepts" [p. 10]) to the moral imperative of leaders to shape the governed into a "people," (pp. 6, 9, 500, 502, and 474: "Because the imperative to constitute a people that feels itself to be a people is politically necessary, it is also a weighty though certainly not an absolute *moral* imperative" [emphasis added])? That the need for nationhood comes along with potential dangers is noted but then more quickly overridden earlier in the book, when Smith compares the nation to political parties: both are "ineradicably human creations, crafted to govern and assist some people more than others. . . . In light of the good they do, we may rightly value them highly and feel great loyalty toward them; but in light of their dangerous tendencies, we should understand them to be imperfect human instruments and not take them as the proper objects of our full trust or ultimate allegiance. *Despite these essential qualifications*, liberal democracies that conceive of political communities in the ways I propose can, I believe, legitimately capture some of the engaging features of ascriptive Americanism and other myths glorifying allegedly transcendent national identities" (p. 11; emphasis added). The need to be a people is so strongly felt and assumed in this text that it is difficult to imagine under what (humanist?) circumstances someone like Smith would suddenly give it up, as opposed, say, to being willing to criticize the nation, at any particular moment in time, in the name of liberal principles.

32. Hence my sympathy with George Shulman's claim in "Race and the Romance of American Nationalism in Martin Luther King, Norman Mailer, and James Baldwin." Regarding Mailer and Baldwin, Shulman says: "Their examples suggest the value in practices of citizenship that defeat idealization but not aspiration." What is the difference between idealization (as in Rorty's idealized nation) and aspiration? "[I]dealization flees actuality while aspiration finds in it gifts to exploit." Thus, idealization produces rage and horror when it is disappointed, which it inevitably is because actuality tends to reassert itself from time to time. Aspiration's hopes are less vulnerable to being dashed.

Bibliography

Adatto, Kiku. *Picture Perfect: The Art and Artifice of Public Image Making*. New York: Basic Books, 1993.

Agamben, Giorgio. *Homo Sacer*. Stanford, Calif.: Stanford University Press, 1998.

Ahmed, Leila. *Women and Gender in Islam: Historical Roots of a Modern Debate*. New Haven: Yale University Press, 1992.

Akenson, Donald Harman. *God's Peoples: Covenant and Land in South Africa, Israel, and Ulster*. Ithaca, N.Y.: Cornell University Press, 1992.

An American in Paris. Directed by Vincente Minnelli. Metro-Goldwyn-Mayer, 1951. Videocassette.

Anderson, Benedict. "Exodus." *Critical Inquiry* 20, no. 2 (winter 1994): 314–327.

Andrews, Geoff, ed. *Citizenship*. London: Lawrence and Wishart, 1991.

Appadurai, Arjun. "Disjuncture and Difference in the Global Cultural Economy." In *Modernity at Large: Cultural Dimensions of Globalization*, 27–47. Minneapolis: University of Minnesota Press, 1996.

Archives parlementaires de 1787 á 1860; recueil complet des débats législatifs et politiques des chambres françaises imprimé par ordre du Sénat et de la Chambre des députés sous la direction de m. J. Mavidal . . . et de m. E. Laurent. Première série (1787 à 1799). Paris: Librairie administratif de P. Dupont, 1875–.

Arendt, Hannah. *The Human Condition*. Chicago: University of Chicago Press, 1958.

————. *The Origins of Totalitarianism*. New York: Harcourt Brace Jovanovich, 1973.

————. *Rahel Varnhagen*. Translated by Richard and Clara Winston. New York: Harcourt Brace Jovanovich, 1974.

Aristotle. *Nicomachean Ethics*. Translated by Terence Irwin. Indianapolis: Hackett, 1985.

————. *Politics*. Translated by Ernest Barker. Oxford: Oxford University Press, 1948.

Assmann, Jan. *Moses, the Egyptian: The Memory of Egypt in Western Monotheism*. Cambridge, Mass.: Harvard University Press, 1997.

Austin, J. L. *How to Do Things with Words*. Cambridge, Mass.: Harvard University Press, 1975.

Aylesworth, Len. "The Passing of Alien Suffrage." *American Political Science Review* 25, no. 1 (February 1931): 114–116.

Backus, Margot Gayle. *The Gothic Family Romance: Heterosexuality, Child Sacrifice, and the Anglo-Irish Colonial Order*. Durham, N.C.: Duke University Press, 1999.

Bakhtin, M. M. *Dialogic Imagination*. Austin: University of Texas Press, 1981.

————. *Speech Genres and Other Late Essays*. Edited by Caryl Emerson and Michael Holquist; translated by Vern W. McGee. Austin: University of Texas Press, 1986.

Bal, Mieke. *Lethal Love: Feminist Literary Readings of Biblical Love Stories*. Indiana Studies in Bible Literature. Bloomington: Indiana University Press, 1987.

Bal, Mieke, ed. *Anti-Covenant: Counter-Reading Women's Lives in the Hebrew Bible*. Sheffield, England: Almond, 1989.

Baldwin, James. *Notes of a Native Son*. Boston: Beacon Press, 1990.

Baldwin, Thomas. "The Territorial State." In *Cambridge Essays in Jurisprudence*, edited by H. Gross and J. R. Harrison, 207–230. Oxford: Clarendon Press, 1992.

Barthes, Roland. *Mythologies*. Translated by Annette Lavers. New York: Hill and Wang, 1972.

Basch, Linda, Nina Glick Schiller, and Cristina Szanton Blanc. *Nations Unbound*. Langhorne, Penn.: Gordon and Breach, 1994.

Bauman, Zygmunt. "Modernity and Ambivalence." *Theory, Culture and Society* 7 (1990): 143–169.

Bean, Frank D., Barry Edmonston, and Jeffrey S. Passel, eds. *Undocumented Migration to the United States: IRCA and the Experience of the 1980s*. Santa Monica, Calif.: Rand Corporation; Washington, D.C.: Urban Institute; distributed by University Press of America, 1990.

Becklund, Laurie. "Likened to Marriage, Sister Cities Boost Global Ties." *Los Angeles Times*, October 12, 1987, 1.

Beer, Samuel. *To Make a Nation: The Rediscovery of American Federalism*. Cambridge, Mass.: Harvard University Press, Belknap Press, 1993.

Behdad, Ali. "Nationalism and Immigration to the United States." *Diaspora* 6, no. 2 (1997): 155–178.

———. *Forgetful Nation: Reflections on Immigration and Cultural Identity in the United States*. Durham: Duke University Press, forthcoming.

Beiner, Ronald, ed. *Theorizing Citizenship*. Albany: State University of New York Press, 1995.

———. *Theorizing Nationalism*. Albany: SUNY Press, 1999.

Bennington, Geoffrey. *Dudding*. Paris: Galilée, 1991.

———. *Legislations: The Politics of Deconstruction*. London: Verso, 1994.

———. *Sententiousness and the Novel: Laying Down the Law*. Cambridge, England: Cambridge University Press, 1985.

Bercovitch, Sacvan. *The American Jeremiad*. Madison: University of Wisconsin Press, 1978.

Berlant, Lauren. "Face of America." In *Disciplinarity and Dissent in Cultural Studies*, edited by Cary Nelson and Dilip Parameshwar Gaonkar. New York: Routledge, 1996.

———. "Poor Eliza." *American Literature* 70, no. 3 (September 1998): 635–668.

———. *The Queen of America Goes to Washington City*. Durham, N.C.: Duke University Press, 1997.

Berlin, Isaiah. "Two Concepts of Liberty." In *Four Essays on Liberty*. Oxford: Oxford University Press, 1984.

Bernasconi, Robert. "Rousseau and the Supplement to the Social Contract: Deconstruction and the Possibility of Democracy." *Cardozo Law Review* 11, no. 5–6 (July/August 1990): 1539–1564.

Bernstein, Harry. "Harry Bridges: Marxist Founder of West's Longshoremen Union." *Los Angeles Times*, March 31, 1990.

Bernstein, Richard. *Freud and the Legacy of Moses*. Cambridge, England: Cambridge University Press, 1998.

Bhabha, Homi. *The Location of Culture*. New York: Routledge, 1994.

Big Night. Directed by Stanley Tucci and Campbell Scott. Rysher Entertainment for Timpano Productions, 1996. Videocassette.

Binder, Frederick M., and David M. Reimers. *All the Nations under Heaven: An Ethnic and Racial History of New York City*. New York: Columbia University Press, 1995.

Bittle, William, and Gilbert Geis. *The Longest Way Home: Chief Alfred C. Sam's Back-to-Africa Movement*. Detroit: Wayne State University Press, 1964.

Bloom, Harold. *The Book of J*, translated by David Rosenberg. New York: Grove Weidenfeld, 1990.

Bloom, Harold, ed. "Interpretive Essay." In *Exodus*. Modern Critical Interpretations. New York: Chelsea House, 1987.

Bock, Gisela, and Susan James, eds. *Beyond Equality and Difference: Citizenship, Feminist Politics, and Female Subjectivity*. London: Routledge, 1992.

Bodnar, John. *The Transplanted: A History of Immigrants in Urban America*. Bloomington: Indiana University Press, 1987.

Boelhower, William Q. *Immigrant Autobiography in the United States: (Four Versions of the Italian American Self)*. Verona: Essedue Edizioni, 1982.

Bolchazy, Ladislaus J. *Hospitality in Early Rome: Livy's Concept of Its Humanizing Force*. Chicago: Ares Publishers, 1977.

Borjas, George. *Friends of Strangers: The Impact of Immigrants on the U.S. Economy*. New York: Basic Books, 1990.

Bosniak, Linda. "Opposing Prop. 187: Undocumented Immigrants and the National Imagination." *Connecticut Law Review* 28 (spring 1996): 555–619.

Botting, Fred. *Gothic*. London: Routledge, 1996.

Bourne, Randolph. "The Jew and Trans-National America." In *War and the Intellectuals: Collected Essays, 1915–1919*, 124–133. New York: Harper and Row, 1964.

———. "Trans-National America." In *War and the Intellectuals: Collected Essays, 1915–1919*. New York: Harper and Row, 1964.

Boyarin, Jonathan. "Another Abraham: Jewishness and the Law of The Father." *Yale Journal of Law and the Humanities*, Summer 1997.

Braidotti, Rosi. *Nomadic Subjects: Embodiment and Sexual Difference in Contemporary Feminist Theory*. New York: Columbia University Press, 1994.

Brennan, Timothy. *At Home in the World: Cosmopolitanism Now*. Cambridge, Mass.: Harvard University Press, 1997.

Brenner, Athalya. "Ruth as Foreign Worker and the Politics of Exogamy." In *Ruth and Esther: A Feminist Companion to the Bible*, 3. 2nd series, edited by Athalya Brenner. Sheffield, England: Sheffield Academic Press, 1999.

Brenner, Athalya, ed. *A Feminist Companion to Ruth*. The Feminist Companion to the Bible, 3. Sheffield, England: Sheffield Academic Press, 1993.

———. *Ruth and Esther: A Feminist Companion to the Bible*, 3. 2nd series. Sheffield, England: Sheffield Academic Press, 1999.

Brimelow, Peter. *Alien Nation: Common Sense about America's Immigration Disaster*. New York: Random House, 1995.

Brontë, Charlotte. *Jane Eyre*. New York: Penguin, 1966.

Brown, Peter, and Henry Shue, eds. *Boundaries: National Autonomy and Its Limits*. Totowa, N.J.: Rowman and Littlefield, 1981.

Brownstein, Ronald, and Richard Simon. "Hospitality Turns into Hostility." *Los Angeles Times*, November 14, 1993, A1, A6.

Brubaker, William Rogers. *Citizenship and Nationhood in France and Germany*. Cambridge, Mass.: Harvard University Press, 1992.

Brubaker, William Rogers, ed. *Immigration and the Politics of Citizenship in Europe and North America*. Lanham, Md.: University Press of America, 1989.

Buber, Martin. "Exodus 19–27." In *Exodus*, edited by Harold Bloom. Modern Critical Interpretations. New York: Chelsea House, 1987.

Burstein, Andrew. *Sentimental Democracy: The Evolution of America's Romantic Self-Image*. New York: Farrar, Straus, and Giroux, 1999.

Butler, Judith. "Kantians in Every Culture?" *Boston Review*, October–November, 1994.

———. "Merely Cultural." *New Left Review* 227 (1998): 33–44.

———. *The Psychic Life of Power*. Stanford, Calif.: Stanford University Press, 1997.

———. "Sovereign Performatives in the Contemporary Scene of Utterance." *Critical Inquiry* 23, no. 2 (winter 1997): 350–377.

Butler, Judith, and Joan Scott, eds. *Feminists Theorize the Political*. New York: Routledge, 1992.

Calavita, Kitty. *Inside the State: The Bracero Program, Immigration and the I.N.S.* New York: Routledge, 1992.

"Canada's Ellis Island." *New York Times*, July 2, 1999, A1, A4.

Carbonnier, Jean. "A beau mentir qui vient de loin ou le mythe du législateur étranger (1)." In *Essais sur les lois*, 227–338. Paris: Râepertoire du notariat Defrâenois, 1995.

Carens, Joseph H. *Culture, Citizenship, and Community: A Contextual Exploration of Justice as Even-Handedness*. Oxford: Oxford University Press, 2000.

Caruth, Cathy. *Unclaimed Experience: Trauma, Narrative, and History*. Baltimore: Johns Hopkins University Press, 1996.

Carvajal, Doreen. "Immigrants Fight Residency Rules Blocking Children in L.I. Schools." *New York Times*, August 7, 1995, A1, B4.

Cavell, Stanley. "The Uncanniness of the Ordinary." In *In Quest of the Ordinary: Lines of Skepticism and Romanticism*, 153–178. Chicago: University of Chicago Press, 1988.

Chambers, Iain. *Migrancy, Culture, Identity*. London: Routledge, 1994.

Chase, Richard. "The Brontës: A Centennial Observance." *Kenyon Review* 9 (Autumn 1947): 486–506.

Cheah, Pheng, and Bruce Robbins, eds. *Cosmopolitics: Thinking and Feeling beyond the Nation*. Minneapolis: University of Minnesota Press, 1998.

Chicago Tribune. "Crackdown on Importing Foreign Brides," February 2, 1997, 2.

Chilsen, Liz, and Sheldon Rampton. *Friends in Deed: The Story of U.S. Nicaraguan Sister Cities*. Madison: Wisconsin Co-ordinating Council on Nicaragua, 1988.

Chiswick, Barry R. *Illegal Aliens: Their Employment and Employers*. Kalamazoo, Mich.: W. E. Upjohn Institute for Employment Research, 1988.

Cioffi, Frank. *Wittgenstein on Freud and Frazer*. Cambridge, England: Cambridge University Press, 1998.

Connolly, William. *The Augustinian Imperative: A Reflection on the Politics of Morality*. Newbury Park, Calif.: Sage Publications, 1993.

———. *The Ethos of Pluralization*. Minneapolis: University of Minnesota Press, 1995.

———. "Freud, Moses, and Secularism." Paper presented at the annual meeting of the American Political Science Association, Atlanta, Georgia, September 1999.

———. *Political Theory and Modernity*. Ithaca, N.Y.: Cornell University Press, 1993.

———. *Brains, Techniques, and Time: The Ethics of Nonlinear Politics*. Minneapolis: University of Minnesota Press, forthcoming.

Connor, Walker. "Nationalism and Its Myth." *International Journal of Comparative Sociology* 33: 48–57.

Constable, Marianne. *The Law of the Other: The Mixed Jury and Changing Conceptions of Citizenship, Law, and Knowledge*. Chicago: University of Chicago Press, 1994.

———. "Sovereignty and Governmentality in Modern American Immigration Law." *Law, Politics and Society* 13 (1993): 249–271.

Coontz, Stephanie. *The Way We Never Were: American Families and the Nostalgia Trap*. New York: Basic Books, 1992.

Copjec, Joan. "The *Unvermögender* Other: Hysteria and Democracy in America." *New Formations*, no. 14 (summer 1991): 27–41.

Crawford, James. *Hold Your Tongue: Bilingualism and the Politics of "English Only."* Reading, Mass.: Addison-Wesley, 1992.

Crawford, James, ed. *Language Loyalties: A Sourcebook on the Official English Controversy*. Chicago: University of Chicago Press, 1992.

Cronon, Edmond David. *Black Moses: The Story of Marcus Garvey and the Universal Negro Improvement Association*. Madison: University of Wisconsin Press, 1955.

Cross, Samuel Hazzard, and Olgerd P. Sherbowitz-Wetzor, eds. and trans. *The Russian Primary Chronicle: Laurentian Text*. Mediaeval Academy of

America Publication, no. 60. Cambridge, Mass.: The Mediaeval Academy of America, 1953.

Crossette, Barbara. "And You Thought the Age of Viceroys Was Over." *New York Times*, May 12, 1996, Week in Review, 3.

Crow, Charles L., "Introduction." In *American Gothic: An Anthology, 1787–1916*, edited by Charles L. Crow. Oxford: Blackwell, 1999.

Crow, Charles L., ed. *American Gothic: An Anthology, 1787–1916*. Oxford: Blackwell, 1999.

Daly, John. "Global Connections: Political Giving in the 1996 Elections by Foreign Agents and U.S. Subsidiaries of Foreign Companies." In Opensecrets.org: Your Guide to Money in American Politics [website]. Washington, D.C.: Center for Responsive Politics, 1997 [cited August 17, 2000]. Available from http://www.opensecrets.org/pubs/global/globalindex.htm.

Daniels, Roger. *Coming to America: A History of Immigration and Ethnicity in American Life*. New York: HarperCollins, 1990.

Daube, David. *Civil Disobedience in Antiquity*. Edinburgh: Edinburgh University Press, 1972.

de Certeau, Michel. *The Writing of History*. Translated by Tom Conley. New York: Columbia University Press, 1988.

Delaney, Carol. *Abraham on Trial: The Social Legacy of Biblical Myth*. Princeton, N.J.: Princeton University Press, 1998.

Delgado, Héctor L. *New Immigrants, Old Unions: Organizing Undocumented Workers in Los Angeles*. Philadelphia: Temple University Press, 1993.

de Pommereau, Isabelle. "Where Immigrants Are Welcome: As Uncle Sam Cuts Benefits to Illegals, Jersey City Declares Itself a Sanctuary." *Christian Science Monitor*, March 4, 1997.

Derrida, Jacques. *Archive Fever: A Freudian Impression*. Translated by Eric Prenowitz. Chicago: University of Chicago Press, 1995.

———. *Glas*. Lincoln: University of Nebraska Press, 1986.

———. *Grammatology*. Baltimore: Johns Hopkins University Press, 1976.

———. *The Politics of Friendship*. Translated by George Collins. London: Verso, 1997.

———. "Signature, Event, Context." In *Limited, Inc*. Evanston, Ill.: Northwestern University Press, 1988.

———. "Des Tours de Babel." In *Difference in Translation*, edited by Joseph F. Graham. Ithaca, N.Y.: Cornell University Press, 1985.

Dinnerstein, Leonard, and David M. Reimers. *Ethnic Americans: A History of Immigration*. New York: Columbia University Press, 1999.

Dobrzynski, Judith H. "For More and More Job Seekers, an Aging Parent Is a Big Factor." *New York Times*, January 1, 1996.

Donaldson, Laura. "The Sign of Orpah: Reading Ruth through Native Eyes." In *Ruth and Esther: A Feminist Companion to the Bible*, 3. 2nd series, edited by Athalya Brenner. Sheffield, England: Sheffield Academic Press, 1999.

Dube, Musa. "The Unpublished Letters of Orpah to Ruth." In *Ruth and Esther: A Feminist Companion to the Bible*, 3. 2nd series, edited by Athalya Brenner. Sheffield, England: Sheffield Academic Press, 1999.

Du Bois, W.E.B. *Dusk of Dawn: An Essay toward an Autobiography of a Race Concept*. New Brunswick, N.J.: Transaction Books, 1984.

Du Maurier, Daphne. *Rebecca*. New York: Doubleday, 1953.

Duncan, Graeme. *Democratic Theory and Practice*. Cambridge, England: Cambridge University Press, 1983.

Dunn, John, ed. *Contemporary Crisis of the Nation State?* Oxford: Blackwell, 1992.

Duplessis, Rachel. *Writing beyond the Ending: Narrative Strategies of Twentieth-Century Women Writers*. Bloomington: Indiana University Press, 1985.

Edmonston, Barry, and Jeffrey S. Passel, eds. *Immigration and Ethnicity: The Integration of America's Newest Arrivals*. Washington, D.C.: Urban Institute Press; distributed by University Press of America, 1994.

Edmundson, Mark. *Nightmare on Main Street: Angels, Sadomasochism, and the Culture of Gothic*. Cambridge, Mass.: Harvard University Press, 1997.

Exum, J. Cheryl, and David J. A. Clines, eds. *The New Literary Criticism and the Hebrew Bible*. Sheffield: Sheffield Academic Press, 1993.

Fanon, Frantz. *A Dying Colonialism*. Translated by Haakon Chevalier. London: Grove Press, 1965.

Fewell, Danna, Nolan and David Gunn. *Compromising Redemption: Relating Characters in the Book of Ruth*. Louisville, Ky.: Westminster/John Knox Press, 1990.

Fiedler, Leslie A. *Love and Death in the American Novel*. New York: Stein and Day, 1966.

Fiorenza, Elisabeth Schüssler. *Bread Not Stone: the Challenge of Feminist Biblical Interpretation*. Boston: Beacon Press, 1984.

Frazer, James. *The Golden Bough: A Study in Magic and Religion*. New York: Simon and Schuster, 1996.

Freud, Sigmund. "Beyond the Pleasure Principle." In *The Standard Edition of the Complete Psychological Works of Sigmund Freud*, edited and translated by James Strachey. Vol. 18. London: Hogarth Press and Institute of Psycho-Analysis, 1953–74.

———. *Civilization and Its Discontents*. New York: W. W. Norton, 1989.

———. "The Moses of Michelangelo." In *The Standard Edition of the Complete Psychological Works of Sigmund Freud*, edited and translated by James Strachey. Vol. 13. London: Hogarth Press and Institute of Psycho-Analysis, 1955.

———. *Moses and Monotheism*. New York: Random House, 1987.

———. *The Psychopathology of Everyday Life*, edited by James Strachey. New York: W. W. Norton, 1989.

———. *Totem and Taboo*. New York: W. W. Norton, 1950.

———. "The Uncanny." In *The Standard Edition of the Complete Psychological Works of Sigmund Freud*, edited and translated by James Strachey, 217–252. Vol. 17. London: Hogarth Press and Institute of Psycho-Analysis, 1955.

Frye, Northrup. *Anatomy of Criticism: Four Essays*. Princeton, N.J.: Princeton University Press, 1957.

Fuchs, Lawrence H. *The American Kaleidoscope: Race, Ethnicity, Civic Culture*. Hanover, N.H.: University Press of New England for Wesleyan University Press, 1990.

Funkenstein, Amos. *Perceptions of Jewish History*. Berkeley and Los Angeles: University of California Press, 1993.

Fuss, Diana. "Interior Colonies: Frantz Fanon and the Politics of Identification." *Diacritics* 24, no. 2/3 (summer/fall 1994): 20–42.

Giddens, Anthony. *The Nation-State and Violence*. Berkeley and Los Angeles: University of California Press, 1985.

Gilbert, Sandra M., and Susan Gubar. *The Madwoman in the Attic: The Woman Writer and the 19th Century Literary Imagination*. Yale University Press, 2000.

Gilman, Sander, Jutta Bermele, Jay Geller, and Valerie D. Greenberg, eds. *Reading Freud's Reading*. New York: New York University Press, 1994.

Girard, René. *Job: The Victim of His People*. Translated by Yvonne Freccero. Stanford, Calif.: Stanford University Press, 1987.

———. *Violence and the Sacred*. Baltimore: Johns Hopkins University Press, 1977.

Giraudon, Virginie. "Cosmopolitanism and National Priority: Attitudes towards Foreigners in France between 1789 and 1794." *History of European Ideas* 13, no. 5 (1991): 591–604.

Girouard, Mark. *Cities and People: A Social and Architectural History*. New Haven: Yale University Press, 1985.

Goddu, Teresa A. *Gothic America: Narrative, History, and Nation*. New York: Columbia University Press, 1997.

Golden, Renny, and Michael McConnell. *Sanctuary: the New Underground Railroad*. Maryknoll, N.Y.: Orbis Books, 1986.

Goldman, Emma. *Living My Life*. New York City: Dover Publications, 1970.

Gordon, Jennifer. "We Make the Road by Walking: Immigrant Workers, the Workplace Project, and the Struggle for Social Change." *Harvard Civil Rights—Civil Liberties Law Review* 30 (1995): 407–50.

Graves, Robert and Raphael Patai. *Hebrew Myths: The Book of Genesis*. New York: Doubleday, 1963.

Greenblatt, Stephen. "A Story Told with Evil Intent." *New York Times*, September 22, 1998.

Greene, Victor R. *American Immigrant Leaders, 1800–1910: Marginality and Identity*. Baltimore: Johns Hopkins University Press, 1987.

Grewal, Inderpal, and Caren Kaplan, eds. *Scattered Hegemonies: Postmodernity and Transnational Feminist Practices*. Minneapolis: University of Minnesota Press, 1994.

Guerin-Gonzales, Camille. "The International Migration of Workers and Segmented Labor: Mexican Immigrant Workers in California Industrial Agriculture, 1900–1940." In *The Politics of Immigrant Workers: Labor Activism and Migration in the World Economy since 1830*, edited by Camille Guerin-Gonzales and Carl Strikwerda. New York: Holmes and Meier, 1993.

Gunn, David. *The Story of King David: Genre and Interpretation*. Sheffield, England: Department of Biblical Studies, University of Sheffield, 1978.

Gunn, David, and Danna Nolan Fewell. *Narrative in the Hebrew Bible*. Oxford: Oxford University Press, 1993.

Hall, Charles W. "Noncitizens Prepare to Vote in Arlington Primary for School Board." *Washington Post*, May 22, 1994.

Hall, John A., ed. *The State of the Nation: Ernest Gellner and the Theory of Nationalism*. Cambridge, England: Cambridge University Press, 1998.

Handelman, Susan. *The Slayers of Moses*. Albany: State University of New York Press, 1982.

Handlin, Oscar. *Race and Nationality in American Life*. Boston: Little, Brown, 1957.

———. *The Uprooted*. Boston: Little, Brown, 1990.

Hargreaves, Alec G., and Michael J. Hefferman, eds. *French and Algerian Identities from Colonial Times to the Present*. Lewiston, Queenston, Lampeter: Edwin Mellen Press, 1993.

Hartsoe, Collen Ivey. *Dear Daughter: Letters from Eve and Other Women of the Bible*. Wilton, Conn.: Morehouse-Barlow, 1981.

Hartz, Louis. *The Founding of New Societies: Studies in the History of the United States, Latin America, South Africa, Canada and Australia*. New York: Harcourt, Brace and World, 1964.

Harvey, Simon, Marian Hobson, David J. Kelley, and Samuel S. B. Taylor. *Reappraisals of Rousseau: Studies in Honor of R. A. Leigh*. Manchester, England: Manchester University Press, 1980.

Heater, Derek. *Citizenship: The Civic Ideal in World History, Politics, and Education*. London: Longman, 1990.

———. *World Citizenship and Government: Cosmopolitan Ideas in the History of Western Political Thought*. New York: St. Martin's Press, 1996.

Heer, D. M., et al. "A Comparative Analysis of the Position of Undocumented Mexicans in the Los Angeles County Work Force in 1980." *International Migration* 30, no. 2 (June 1980): 101–26.

Held, David. "The Development of the Modern State." In *Formations of Modernity*, edited by S. Hall and B. Gieben. Cambridge: Polity Press, 1992.

———. *Political Theory Today*. Stanford, Calif.: Stanford University Press, 1991.

Herbert, Ulrich. *A History of Foreign Labor in Germany, 1880–1980: Seasonal Workers, Forced Laborers, Guest Workers*. Translated by W. Templar. Ann Arbor: University of Michigan Press, 1990.

"Here Come the Brides: In Japan, They're the Newest Import—and They're Forcing a Re-examination of Attitudes." *Newsday* (New York), March 3, 1997, Part II, B04, Queens Edition.

Herodotus. *Histories*. Translated by Robin Waterfield. Oxford: Oxford University Press, 1998.

Heschel, Susannah, ed. *On Being a Jewish Feminist*. New York: Schocken, 1983.

Higham, John. *Multiculturalism in Disarray*. Berlin: John-F.-Kennedy-Institut für Nordamerikastudien, 1992.

———. *Send These to Me: Immigrants in Urban America*. Baltimore: Johns Hopkins University Press, 1984.

———. *Strangers in the Land: Patterns of American Nativism, 1860–1925*. New Brunswick, N.J.: Rutgers University Press, 1988.

Hochschild, Jennifer. *Facing Up to the American Dream: Race, Class, and the Soul of the Nation*. Princeton, N.J.: Princeton University Press, 1995.

Hoffman, E.T.A. "The Sandman." In *Selected Writings of E.T.A. Hoffman*, edited and translated by Leonard J. Kent and Elizabeth C. Knight, 137–167. Vol. 1. Chicago: University of Chicago Press, 1969.

Hoffman, Stanley, and David P. Fidler, eds. *Rousseau on International Relations*. Oxford: Clarendon Press, 1991.

Hollifield, James. *Immigrants, Markets, and States: The Political Economy of Postwar Europe*. Cambridge, Mass.: Harvard University Press, 1992.

Hollinger, David. *Postethnic America: Beyond Multiculturalism*. New York: Basic Books, 1995.

Holmes, Steven. "Anti-Immigrant Mood Moves Asians to Organize." *New York Times*, January 3, 1996, A1, A11.

Holst-Warhaft, Gail. *Dangerous Voices: Women's Laments in Greek Literature*. New York: Routledge, 1992.

Holston, James, and Arjun Appadurai. "Cities and Citizenship." *Public Culture* 8 (1996): 187–204.

Holtzmann, Steven H., and Christopher M. Leich. *Wittgenstein: To Follow a Rule*. London, Boston, and Henley: Routledge and Kegan Paul, 1991.

Honig, Bonnie. "Declarations of Independence: Arendt and Derrida on the Problem of Founding a Republic." *American Political Science Review* 85, no. 1 (March 1991): 97–113.

———. "Difference, Dilemmas, and the Politics of Home." In *Democracy and Difference: Contesting the Boundaries of the Political*, edited by Seyla Benhabib. Princeton, N.J.: Princeton University Press, 1996.

Honig, Bonnie. "My Culture Made Me Do It." In *Is Multiculturalism Bad for Feminism?* edited by Joshua Cohen, Matthew Howard, and Martha C. Nussbaum. Princeton, N.J.: Princeton University Press, 1999.

———. *Political Theory and the Displacement of Politics.* Ithaca, N.Y.: Cornell University Press, 1993.

———. "Toward an Agonistic Feminism: Hannah Arendt and the Politics of Identity." In *Feminists Theorize the Political,* edited by Judith Butler and Joan Scott, 215–235. New York: Routledge Press, 1992.

Honig, Bonnie, ed. *Feminist Interpretations of Hannah Arendt.* University Park, Penn.: Pennsylvania State University Press, 1995.

"Hospitality Is Their Business." *New York Times,* March 21, 1996, D1 and D9.

Howard, Jacqueline. *Reading Gothic Fiction: A Bahktinian Approach.* Oxford: Clarendon Press, 1994.

Howe, Irving. *The World of Our Fathers: The Journey of the East European Jews to America and the Life They Found and Made.* New York: Schocken Books, 1990.

Hubbard, Robert L. *The Book of Ruth.* Grand Rapids, Mich.: William B. Eerdmans, 1988.

Hufton, Olwen, ed. *Historical Change and Human Rights.* New York: Basic Books, 1995.

Hugo, Victor. "Boaz Asleep." In *The Complete Works of Victor Hugo: Poems,* 97–100. London: Hawarden Press, n.d.

———. "Booz Endormi." In *Poémes,* choisis et présentés par Jean Gaudon, 360–363. Paris: Flammarion, 1985.

Hurston, Zora Neale. *Moses, Man of the Mountain.* Urbana: Illini Books; University of Illinois Press, 1984.

Ignatiev, Noel. *How the Irish Became White.* New York: Routledge, 1995.

Invasion of the Body Snatchers. Directed by Don Siegel. Allied Artists Pictures, 1956. Videocassette.

Irigaray, Luce. *Speculum of the Other Woman.* Ithaca, N.Y.: Cornell University Press, 1985.

Ishay, Micheline. *Internationalism and Its Betrayal.* Minneapolis: University of Minnesota Press, 1995.

Jabes, Edmond. *A Foreigner Carrying in the Crook of His Arm a Tiny Book.* Translated by Rosemarie Waldrop. Hanover, N.H.: University Press of New England for Wesleyan University Press, 1993.

Johnson, Barbara. "Moses and Intertextuality: Sigmund Freud, Zora Neale Hurston, and the Bible." In *Poetics of the Americas: Race, Founding, and Textuality,* edited by Bainard Cowan and Jefferson Humphries, 15–29. Baton Rouge: Louisiana State University Press, 1997.

Johnson, Daniel M. *Black Migration in America: A Social Demographic History.* Durham, N.C.: Duke University Press, 1981.

Johnston, Steven. *Encountering Tragedy: Rousseau and the Project of Democratic Order.* Ithaca, N.Y.: Cornell University Press, 1999.

Judaism: A Quarterly Journal. Issue no. 169, 43, no. 1 (Winter 1994).

Kallen, Horace Meyer. *Culture and Democracy in the United States.* New York: Boni and Liveright, 1924.

Kant, Immanuel. *Groundwork of the Metaphysics of Morals.* Indianapolis: Bobbs Merrill, 1959.

———. *Observations on the Feeling of the Beautiful and the Sublime.* Translated by John Goldthwait. Berkeley and Los Angeles: University of California Press, 1991.

Kaplan, Morris B. "Refiguring the Jewish Question: Arendt, Proust, and the Politics of Sexuality." In *Feminist Interpretations of Hannah Arendt,* edited by Bonnie Honig, 105–133. University Park, Penn.: Pennsylvania State University Press, 1995.

Kaplan, Rosa Felsenburg. "The Noah Syndrome." In *On Being a Jewish Feminist,* edited by Susannah Heschel. New York: Schocken, 1983.

Karlin-Neumann, Patricia. "The Journey toward Life." In *Reading Ruth: Contemporary Women Reclaim a Sacred Story,* edited by Judith A. Kates and Gail Twersky Reimer. New York: Ballantine, 1994.

Kates, Judith A. "Women at the Center: *Ruth* and Schavuoth." In *Reading Ruth: Contemporary Women Reclaim a Sacred Story,* edited by Judith A. Kates and Gail Twersky Reimer. New York: Ballantine, 1994.

Kates, Judith A., and Gail Twersky Reimer, eds. *Reading Ruth: Contemporary Women Reclaim a Sacred Story.* New York: Ballantine, 1994.

Keck, Margaret E., and Kathryn Sikkink. *Activists Beyond Borders.* Ithaca, N.Y.: Cornell University Press, 1998.

Keenan, Alan. *The Democratic Question: On the Rule of the People and the Paradoxes of Political Freedom.* Minneapolis: University of Minnesota Press, forthcoming.

Keller, Werner. *The Bible as History.* 2nd rev. ed. New York: Bantam Books, 1980.

Kennedy, John F. *A Nation of Immigrants.* New York: Harper and Row, 1986.

Kenner, Hugh. "Between Two Worlds." *New York Times,* April 14, 1996, Book Review, 14.

Kilgour, Maggie. *The Rise of the Gothic Novel.* London: Routledge, 1995.

King, Anthony D. *Culture, Globalization, and the World System.* Minneapolis: University of Minnesota Press, 1997.

King, Katie. "Lesbianism in Multicultural Reception: Global Gay, Local Homo." *Camera Obscura* 28 (1992): 78–99.

Kohn, Hans. *Pan-Slavism: Its History and Ideology.* Notre Dame, Ind.: University of Notre Dame Press, 1953.

Koven, Ronald. "The French Melting Pot." *France Magazine*, fall 1991.

Kramer, Lloyd. *Lafayette in Two Worlds: Public Cultures and Personal Identities in an Age of Revolutions*. Chapel Hill: University of North Carolina Press, 1996.

Kristeva, Julia. *Nations without Nationalism*. Translated by Leon S. Roudiez. New York: Columbia University Press, 1993.

———. *Strangers to Ourselves*. Translated by Leon S. Roudiez. New York: Columbia University Press, 1991.

Kymlicka, Will. *Multicultural Citizenship: A Liberal Theory of Minority Rights*. New York: Oxford University Press, 1995.

Labovitz, Priscilla. "Immigration: Just the Facts." *New York Times*, March 25, 1996, Op. Ed.

Lacan, Jacques. *Écrits: A Selection*. Translated by Alan Sheridan. New York: W. W. Norton, 1977.

Laclau, Ernesto. *Emancipations*. London: Verso, 1996.

Laclau, Ernesto, and Chantal Mouffe. *Hegemony and Socialist Strategy*. Translated by Winston Moore and Paul Commack. London: Verso, 1985.

Lacocque, Andre. *The Feminine Unconventional: Four Subversive Figures in Israel's Tradition*. Minneapolis: Fortress Press, 1990.

Lakenbacher, X. X. "Note sur l'ardat-lili." *RA* 65m (1971): 119–154.

Lane, A. T. *Solidarity or Survival? American Labor and European Immigrants, 1830–1924*. New York and London: Greenwood Press, 1987.

Larkin, Katrina J. A. *Ruth and Esther*. Old Testament Guides. Sheffield: Sheffield Academic Press, 1996.

Larmore, Charles. "Pluralism and Reasonable Disagreement." *Social Philosophy and Policy*, winter 1994, 61–79.

Laslett, John H. M. "Labor Party, Labor Lobbying, or Direct Action? Coal Miners, Immigrants, and Radical Politics in Scotland and the American Midwest, 1880–1924." In *The Politics of Immigrant Workers*, edited by Camille Guerin-Gonzales and Carl Strikwerda. New York: Holmes and Meier, 1993.

Lazreg, Marnia. *The Eloquence of Silence: Algerian Women in Question*. London: Routledge, 1995.

Levi-Strauss, Claude. *Myth and Meaning: Five Talks for Radio*. Toronto: University of Toronto Press, 1978.

Levinson, Sanford. *Constitutional Faith*. Princeton, N.J.: Princeton University Press, 1988.

Lincoln, Abraham. "The Perpetuation of Our Political Institutions." In Richard N. Current, ed., *The Political Thought of Abraham Lincoln*. New York: Macmillan, 1967.

Lind, Michael. *The Next American Nation: The New Nationalism and the Fourth American Revolution*. New York: Free Press, 1995.

Lissak, Rivka Shpak. *Liberal Progressives and Immigration Restriction, 1896–1917*. Jerusalem: American Jewish Archives, 1992.

————. *Pluralism and Progressives: Hull House and the New Immigrants, 1890–1919*. Chicago: University of Chicago Press, 1989.

Littlefield, Daniel F. *The Chickasaw Freedmen: A People without a Country*. Westport, Conn.: Greenwood Press, 1980.

Littlefield, Henry M. "The Wizard of Oz: Parable on Populism." *American Quarterly* 16, no. 1 (spring 1964): 47–58.

Loo, Tina, and Carolyn Strange. "The Travelling Show Menace: Contested Regulation in Turn-of-the-Century Ontario." *Law and Society Review* 29, no. 4 (1995): 639–667.

Low, Victor. *The Unimpressible Race: A Century of Educational Struggle by the Chinese in San Francisco*. San Francisco: East/West Publishing, 1982.

Lyons, Eugene. *The Life and Death of Sacco and Vanzetti*. New York: Da Capo Press, 1970.

MacAndrew, Elizabeth. *The Gothic Tradition in Fiction*. New York: Columbia University Press, 1979.

MacCannell, Juliet Flower. *Regime of the Brother: After the Patriarchy*. London: Routledge, 1991.

MacEoin, Gary, ed. *Sanctuary: A Resource Guide for Understanding and Participating in the Central American Refugee's Struggle*. San Francisco: Harper and Row, 1985.

Machiavelli, Niccolò. *Discourses on the First Decade of Titus Livius*. In *Machiavelli: The Chief Works and Others*, translated by Allan Gilbert. Durham, N.C.: Duke University Press, 1989.

MacIntyre, Alasdair. *After Virtue: A Study in Moral Theory*. Notre Dame, Ind.: University of Notre Dame Press, 1984.

Madison, James. "Charters." In *The Writings of James Madison*, edited by Gaillard Hunt. New York: G. P. Putnam's Sons, 1906.

————. *The Debates in the Federal Convention of 1787 Which Framed the Constitution of the United States of America*. New York: Oxford University Press, 1920.

Mann, Michael, ed. *The Rise and Decline of the Nation State*. Oxford: Blackwell, 1990.

Marlowe, Lara. "Left's Promise Brings Illegal Aliens Out in Force." *The Irish Times*, July 25, 1997, World News, 9.

————. "The Rise of the Sans Papiers." *Irish Times*, February 20, 1997, 15.

————. "Voices of Left Sound Faintly through Uproar on Immigration." *Irish Times*, April 9, 1998, World News, 14.

Marshall, Ray. "Economic Factors Influencing the International Migration of Workers." In *Views across the Border*, edited by Stanley Ross. Albuquerque: University of New Mexico Press, 1978.

Martin, Robert K., and Eric Savoy, eds. *American Gothic: New Interventions in a National Narrative*. Iowa City: University of Iowa Press, 1998.

McKinlay, Judith. "A Son Is Born to Naomi: A Harvest for Israel." In *Ruth and Esther: A Feminist Companion to the Bible*, 3. 2nd series, edited by Athalya Brenner. Sheffield, England: Sheffield Academic Press, 1999.

McMillan, Penelope. "Finally an American: 'Born Rebel' Becomes a Citizen at 75 after Battling McCarthy Era Deportation Proceeding since 1956." *Los Angeles Times*, August 9, 1985.

Mehta, Uday. *The Anxiety of Freedom: Imagination and Individuality in Locke's Political Thought*. Ithaca, N.Y.: Cornell University Press, 1992.

———. "Liberal Exclusion." *Politics and Society* 18 (1990): 427–453.

Melville, Herman. *White Jacket, or The World in a Man-of-War*. New York: The Library of America, 1983.

Meyers, Carol. *Discovering Eve: Ancient Israelite Women in Context*. New York: Oxford University Press, 1988.

Migration News Sheet, November 1994.

Mill, John Stuart. "On Individuality." In *On Liberty*. New York: Norton, 1975.

Miller, David. *On Nationality*. Oxford: Oxford University Press, 1996.

Mills, Marja. "Sanctuary Push Turns to Rights." *Chicago Tribune*, January 27, 1989.

Mississippi Masala. Directed by Mira Nair. Mirabai, 1992. Videocassette.

Modleski, Tania. *Loving with a Vengeance: Mass-Produced Fantasies for Women*. Hamden, Conn.: Archon Books, 1982.

Moers, Ellen. *Literary Women*. Garden City, N.Y.: Doubleday and Company, 1976.

"More U.S. Men Look for Love Overseas." *Columbus Dispatch*, December 30, 1996, 2C.

Morrison, Toni. "On the Backs of Blacks." In *Arguing Immigration*, edited by Nicolaus Mills. New York: Simon and Schuster, 1994.

———. *Playing in the Dark: Whiteness and the Literary Imagination*. Cambridge, Mass.: Harvard University Press, 1992.

Morse, Rob. "Thinking Globally, Acting Symbolically." *San Francisco Examiner*, February 7, 1991, A3.

Moruzzi, Norma. "A Problem with Headscarves: Contemporary Complexities of Political and Social Identity." *Political Theory* 22 (1994): 653–672.

———. "Veiled Agents: Feminine Agency and Masquerade in the Battle of Algiers." In *Negotiating at the Margins: The Gendered Discourse of Power and Resistance*, edited by S. Fisher and K. Davis, 255–277. New Brunswick, N.J.: Rutgers University Press, 1993.

Narayan, Uma. "Male Order Brides: Immigrant Women, Domestic Violence, and Immigration Law." *Hypatia* 10, no. 1 (winter 1995):104–119.

Nelson, Cary, and Dilip Parameshwar Gaonkar, eds. *Disciplinarity and Dissent in Cultural Studies*. New York: Routledge, 1996.

Newman, Barry. "Foreign Legions: Lots of Noncitizens Feel Right at Home in U.S. Political Races." *Wall Street Journal*, October 31, 1997, A1.

Newsom, Carol, and Sharon Ringe, eds. *Women's Bible Commentary*. Louisville, Ky.: Westminster John Knox Press, 1992.

New York Times, March 17, 1997, Letter to the Editor.

New York Times. "U.S. Surveys Find Farm Work Pay Down for 20 years,"March 31, 1997.

Niederlander, William. *The Schreber Case: Psychoanalytic Profile of a Paranoid Personality*. Hillsdale, N.J.: Analytic Press, 1984.

Noiriel, Gérard. *The French Melting Pot: Immigration, Citizenship, and National Identity*. Minneapolis: University of Minnesota Press, 1996.

———. "Immigration: Amnesia and Memory." *French Historical Studies* 19, no. 2 (fall 1995): 367–380.

Nolte, Carl. "S.F. Labor Leader Harry Bridges Dies: Founder and Leader of Longshoremen's Union." *San Francisco Chronicle*, March 31, 1990.

Oakley, S. P. "Notes on Livy." *Classical Quarterly* 44, no. 1 (1994): 171.

Okin, Susan Moller, with respondents. *Is Multiculturalism Bad for Feminism?*, edited by Joshua Cohen, Matthew Howard, and Martha C. Nussbaum. Princeton, N.J.: Princeton University Press, 1999.

Oliver, Kelly. Review of *Nations without Nationalism* by Julia Kristeva. *Ethics* 104, no. 4 (July 1994): 939.

Ostling, Richard. "A Defeat for Sanctuary: Church Activists Are Convicted of Smuggling Illegal Aliens." *Time Magazine*, May 12, 1986, 82.

Ostriker, Alicia Suskin. *Feminist Revision and the Bible*. Oxford: Blackwell, 1993.

Ostrom, Carol M. "Sanctuary Resolution Called Strongest in Nation." *Seattle Times*, January 14, 1986, B2.

Ostrow, Ronald. "Big Cities Criticized for Failing to Cooperate with INS Policy: Sen. Roth Says Many, Like Los Angeles, Are 'Hypocritical' for Complaining of Influx of Illegal Immigrants While Refusing to Help Prosecute." *Los Angeles Times*, November 11, 1993.

Ozick, Cynthia. *Metaphor and Memory: Essays*. New York: Alfred A. Knopf, 1989.

———. "Ruth." In *Reading Ruth: Contemporary Women Reclaim a Sacred Story*, edited by Judith A. Kates and Gail Twersky Reimer. New York: Ballantine, 1994.

Padover, Saul K., ed. *The Forging of American Federalism: Selected Writings of James Madison*. New York: Harper and Row, 1953.

Pangle, Thomas. "Interpretive Essay." In *The Laws of Plato*. New York: Basic Books, 1980.

Pardes, Ilana. *Countertraditions in the Bible: A Feminist Approach*. Cambridge, Mass.: Harvard University Press, 1992.

Parekh, Bhikhu. "The Rushdie Affair: Research Agenda for Political Philosophy." *Political Studies* 38, no. 4: 695–709.

Parekh, Bhikhu. "Three Theories of Immigration." In *Strangers and Citizens: A Positive Approach to Migrants and Refugees*, edited by Sarah Spencer, 91–110. London: Oran River Press, 1994.

Park, Robert, and Herbert Miller. *Old World Traits Transplanted*. New York and London: Harper and Brothers, 1921.

Parker, Kunal. "Making Blacks Foreigners: The Legal Construction of Former Slaves in Post-Revolutionary Massachusetts." Paper on file with author.

Patterson, Orlando. *Freedom*. New York: Basic Books, 1991.

Paul, Robert A. *Moses and Civilization: The Meaning Behind Freud's Myth*. New Haven: Yale University Press, 1996.

Paulson, Ronald. *Representations of Revolution, 1789–1820*. New Haven: Yale University Press, 1983.

Pavić, Milorad. *Dictionary of the Khazars: a Lexicon Novel in 100,000 Words*. Translated by Christina Privićević Zorić. London: H. Hamilton, 1988.

Perez-Bustillo, Camilo. "What Happens When English Only Comes to Town? A Case Study of Lowell, Massachusetts." In *Language Loyalties: A Sourcebook on the Official English Controversy*, edited by James Crawford. Chicago: University of Chicago Press, 1992.

Pitkin, Hanna Fenichel. *Attack of the Blob: Hannah Arendt's Concept of the Social*. Chicago: University of Chicago Press, 1998.

Plato. *The Works of Plato, His Fifty-Five Dialogues, and Twelve Epistles*. Translated by Floyer Sydenham and Thomas Taylor. London: R. Wilks, Chancery-Lane, 1804.

Porter, Joshua Roy. *Moses and Monarchy: A Study in the Biblical Tradition of Moses*. Oxford: Blackwell, 1963.

Portes, Alejandro, and Rubén G. Rumbaut. *Immigrant America: A Portrait*. Berkeley and Los Angeles: University of California Press, 1990.

Pozzetta, George E., ed. *The Work Experience: Labor, Class and the Immigrant Enterprise*. New York: Garland Publishing, 1991.

The Prince of Egypt. Directed by Simon Wells and Steve Hickner. Disney, 1998. Videocassette.

Pritsak, Omeljan. *The Origin of Rus': Volume One, Old Scandinavian Sources Other than the Sagas*, 3–7. Cambridge, Mass.: Harvard University Press, 1981.

Punter, David. *The Literature of Terror: A History of Gothic Fictions from 1765 to the Present Day*. 2nd ed. New York: Longman, 1996.

Radcliffe, S. A. "Ethnicity, Patriarchy, and Incorporation into the Nation: Female Migrants as Domestic Workers in Peru." *Environment and Planning D, Society and Space* 8 (1990): 379–393.

Raglan, Lord. "The Hero: A Study in Tradition, Myth, and Drama, Part II." In *In Quest of the Hero*, edited by Robert A. Segal. Princeton, N.J.: Princeton University Press, 1990.

Rancière, Jacques. *Dis-agreement: Politics and Philosophy*. Translated by Julie Rose. Minneapolis: University of Minnesota Press, 1999.

Rank, Otto. "The Myth of the Birth of the Hero." In *In Quest of the Hero*, edited by Robert A. Segal. Princeton, N.J.: Princeton University Press, 1990.

Raskin, Jamin. "Legal Aliens, Local Citizens: The Historical, Constitutional, and Theoretical Meanings of Alien Suffrage." *University of Pennsylvania Law Review* 141 (April 1993): 1391–1469.

Reagon, Bernice Johnson. "Coalition Politics: Turning the Century." In *Home Girls: A Black Feminist Anthology*, edited by Barbara Smith. New York: Kitchen Table—Women of Color Press, 1983.

Rebecca. Directed by Alfred Hitchcock. David O. Selznick, 1940. Videocassette.

Reece, Steve. *The Stranger's Welcome: Oral Theory and the Aesthetics of the Homeric Hospitality Scene*. Ann Arbor: University of Michigan Press, 1993.

Reimer, Gail Twersky. "Her Mother's House." In *Reading Ruth: Contemporary Women Reclaim a Sacred Story*, edited by Judith A. Kates and Gail Twersky Reimer. New York: Ballantine, 1994.

Reinhard, Kenneth, and Julia Lupton. "Shapes of Grief: Freud, *Hamlet*, and Meaning." *Genders* 4 (spring 1989): 50–67.

Review of *Culture and Imperialism*. *19th Century Contexts* 18, no. 1 (1994): 93–112.

Review of *The Next American Nation* by Michael Lind. *New York Times Book Review* (summer 1995).

Rhys, Jean. *Wide Sargasso Sea*. New York: Norton, 1966.

Riasanovsky, Nicholas V. *A History of Russia*. 6th ed., 23–28, 450–451. New York: Oxford University Press, 2000.

Richter, David H. *Progress of Romance: Literary Historiography and the Gothic Novel*. Columbus: Ohio State University Press, 1996.

Ringe, Donald A. *American Gothic: Imagination and Reason in Nineteenth-Century Fiction*. Lexington: University Press of Kentucky, 1982.

Ritter, Gretchen. "Silver Slippers and a Golden Cap: L. Frank Baum's *The Wonderful Wizard of Oz* and Historical Memory in American Politics." *Journal of American Studies* 31, no. 2 (1997): 171–202.

Rivera-Batiz, Francisco, Selig L. Sechzer, and Ira Gang, eds. *U.S. Immigration Policy Reform in the 1980s*. New York: Praeger, 1991.

Robbins, Bruce. *Feeling Global: Internationalism in Distress*. New York: New York University Press, 1999.

———. "Introduction, Part I: Actually Existing Cosmopolitanism." In *Cosmopolitics: Thinking and Feeling beyond the Nation*, edited by Pheng Cheah and Bruce Robbins. Minneapolis: University of Minnesota Press, 1998.

Rogin, Michael. *Ronald Reagan, the Movie: And Other Episodes in American Political Demonology*. Berkeley and Los Angeles: University of California Press, 1987.

Rogoff, Irit. "From Ruins to Debris: The Feminization of Fascism in German-History Museums." In *Museum Culture: Histories, Discourses, Spectacles*, edited by Daniel J. Sherman and Irit Rogoff, 223–249. Minneapolis: University of Minnesota Press, 1994.

Rorty, Richard. *Achieving Our Country: Leftist Thought in Twentieth-Century America*. Cambridge, Mass.: Harvard University Press, 1998.

———. *Irony, Contingency, Solidarity*. Cambridge, England: Cambridge University Press, 1989.

———. *Philosophy and Social Hope*. New York: Penguin, 1999.

Rose, Gillian. *Judaism and Modernity: Philosophical Essays*. Oxford: Blackwell, 1993.

Rosen, Robert N. *A Short History of Charleston*. Charleston, S.C.: Peninsula Press, 1992.

Rosenberg, David, ed. *Congregation: Contemporary Writers Read the Jewish Bible*. New York: Harcourt Brace Jovanovich, 1987.

Rothstein, Richard. "Immigration Dilemmas." In *Arguing Immigration*, edited by Nicolaus Mills. New York: Simon and Schuster, 1994.

Rouner, Leroy S., ed. *Human Rights and the World's Religions*. Notre Dame, Ind.: University of Notre Dame Press, 1988.

Rousseau, Jean-Jacques. *The Collected Writings of Rousseau*, edited by Roger D. Masters and Christopher Kelly. Translated by Judith R. Bush, Christopher Kelly, and Roger D. Masters. Hanover, N.H.: Published for Dartmouth College by University Press of New England, 1990.

———. *Discourse on the Origin of Inequality (Second Discourse)*, edited by Roger Masters. Published for Dartmouth College by University Press of New England, 1992.

———. "Discourse on the Virtue Most Necessary for a Hero." In *The Collected Writings of Rousseau*, edited by Roger D. Masters and Christopher Kelly. Translated by Judith R. Bush, Christopher Kelly, and Roger D. Masters. Vol. 4. Hanover, N.H.: Published for Dartmouth College by University Press of New England, 1990.

———. *Du Contrat Social*, II.7. Paris: Bordas, 1972.

———. *Geneva Manuscript*. In *The Collected Writings of Rousseau*, edited by Roger D. Masters and Christopher Kelly. Translated by Judith R. Bush, Christopher Kelly, and Roger D. Masters. Vol. 4. Hanover, N.H.: Published for Dartmouth College by University Press of New England, 1990.

———. *The Government of Poland*. Translated by Willmore Kendall. Indianapolis: Hackett, 1985.

———. *On the Social Contract.* Translated and edited by Donald A. Cress. Indianapolis: Hackett, 1987.

Rudnytsky, Peter L., ed. *Transitional Objects and Potential Spaces: Literary Uses of D. W. Winnicott.* New York: Columbia University Press, 1993.

Rushdie, Salman. *The Wizard of Oz.* London: BFI, 1992.

Russ, Joanna. "Somebody Is Trying to Kill Me and I Think It's My Husband: The Modern Gothic." *Journal of Popular Culture* 6 (1973): 666–691.

Saccamano, Neil. "Rhetoric, Consensus, and the Law in Rousseau's *Contrat social.*" *MLN* 107 (1992): 730–751.

Sacks, Peter. *The English Elegy: Studies in Genre from Spenser to Yeats.* Baltimore: Johns Hopkins University Press, 1985.

Sacramento Bee. "Berkeley Weighs Sister-City Tie." April 15, 1996, A4.

Sage, Victor, ed. *The Gothick Novel: A Casebook.* London: Macmillan, 1990.

Salomon, Lester. "The Rise of the Nonprofit Sector." *Foreign Affairs* 73, no. 4: 109–122.

Salzinger, Leslie. "A Maid by Any Other Name: The Transformation of 'Dirty Work' by Central American Immigrants." *In Ethnography Unbound: Power and Resistance in the Modern Metropolis,* edited by Michael Burawoy et al., 139–160. Berkeley and Los Angeles: University of California Press, 1991.

Sandel, Michael. *Democracy's Discontents.* Cambridge, Mass.: Harvard University Press, Belknap Press, 1996.

———. *Liberalism and the Limits of Justice.* Cambridge, England: Cambridge University Press, 1982.

Santner, Eric. *My Own Private Germany: Daniel Paul Schreber's Secret History of Modernity.* Princeton, N.J.: Princeton University Press, 1996.

———. *On the Psychotheology of Everyday Life.* Chicago: University of Chicago Press, forthcoming.

———. *Stranded Objects: Mourning, Memory, and Film in Postwar Germany.* Ithaca, N.Y.: Cornell University Press, 1990.

Sassen, Saskia. *Losing Control? Sovereignty in an Age of Globalization.* New York: Columbia University Press, 1996.

Sasson, Jack M. *Ruth: A New Translation with a Philological Commentary and Formalist-Folklorist Interpretation.* Sheffield, England: JSOT Press, 1989.

Schlesinger, Arthur. *The Disuniting of America.* New York: Norton, 1993.

Schmitt, Cannon. *Alien Nation: Nineteenth-Century Gothic Fictions and English Nationality.* Philadelphia: University of Pennsylvania Press, 1997.

Schuck, Peter H. *Citizens, Strangers, and In-Betweens: Essays on Immigration and Citizenship.* Boulder, Col.: Westview Press, 1998.

———. "Membership in the Liberal Polity: The Devaluation of American Citizenship." In *Immigration and the Politics of Citizenship in Europe and North America,* edited by William Rogers Brubaker. Lanham, Md.: University Press of America, 1989.

Schuck, Peter H. "The Status and Rights of Undocumented Aliens in the U.S." In *Citizenship without Consent: Illegal Aliens in the American Polity*. New Haven: Yale University Press, 1985.

———. "The Status and Rights of Undocumented Aliens in the United States." *International Migration* 25, no. 2 (June 1987): 125–139.

Schuck, Peter, and Rogers Smith. *Citizenship without Consent: Illegal Aliens in the American Polity*. New Haven: Yale University Press, 1985.

Sedgwick, Eve Kosofsky. *The Coherence of Gothic Conventions*. New York: Arno Press, 1980.

Seery, John. *Political Returns: Irony in Politics and Theory: From Plato to the Antinuclear Movement*. Boulder, Colo.: Westview Press, 1990.

Shane. Directed by George Stevens. Paramount, 1953. Videocassette.

Shapiro, Michael. *Cinematic Political Thought: Narrating Race, Nation and Gender*. New York: New York University Press, 1999.

Shell, Marc. *Children of the Earth: Literature, Politics, and Nationhood*. New York: Oxford University Press, 1993.

Shulman, George. "Race and the Romance of American Nationalism in Martin Luther King, Norman Mailer, and James Baldwin." In *Political Theory and Cultural Studies*, edited by Jodi Dean. Ithaca, N.Y.: Cornell University Press, 2000.

Simmel, Georg. *The Sociology of Georg Simmel*. Translated and edited by Kurt H. Wolff. Glencoe, Ill.: Free Press, 1950.

Singh, Nikhil. "Culture/Wars: Recoding Empire in an Age of Democracy." *American Quarterly* 50, no. 3 (September 1998): 471–522.

Smith, David Horton. "Voluntary Inter-Cultural Exchange and Understanding Groups: The Roots of Success in U.S. Sister City Programs." *International Journal of Comparative Sociology* 31, no. 3–4 (September–December 1990): 177–192.

Smith, David Horton, and Burt R. Baldwin. "Voluntary Group Prevalence among U.S. States: Factors Affecting the Distribution of Intercultural Understanding Groups (Sister City Programs." *International Journal of Comparative Sociology* 31, no. 1–2 (January–April 1990): 79–85.

Smith, Paul. *Clint Eastwood*. Minneapolis: Minnesota University Press, 1993.

Smith, Robert. "The Flower Sellers of Manhattan." *NACLA Report on the Americas* 30, no. 3 (November–December 1996).

Smith, Rogers. "Beyond Tocqueville, Myrdal and Hartz: The Multiple Traditions Thesis in America." *American Political Science Review* 87, no. 3 (September 1993): 549–566.

———. *Civic Ideals: Conflicting Visions of Citizenship in U.S. History*. New Haven: Yale University Press, 1997.

———. Response to "Beyond Tocqueville, Please!" by Jacqueline Stevens. *American Political Science Review* 89, no. 4 (December 1995): 990–995.

Solovyev, Vladimir. *The Justification of the Good: An Essay on Moral Philosophy*. Translated by Nathalie A. Duddington. New York: Macmillan, 1918.

Sophocles. *Antigone*. Translated by Robert Fagles. New York: Penguin, 1984.

Sowell, Thomas. *Migrations and Cultures: A World View*. New York: Basic Books, 1996.

Spivak, Gayatri Chakravorty. "Acting Bits/Identity Talk." *Critical Inquiry* (Spring 1992): 770–803.

——. *A Critique of Postcolonial Reason: Toward a History of the Vanishing Present*. Cambridge, Mass.: Harvard University Press, 1999.

——. *Outside in the Teaching Machine*. New York: Routledge, 1993.

Stern, Julia A. "Excavating Genre in *Our Nig*." *American Literature* 67, no. 3 (September 1995): 439–466.

——. *The Plight of Feeling: Sympathy and Dissent in the Early American Novel*. Chicago: University of Chicago Press, 1997.

Stevens, Jacqueline. "Beyond Tocqueville, Please!" *American Political Science Review* 89, no. 4 (December 1995): 987–990.

——. *Reproducing the State*. Princeton, N.J.: Princeton University Press, 1999.

Strandberg, Victor. *Greek Mind/Jewish Soul: The Conflicted Art of Cynthia Ozick*. Madison: University of Wisconsin Press, 1994.

Strictly Ballroom. Directed and written by Baz Luhrman. Rank/M&A/Australian Film Finance Corp., 1992. Videocassette.

Sundquist, Eric. *Faulkner: The House Divided*. Baltimore: Johns Hopkins University Press, 1983.

"Swedish Bank Merger Flurry Seen Continuing." *Reuter European Business Report*, February 18, 1997.

Takaki, Ronald. *In a Different Mirror: A History of Multicultural America*. Boston: Little, Brown, 1993.

Thomsen, Vilhelm. *The Relations between Ancient Russia and Scandinavia and the Origins of the Russian State*. New York: Burt Franklin, 1877.

Tocqueville, Alexis de. *Democracy in America*, edited by J. P. Mayer. Translated by George Lawrence. Garden City, N.Y.: Doubleday, 1969.

Todorov, Tzvetan. *The Fantastic: A Structural Approach to a Literary Genre*. Translated by Richard Howard. Ithaca, N.Y.: Cornell University Press, 1973.

Toll, Katharine. "Making Roman-ness and the *Aeneid*." *Classical Antiquity* 16, no. 1 (April 1997): 34–56.

Trible, Phyllis. *God and the Rhetoric of Sexuality*. Philadelphia: Fortress Press, 1978.

——. *Texts of Terror: Literary-Feminist Readings of Biblical Narratives*. Philadelphia: Fortress Press, 1984.

Trumpener, Katie. *Bardic Nationalism: The Romantic Novel and the British Empire*. Princeton, N.J.: Princeton University Press, 1997.

Tully, James. *Strange Multiplicity: Constitutionalism in an Age of Diversity*. Cambridge, England: Cambridge University Press, 1995.

Ungar, Sanford. *Fresh Blood: The New American Immigrants*. New York: Simon and Schuster, 1995.

Van Houten, Christiana de Groot. *The Alien in Israelite Law*. Sheffield, England: JSOT Press, 1991.

Van Zyl, A. H. *The Moabites*. Leiden: E. J. Brill, 1960.

Villapando, Venny. "The Business of Selling Mail Order Brides." In *Making Waves: An Anthology of Writing by and about Asian American Women*, edited by Asian Women of California. Boston: Beacon Press, 1989: 318–326.

Virgil. *Aeneid*. Translated by Robert Fitzgerald. New York: Vintage, 1990.

Visvanathan, Shiv. "From the Annals of the Laboratory State." *Alternatives: A Journal of World Policy* 12 (1987).

Vogel, Ursula, and Michael Moran, eds. *The Frontiers of Citizenship*. Houndmills, Basingstoke, Hampshire, England: Macmillan, 1991.

Wachtel, Andrew. *An Obsession with History: Russian Writers Confront the Past*. Stanford, Calif.: Stanford University Press, 1994.

Walby, Sylvia. "Woman and Nation." *International Journal of Comparative Sociology* 33, no. 1–2 (1992): 91–100.

Walsh, Diana. "Ballot Plan Would Let Noncitizens Vote in S.F." *San Francisco Examiner*, April 23, 1996.

———. "Judge Rules against Plan to Let Noncitizens Vote." *San Francisco Chronicle*, May 1, 1996.

Walzer, Michael. "The Communitarian Critique of Liberalism." *Political Theory* 18, no. 1 (February 1990): 6–23.

———. "Nations and Universe." *The Tanner Lectures on Human Values*. Vol. 11. Salt Lake City: University of Utah Press, 1990.

———. *On Toleration*. New Haven: Yale University Press, 1997.

———. "Philosophy and Democracy." *Political Theory* 9, no. 3 (1981): 379–399.

———. "Political Alienation and Military Service." In *Obligations*, edited by Michael Walzer. Cambridge, Mass.: Harvard University Press, 1970.

———. *Spheres of Justice: A Defense of Pluralism and Equality*. New York: Basic Books, 1983.

———. *What It Means to Be an American*. New York: Marsilio, 1992.

Walzer, Michael, ed. *Obligations*. Cambridge, Mass.: Harvard University Press, 1970.

Walzer, Michael, et al. *The Politics of Ethnicity*. Cambridge, Mass.: Harvard University Press, Belknap Press, 1982.

Warner, Marina. *Managing Monsters: Six Myths of Our Time*. The 1994 Reith Lectures. London: Vintage, 1994.

Warner, Michael. *The Trouble with Normal: Sex, Politics and the Ethics of Queer Life*. New York: Free Press, 1999.

Waters, Mary. *Ethnic Options: Choosing Identities in America*. Berkeley and Los Angeles: University of California Press, 1990.

Weber, Max. *Sociology of Religion*. Boston: Beacon Press, 1963.

Weber, Samuel. "In the Name of the Law." *Cardozo Law Review* 11, no. 5–6 (July–August 1990): 1515–1538.

Weintraub, Sidney, and Stanley R. Ross. *"Temporary" Alien Workers in the United States: Designing Policy from Fact and Opinion*. Boulder, Col.: West-view Press, 1982.

Weir, Robert M. *Colonial South Carolina: A History*. Millwood, N.Y.: KTO, 1983.

Werbner, Pnina, and Tariq Modood, eds. *Debating Cultural Hybridity: Multi-Cultural Identities and the Politics of Anti-Racism*. Oxford: Zed Books, 1997.

White, Hayden. *Metahistory: The Historical Imagination in 19th-Century Europe*. Baltimore: Johns Hopkins University Press, 1973.

Wildavsky, Aaron. *The Nursing Father: Moses as a Political Leader*. Tuscaloosa: University of Alabama Press, 1984.

Wills, Gary. *Cincinnatus: George Washington and the Enlightenment*. Garden City, N.Y.: Doubleday, 1984.

Wingrove, Elizabeth. *Rousseau's Republican Romance*. Princeton, N.J.: Princeton University Press, 2000.

Winnick, Lewis. "America's 'Model Minority.' " *Commentary* 90, no. 2 (August 1990): 22–29.

Winnicott, D. W. *Playing and Reality*. London: Tavistock, 1971.

Wittgenstein, Ludwig. *Philosophical Investigations*, translated by G.E.M. Anscombe. New York: Macmillan, 1968.

————. *Philosophical Occasions, 1912–1951*, edited by James C. Klagge and Alfred Nordmann. Indianapolis: Hackett, 1993.

The Wizard of Oz. Directed by Victor Fleming. Metro-Goldwyn-Mayer, 1939.

Wolfe, Alan. "The Return of the Melting Pot." *New Republic*, December 31, 1990.

Woodhull, Winifred. *Transfigurations of the Maghreb: Feminism, Decolonization, and Literatures*. Minneapolis: University of Minnesota Press, 1993.

Wright, George R. "Federal Immigration Law and the Case for Open Entry." *Loyola of Los Angeles Law Review* 27 (June 1994): 1264.

Yerushalmi, Yosef Hayim. *Freud's Moses: Judaism Terminable and Interminable*. New Haven: Yale University Press, 1991.

Zeitlin, Froma. *Playing the Other: Gender and Society in Classical Greek Literature*. Chicago: University of Chicago Press, 1996.

Zelinsky, Wilbur. "The Twinning of the World: Sister Cities in Geographical and Historical Perspective." *Annals of the Association of American Geographers* 81, no. 1 (1991): 1–31.

Zenkovsky, Serge. *Medieval Russia's Epics, Chronicles and* Tales. New York: Dutton, 1974.

Zerilli, Linda. *Signifying Woman: Culture and Chaos in Rousseau, Burke, and Mill.* Ithaca, N.Y.: Cornell University Press, 1995.

———. "This Universalism Which Is Not One." Review of *Emancipation(s)* by Ernesto Laclau. *Diacritics* 28, no. 2 (summer 1998): 3–20.

Zizak, Slavoj. *Tarrying with the Negative: Kant, Hegel, and the Critique of Ideology.* Durham, N.C.: Duke University Press, 1993.

Index

Basch, Linda, 2
Behdad, Ali, 76–77, 79, 154nn.7, 10
Beiner, Ronald, 130n.30, 131n.32
Bennington, Geoffrey, 36, 37, 136n.27,
 140n.49, 142n.57
Bercovitch, Sacvan, 153n.4
Berlant, Lauren, 135n.19
Berlin, Isaiah, 142n.56
Blanc, Christina Szanton, 2
Bloom, Harold, 23
Bourne, Randolph, 156n.26, 164n.84
Boyarin, Jonathan, 137n.31
Bridges, Harry, 81, 155n.17
Brimelow, Peter, 123n.2, 127n.20
Burstein, Robert, 167n.14

Cameron, Norman, 111
Canada: aboriginals, 105–106; immigrants
 in, 126–127n.20
Carbonnier, Jean, 125n.10, 130n.29,
 135n.16
Carens, Joseph H., 165n.88
Catherine the Great (queen of Russia),
 5–6
Chambers, Iain, 2
Chosen People, 7, 46, 47–48, 59
Cioffi, Frank, 126n.18
citizenship: for children, 161n.61, 161–
 162n.65; and consent, 71, 74–75, 84,
 159n. 54, 159–160n.55, 160n.60,
 162n.70, 164n.82; devaluation of,
 161n.62; and marriage, 159n.44; and
 residency requirements, 163n.77
*Citizenship without Consent: Illegal
 Aliens in the Polity* (Schuck and Smith),
 9, 92–98
Civic Ideals (Smith), 11, 129nn.24–25,
 130n.28, 171–172n.31
Civilization and Its Discontents (Freud),
 138n.36
Connolly, William, 36–37, 140n.44,
 142n.57, 166n.4
consent, 59, 71, 74, 75, 79, 84, 92–
 98, 159n.54, 160n.60, 162n.70,
 164n.82
constitutive outside, 124n.6
Copjec, Joan, 139n.38, 169n.15

cosmopolitanism: democratic, 40, 72, 79,
 102–106, 122; and internationalism,
 131n.32, 149n.61, 164n.85; and maternalism, 150–151n.75; rooted cosmopolitanisms, 63, 164n.87; vs. nationalism,
 10, 13–14, 62–67, 104, 164–165n.87
Culture, Citizenship, and Community
 (Carens), 165n.88

David (king): line of, 3, 10, 42, 44, 45, 55–
 57; and Goliath, 147n.44; and Ruth, 42,
 44, 45, 55
democracy: and conquest, slavery, and
 expansion, 75–76; denationalization of,
 101–102, 105–106; dependence on social unity, 1, 18–19, 24; and ethnicity,
 82–86; and foreignness; 38–40;
 genres of, 107–120; and kinship
 relations, 72
Democracy in America (de Tocqueville),
 99, 153n.1
democratic cosmopolitanism. *See* cosmopolitanism
Déroin, Jeanne, 100
Derrida, Jacques, 1, 22, 53, 54, 78, 87, 91,
 120, 140nn.45–46, 146n.33, 147n.37
Dis-agreement (Rancière), 100
du Maurier, Daphne, 113
Duplessis, Rachel, 98

Edmundson, Mark, 170nn. 21, 23, 25,
 171n.26
emigration statistics, 85, 157n.30
ethnic communities, 80–86, 152n.87
expatriation rights, 92
exposure myths, 26, 138n.32

Facing Up to the American Dream
 (Hochschild), 153n.3
Fanon, Frantz, 65
father: ambivalence toward the father,
 111–112; law of the natural father, 28–
 29; ideal father, 139n.38; slain father,
 26, 28, 29, 35, 137n.31; splitting of the
 father-imago, 142n.55
female gothic. *See* gothic romance genre

and renationalization of the state, 10, 164n.87

Nations Unbound (Basch, Schiller, and Blanc), 2

Nations without Nationalism (Kristeva), 62, 150n.75

naturalization, 92–95

Nicomachean Ethics (Aristotle), 53

Niederland, William, 142n.55

Noiriel, Gerard, 127n.20, 156n.29

Noonan, Peggy, 139n.38

Notes of a Native Son (Baldwin), 121

Oedipus, 3, 145n.16

Okin, Susan, 159n.45

On the Social Contract (Rousseau), 3–4, 7, 9, 18–25, 28, 36–37, 107, 110–111, 171n.30

Origins of Totalitarianism (Arendt), 149n.53

Orpah (Moabite), 48–50, 64, 146n.28, 146n.36; normality vs. singularity of her character, 43, 47, 48–50; as personification of Ruth's Moabite character, 47, 144n.15; separation from Ruth, 58, 68–69, 71, 114

outsiders, 3, 4; and cultural unanimity, 33; depiction as criminals, 8; as scapegoats, 35–36. *See also* scapegoats

Ozick, Cynthia, 45–46, 48–55, 61, 151n.82

Pangle, Thomas, 124–125n.8, 133n.14

Parekh, Bhikhu, 3, 124n.7

Parker, Kunal M., 153n.5, 163n.77

Pateman, Carole, 128n.24

paternal authority. *See* father

Paulson, Ronald, 169n.15

Plato, 3, 124n.8, 133n.14

Political Theory and Modernity (Connolly), 142n.57

Politics of Friendship (Derrida), 53

Portes, Alejandro, 124n.7

postnational politics, 2, 128n.23. *See also* nationalism vs. cosmopolitanism

Pratt, Minnie Bruce, xiii

Pritsak, Omeljan, 5–6

Rancière, Jacques, vii, 100

Rank, Otto, 26

Reagon, Bernice Johnson, 83, 107, 120–121

Rebecca (Du Maurier), 113

Reimer, Gail Twersky, 147n.47

renationalization of the democratic state, 115–120

Reproducing the State (Stevens), 143n.62, 149n.61

The Republic (Plato), 3

right to have rights, 61, 149n.53

Robbins, Bruce, 164n.85

Rogin, Michael, 130n.28, 162n.67

romance genre: myths regarding birth and adoption, 26. *See also* gothic romance genre

Rome, its origin stories, 135n.17

Rorty, Richard, 115–120, 165n.4, 171n.29

Rousseau, Jean-Jacques, 7, 9, 107; alienness of the law and general willing, 30–31, 74, 113; conditions for democracy, 135n.22; and cosmopolitanism, 14; the foreign lawgiver, 3–4, 13–14, 18–25, 26, 37–38, 133–134n.15; general willing and the law; 19–20, 29–31, 74, 133nn.10, 11, 142n.57; law of the natural father, 28–29; on Machiavelli, 171n.30; self-identity, need for, 140n.46; views on Moses as lawgiver, 26

Rumbaut, Rubén G., 124n.7

Rushdie, Salman, 15–16, 131–132nn.1, 2, 3, 6

Russ, Joanna, 166nn.5, 7, 167nn.12, 13

Russia, its origin stories, 5–6, 57

Ruth: and Abraham, 147–148n.48; as disruptor of social order, 45–46; as foreign-founder, 3, 10, 41–42, 144n.11; foreignness of, 7, 71, 147n.46; as model convert, 45–48, 48–55; as model immigrant, 45–48, 55–58; and motherhood, 147n.42, 147n.47; and Naomi, 43–44, 52–54, 78, 146n.36, 151n.82; and Orpah, 49, 68–69, 71, 146n.36; as seductress (as a Lillith), 51–52, 110; as taker, 60–62, 148n.49

Ruth, Book of: biblical story of, 42–46; as conversion story, 9, 45–48, 48–55; as foreign-founding myth, 3, 10, 41–70, 144n.11; gothic reading of, 109–110; Kristeva's reading of, 4, 11, 42, 45, 52–58, 62, 148n.48; Lacocque's reading of, 55; as mourning narrative, 68–71, 152n.88; Naomi as transitional object, 67, 151n.82; Ozick's reading of, 45, 46, 48–55, 61, 151n.82; Trible's reading of, 60–61, 148–149n.51

Saccamano, Neil, 37, 55
Sacco and Vanzetti, 81, 154n.12
Sacks, Peter, 68
sacrificial crises, 33–34, 39, 43, 141n.50; and the judicial system, 143n.61; Moabite sacrifice rituals, 144n.13
Salomon, Lester, 163n.80
Sandel, Michael, 133n.9
Santner, Eric, 67–70, 128n.22, 142n.55
Sasson, Jack M., 144n.15
scapegoats and scapegoating, 12, 33–38, 40, 46–47, 57, 140–141nn.48, 50, 142n.56
Schiller, Nina Glick, 2
Schlesinger, Arthur, 123n.2, 154n.14, 156n.26
Schuck, Peter, 8,9,92, 93, 96–98, 161n.62
Seery, John, 165n.4
separation and transition issues, 67–71, 151n.83
Shane (film), 9, 22–23, 28, 35, 36, 142n.55
Shih, Marty, 81
Shulman, George, 172n.32
sister-cities, 72, 152n.91
Smith, Rogers, 8, 9, 76–77, 119–120, 130n.31, 142n.59, 171–172n.31; ascriptive mythology critic, 12, 128–129n.24; and consent, 92–93, 96–98; critic of American exceptionalism, 162n.66; liberalism and sexual inequality, 128–129n.24; multiple traditions thesis, 11–12, 119, 130n.28

Social Contract. See On the Social Contract (Rousseau)
social unity: and democracy, 1, 18–19, 24, 123n.2; among Israelites, 43; role of the outsider/scapegoat, 33, 140n.48
Solovyev, Vladimir Sergeyevich, 6, 57–58, 125n.16
Spivak, Gayatari, 106, 114, 120, 151n.76
Stern, Julia, 169n.15
Stevens, Jacqueline, 143n.62, 149n.61
Strange, Carolyn, 124n.6
Strange Multiplicity (Tully), 123n.2, 124n.3
Strangers to Ourselves (Kristeva), 45, 46, 56–58, 148n.48
Strictly Ballroom (film), 9, 86–89, 95, 157–158n.34
suffrage. *See* voting rights

Takaki, Ronald, 156n.21
taking, 8, 29, 39, 60–62, 79, 90, 99–101, 118, 160n.60
Tocqueville, Alexis de, 11, 73, 99–100, 139n.38, 153n.1
Totem and Taboo (Freud), 28
transitional objects, and the Book of Ruth, 63, 67–71, 151n.82
Trible, Phyllis, 60–61, 149n.51
Tully, James, 123n.2, 124n.3

Van Zyl, A. H., 144n.13
veiling, 62, 64–66, 150nn.70–73, 151n.77
violence: toward the father, 28–29, 38; against immigrants, 101; of the Mosaic founding, 27, 138–139n.37; ritual violence, 126n.18; of Rousseauvian democracy, 139; stereotype of violent immigrant, 77. *See also* sacrificial crises

xenophilia, 2, 46, 74–76, 77, 78, 80–81, 84, 90–91, 124n.7
xenophobia, 1–2, 11–12, 18, 30, 38, 46, 76–78, 80–81, 84, 90–92, 97, 140n.48, 154n.10, 156n.26